MEMOIR

ON MAPS ILLUSTRATING

THE ANCIENT GEOGRAPHY KASMIR

MEMOIR

ON MAPS ILLUSTRATING

THE ANCIENT GEOGRAPHY KASMIR

M.A. STEIN, PH.D.

Principal, Madrasah College, Calcutta.

Journal of the Asiatic Society of Bengal, Vol. LXVIII, Part I., Extra-Number 2.—1899.

GYAN

Published by

GYAN

Gyan Publishing House
5, Ansari Road
Daryaganj, New Delhi-110002
Phone: 011-47034999, 9811692060
E-mail: books@gyanbooks.com

Distribution Network
gyanbooks.com
India, USA, Canada, UK, Australia, France

ISBN : 978-81-212-2632-5 (HB)
First Published, 1899

2nd Impression 2021

Printed at: Gyan Press, Delhi.

The Ancient Geography, Kasmir
Author: M.A. Stein

MEMOIR

ON MAPS ILLUSTRATING

THE ANCIENT GEOGRAPHY

KASMIR.

M. A. STEIN, Ph.D.

PRINCIPAL, MADRASAH COLLEGE, CALCUTTA.

JOURNAL OF THE ASIATIC SOCIETY OF BENGAL, VOL. LXVIII,
PART I., EXTRA-NUMBER 2.—1899.

CALCUTTA
PRINTED AT THE BAPTIST MISSION PRESS
AND PUBLISHED BY THE
ASIATIC SOCIETY, 57, PARK STREET.
1899.

N.B.—For Table of Contents and List of Abbreviations see pp. 223-231.

JOURNAL

OF THE

ASIATIC SOCIETY OF BENGAL.

Part I.—HISTORY, LITERATURE, &c.

Extra-Number 2.—1899.

Memoir on Maps illustrating the Ancient Geography of Kaśmīr.—

By M. A. Stein, Ph.D.

CHAPTER I.

INTRODUCTORY.

Ancient topography in Kaśmīr Chronicle.

1. The maps accompanying this memoir are primarily intended to show the results which a detailed study of Kalhaṇa's Rājataraṅgiṇī has furnished regarding the early topography of Kaśmīr and the adjacent territories. From the first when engaged in preparing a critical edition of that text,[1] the earliest and most important of the Sanskrit Chronicles of Kaśmīr, I had realized that an exact identification of the very numerous old localities mentioned in it was indispensable for a correct understanding of the narrative. This conviction forced itself even more strongly upon me in the course of the labours I devoted to the preparation of the commentated translation of the work which is now passing through the press.[2]

[1] *Kalhaṇa's Rājataraṅgiṇī* or *Chronicle of the Kings of Kaśmīr*, Bombay Education Society's Press, 1892, pp. xx and 296, 4to.

[2] To be published, with a Historical Introduction, by Messrs. A. Constable and Co., London, in two volumes, 4to.

Many of the questions thus raised were so detailed and intricate that it would have been manifestly impossible to attempt their solution without carefully studying on the spot those topographical facts which alone could elucidate them. It was, therefore, fortunate for my researches in this direction that I was able during successive years to make a series of antiquarian tours in Kaśmīr. These acquainted me not only with the extant ancient remains of the Valley, but also with its actual topography and that of the neighbouring mountain regions.[1] I cannot feel too grateful for the advantage I thus enjoyed. It has allowed me in more than one case to fix with certainty the position of important ancient sites, which no amount of philological acriby would have sufficed to locate correctly.

Preparation of Maps.

2. In order to place before the student of the Kaśmīr Chronicle the results of these researches, as well as the evidence on which they were based, the preparation of maps appeared necessary that would show the modern topography of the country in full detail together with the ancient sites and local names identified. While considering the means for the execution of such maps I received in the autumn of 1896 the generous offer of the Asiatic Society of Bengal to bear the cost connected with their preparation, on the understanding that the maps would be published also in the Society's Journal with a separate explanatory memoir. I accepted this offer all the more readily as it gave me the desired opportunity of treating the subject of the early geography of Kaśmīr in a connected form and before a larger public. For the liberal assistance thus rendered to me, I wish to record here my sincere thanks. I owe special obligations to Dr. G. A. Grierson, C.S., C.I.E., and Dr. A. F. R. Hoernle, C.I.E., whose kind offices were mainly instrumental in securing the above arrangement.

The successful execution of the maps as now published was rendered possible by the ready co-operation of Colonel J. Waterhouse, I.S.C., late Assistant Surveyor General, in charge of the Lithographic and Photographic Office of the Survey of India Department. The preparation of a new ground map to show on a sufficiently large scale the details of the modern topography of Kaśmīr would have cost much trouble and entailed very heavy, almost prohibitory, expense. At the same time it had to be considered that there were no other materials available for such a map but those supplied by the Trigonometrical

[1] The tours referred to occupied the greatest part of my summer vacations in 1888, 1889, 1891, 1892, 1894 and were supplemented by shorter visits to particular sites during the summers of 1895–96.

Survey operations in Kaśmīr, 1856–60, which had been embodied on the scale of 4 miles to 1 inch in the corresponding sheets of the 'Atlas of India.'

It hence appeared to me the most convenient plan to use as a ground-map a mechanical reproduction of that portion of the 'Atlas of India' which contains Kaśmīr and the adjacent territories. Over this ground-map the entries relating to the ancient topography of the country could be printed in a distinguishing colour. This plan having received Colonel Waterhouse's approval, the required portions of the engraved plates containing Sheets 27 and 28 of the 'Atlas,' were transferred to the stone and the copies of the larger map reproduced from the latter by lithography. A similar process was used for the smaller map showing the capital, S'RĪNAGAR, and its environs on the enlarged scale of 1 mile to 1 inch. But in this case the original map which was not engraved but only zincographed, had to be retraced on the stone.[1]

In the case of either map the entries marking ancient sites and names were printed in red over the ground-map from a separate stone. In order to distinguish at a glance the old local names in the Rājataraṅgiṇī from those known only to the later Chronicles and other sources, the former were shown in GROTESQUE type and the latter in *Italic*.

By following the method here briefly explained it was possible to provide maps which exhibit in all needful detail the latest and most authentic survey of Kaśmīr and at the same time show clearly all important features of the old topography. The success of the technical execution is due mainly to the great care and attention bestowed on it by Colonel WATERHOUSE and his staff. For this as well as much valuable advice accorded to me in connection with the work I may be allowed to offer here my grateful acknowledgments.

Arrangement of memoir.

3. It has already been stated that the maps here presented are in the first place intended to illustrate those data of the ancient geography of Kaśmīr which are contained in KALHAṆA's Chronicle. But in addition to the old local names and sites taken from this our most important source of information those mentioned in the later Sanskrit Chronicles and other Kaśmīrian texts have also been inserted as far as they can claim antiquity and interest. These maps may, therefore, equally well serve to illustrate a comprehensive account of the historical topography of Kaśmīr, such as I shall attempt to give here, up to the close of the Hindu epoch.

1 The original of this smaller ground-map had appeared as an inset in the "*Map of Jummoo, Kashmir and Adjacent Territories*," 4 miles to 1 inch, published by the Survey of India, 1861.

In treating this subject it appears to me most convenient to examine first the sources of information from which our knowledge regarding the ancient topography of Kaśmīr is drawn. I shall next proceed to notice what we can learn from these sources as to the general physical features of Kaśmīr geography and their bearing on the historical and economical conditions of the country during the Hindu period. In the last chapter I intend to discuss the political divisions of the territory and to indicate briefly the information available to us regarding the particular places of historical or religious interest.

Most of the data upon which this account of the old topography of Kaśmīr is based, are contained in Kalhaṇa's Chronicle, and have therefore already been explained by me in the notes which accompany my translation of that work. In order to avoid unnecessary repetition I shall refer to these notes for all such detailed evidence as could not conveniently be set forth within the limits of the present paper.

Earlier publications.

4. Before, however, closing these preliminary remarks it is necessary to refer briefly to those few publications in which facts bearing on the old topography of Kaśmīr have received an earlier treatment.

In view of what has been said above we naturally turn first to the works which have dealt directly with the interpretation of the Rājataraṅgiṇī. Dr. WILSON who was the first European to study the Chronicle in the original, published an abstract of the contents of the first six Books as early as 1825.[1] He seems to have fully realized the importance of an accurate and sober examination of the geographical questions connected with the narrative. The textual materials at his disposal were, however, extremely defective, and European knowledge of Kaśmīr restricted at the time solely to the accounts of BERNIER and FORSTER. He could hence scarcely do more than indicate the more or less corrupt modern equivalents by which the Persian Chronicles render some of the Kaśmīr local names taken from Kalhaṇa's account. The judgment and accuracy with which Dr. Wilson discussed the Chronicle's notices of countries and places situated outside Kaśmīr and better known at that time, shows sufficiently that only the defective character of the available materials prevented that distinguished Sanskrit scholar from doing justice to the task.

The elaborate commentary with which Mr. TROYER accompanied his French translation of the Rājataraṅgiṇī,[2] does not represent any material advance beyond the contents of Wilson's Essay. Yet Mr. Troyer

[1] *An Essay on the Hindu History of Cashmir*, in *Asiatic Researches*, vol. xv., 1825, pp. 1 *sqq*.

[2] *Râdjataranginî ou Histoire des rois du Kachmîr*, Paris, 1840–52.

had already the whole text of the Chronicle to refer to, and in the meantime a considerable amount of information about Kaśmīr had become available through the works of travellers like Moorcroft, Jacquemont, Vigne, Von Hügel, and others. The serious shortcomings which characterize Mr. Troyer's labors notwithstanding his patient devotion to the task, have already been fully indicated by Prof. Bühler.[1] Detailed reference to the defects of the topographical notes is hence unnecessary.

The English translation of the Chronicle published in the years 1879-87 by Babu Jogesh Chunder Dutt makes no attempt whatever to elucidate the many points of topographical interest. Though the translation itself is decidedly better than that of Mr. Troyer, yet it necessarily shares the defects arising from the use of the same corrupt text. Both versions strikingly demonstrate the importance of topographical researches by the frequent instances in which the translators have mistaken local names for words of ordinary meaning or *vice versâ.*[2]

The advantages offered for enquiries of this kind by a personal acquaintance with the country were fully illustrated by the valuable contributions which General (then Captain) Cunningham was able to make to our knowledge of ancient Kaśmīr in connection with his visit to the Valley in November 1847. Though his stay was short and primarily devoted to a survey of the more conspicuous of the temple-ruins still extant, he succeeded in identifying correctly a number of important ancient sites such as *Purāṇādhiṣṭhāṇa* 'the old capital,' *Jyeṣṭheśvara, Mārtāṇḍa, Padmapura, Pattana, Khonamuṣa.*[3]

General Cunningham subsequently had occasion to discuss comprehensively these localities in his *Ancient Geography of India*, a work which, notwithstanding its deficiencies in detail, amply testifies to the great antiquarian experience and natural acumen of its author. The chapter on the "Kingdom of Kashmir"[4] utilizes the evidence afforded by the Chinese sources and Alberūnī, and indicates correctly the old names of the petty hill states to the south and south-east of Kaśmīr (*Rājapurī, Vallāpura, Campā, Kāṣṭhavāṭa*). It further adds to the identifications already mentioned equally important notes on *Pravarapura*, the present Śrīnagar, *Vijayeśvara, Huṣkapura, Juṣkapura, Jayapura.* If General Cunningham was less successful in his attempts at

1 See *Report on a tour in search of Sanskrit Manuscripts made in Kashmir, J. Bo. B. R. A. S.* 1877, pp. 55 *sqq.*

2 For some of the imaginary territories and places which figure in these translations, see *Vienna Oriental Journal*, 1898, pp. 67 *sqq.*

3 See his *Essay on the Arian Order of Architecture as exhibited in the temples of Kashmir, J. A. S. B.*, 1848, pp. 242–327.

4 See *Ancient Geography of India*, 1871, pp. 89–103, 128–141.

locating *Parihāsapura* and some other ancient sites, this may fairly be attributed to his inability to consult the Sanskrit sources in the original.[1]

Professor LASSEN's "Indische Alterthumskunde" gives an extensive analysis of the historical contents of Kalhaṇa's work.[2] But his explanations as to the ancient localities mentioned are generally only there well-founded where they are based on General Cunningham's researches. Ancient territories and places are often connected with modern localities merely on the ground of a faint resemblance of the names and without sufficient internal evidence. This tendency has frequently led that distinguished scholar to ignore the narrow territorial limits within which most of the local and ethnic names occurring in the later portion of Kalhaṇa's narrative have to be looked for. It is only natural that identifications of real (or imaginary) localities which transferred the scene of contemporary events described by Kalhaṇa to territories so distant as Lahore, Eastern Afghānistān or Ajmīr,[3] have helped to produce a very ill-focussed picture of the political power and extent of the Kaśmīr kingdom in those later times.

The merit of having definitely shown the right methods and means for re-constructing the ancient geography of Kaśmīr belongs to Professor BÜHLER. This great scholar by whose lamented death so many branches of Indian research have suffered irreparable loss, had in the masterly

[1] If particular proof were wanted to show that a through acquaintance with the modern topography of a country is in itself not sufficient to lead to useful results in regard to its historical geography, Mr. VIGNE's work, *Travels in Kashmir, Ladak, Iskardo,* (London, 1842, two Vols.) would supply it. This estimable artist and traveller evidently took a great deal of interest in the antiquities of the country which he traversed in many directions. His book, however, as far as the old geography of Kaśmīr is concerned, furnishes scarcely anything more than a series of amusingly naïve etymologies of local names. Thus *Hür^apōr* (Sūrapura) is "the Diamond City," *Pāndrēṭhan* (Purāṇādhiṣṭhāna) the place of the 'Pandus and Duryndun' (*i. e.*, Duryodhana), Sōpūr (Suyyapura) 'the Golden City,' etc.; see i. p. 267, ii. pp. 37, 157.

Mr. Vigne is responsible for the strange derivation of the name of the Kaśmīr capital, *Śrīnagar* (Śrīnagara), or as he spells it, 'Siri-Nagur,' from "*Surya Nagur,* the city of the sun" (p. ii. 137). Judging from the persistence with which the error has been copied by a succession of modern writers on Kaśmīr, this etymology bids fair to establish itself as a piece of orthodox creed with European visitors to the Valley.

[2] See *Indische Alterthumskunde* (second ed.), ii pp. 885–915; iii. pp. 984–1128.

[3] I refer to locations like those of *Lohara* (Loh^arin) at Lahore; of the [imaginary] province *Kampanā* in eastern Afghānistān; of the *Lavanya* tribe near the Sambhar salt lake; of the feudal chief *Koṣṭheśvara* at Kōṭgaṛh on the Satlej, etc.; comp. *Ind. Alterth.* iii. pp. 1057, 1041, 1069, 1105, and for the supposed territorial extent of the Kaśmīr state, iii. p. 1119.

report on his Kaśmīr tour lucidly set forth the work that remained to be done in connection with the Rājataraṅgiṇī.[1] He had there shown that for a full comprehension of its contents a minute study of the ancient geography of Kaśmīr was indispensable. He was the first to call attention to the ample materials which are offered for such a study by the later Sanskrit Chronicles, the Nīlamatapurāṇa and other Kaśmīrian texts. But he also realized that "some of the geographical questions would probably require a final re-examination in Kaśmīr."

Other labors prevented my lamented master from undertaking this task himself. But the most graphic and accurate notices which his Report gives of those sites in the Valley he had himself been able to visit,[2] prove convincingly—if any proof were needed—that no important point connected with the old topography of the country could easily have escaped his attention. The particular identifications first made by Prof. Bühler will be duly mentioned in their proper places. It was a source of true satisfaction to me that I was able during my last year's visit to Europe to present personally the departed with the first clean copies of the maps now published. That the results recorded in them were such as obtained his approval, will always appear to me the highest reward for the labour their preparation and the preceding researches had cost me.

[1] See *Report on a tour in search of Sanskrit manuscripts made in Kashmir*, Bombay, 1877, p. 58.

[2] See *loc. cit.*, pp. 4–18.

CHAPTER II.

ACCOUNTS OF OLD KAŚMĪR.

SECTION I.—CLASSICAL NOTICES.

5. Our sources for the early geography of Kaśmīr may be conveniently divided into foreign notices and indigenous records. As the information supplied by the former is on the whole earlier in date though by no means more precise or important, we shall commence our review with them. Having learned what little the outer world knew or recorded of the secluded alpine land, we shall appreciate all the more the imposing array of Kaśmīrian authorities which offer themselves as our guides in and about the Valley. With the foreign accounts but in a kind of intermediate position we may class those Indian texts the authors of which may have possessed some more detailed information of Kaśmīr, but have not thought it necessary to vouchsafe it to us.

Alexander's invasion.

It is significant for the isolated position which its mountain barriers assured to Kaśmīr, that we do not find any mention of the country in those accounts to which we are accustomed to look for the first truly historical notices of the North-West of India. I mean the relations of Alexander's invasion. The march from Taxila to the Hydaspes (Jehlam) took the Macedonian forces along a line of route which lay comparatively near to the confines of Kaśmīr. Yet there is no notice in the accounts of Alexander's expedition which can be shown to imply even a hearsay knowledge of the Kaśmīr Valley. On the other hand the names of the neighbouring territories on the West and South have long ago been recognized in the names of their rulers *Arsakes* and

Abisares. These names clearly represent ethnic appellations derived from *Uraśā* (Ptolemy's Οὔαρσα) and *Abhisāra.*[1]

The only certain reference to Kaśmīr which classical literature has preserved for us, is found in PTOLEMY'S Geography. There can be no doubt that D'Anville was right in recognizing its name in that of the region of Κασπειρία situated 'below the sources of the Bidaspes (Vitastā) and of the Sandabal (Candrabhāgā) and of the Adris (Irāvatī)'.[2] Ptolemy mentions this territory correctly enough between that of the *Daradrai* or Dards on the Indus and *Kylindrine* or the land of the Kulindas on the Hyphasis (Biās) and eastwards. In his subsequent detailed description of Indian territories, however, he makes the region 'held by the Kaspeiræans' extend eastwards from the land of the Pandoouoi on the Bidaspes as far as Mount Ouïndion or the Vindhya.[3]

Ptolemy's Kaspeiria.

It is clear that the limits here indicated which would embrace a great portion of the present Panjāb with parts of the North-West Provinces and Central India, can have nothing to do with Kaśmīr. It has been suggested that Ptolemy's statement refers to a period when the power of the dynasty ruling over Kaśmīr actually extended over the wide territories above indicated.[4] The assumption, put into a form more in keeping with historical probability, would be that Kaśmīr was then subject to a great foreign dominion the rulers of which, for one reason or the other, were in Ptolemy's source designated from this part of their realm.

However this may be, it is curious to note that we meet with the name Κάσπειρα also in the long list of cities located within the region belonging to the Kaspeiræans. The geographical position assigned to it by Ptolemy's table (or map) would bring Kaspeira close to the junction of the Hydaspes and Zaradros (Satlej), *i.e.*, the neighbourhood of Multān.[5] Yet it seems difficult to believe that the information originally underlying this entry referred to any other locality but Kaśmīr.[6]

1 See LASSEN. *Ind. Alt.*, ii. p. 174; WILSON, *Essay*, p. 116; also my notes on *Rājatar.* i. 180; v. 217.

2 See Ptolemy VII. i. 42 and pp. 21, 40 *sq.* in *Antiquité Géographique de l'Inde, par M. D'Anville, Premier Géographe du Roi*, etc, Paris, 1775.—The accuracy and sound judgment displayed in this work fully justify the great fame it has enjoyed.

3 Ptolemy, VII. i. 47.

4 Compare, *e.g.*, LASSEN, *Ind. Alt.* ii. p. 898; V. DE St. MARTIN, *Mémoires de l'Académie des Inscriptions*, Sav. étrang., Ire Série, t. v., p. 380.

5 See the old map reproduced in DR. MCCRINDLE'S *Ancient India as described by Ptolemy*, Bombay, 1885.

6 This had been rightly seen already by D'ANVILLE. He points out, p. 40, that the error in latitude implied by Ptolemy's position of Kaspeira (if Srīnagar

It would be useless to attempt to seek now for an explanation of the erroneous location. The researches of the most competent scholars have amply proved how little reliance can be placed on the apparent exactness of Ptolemy's latitudes and longitudes in the Asiatic portion of his work.[1] None of the other city names in the same list can be connected with Kaśmīr. Nor is the identification of any one of them certain, expect that of Μόδουρα ἡ τῶν Θεῶν, the sacred Mathurā. This alone suffices to show how far away from Kaśmīr we are liable to be taken.

The value of Ptolemy's notice of *Kaspeiria* lies mainly in the fact that it presents us with an accurate enough transcription of that form of the country's name which on independent phonetic evidence we must assume as an intermediate stage between the Sanskrit *Kaśmīra* and the modern Kaśmīri form *Kaśīr*. The explanations given below (§ 36) will show that a well-established phonetic law presupposes a form **Kaśvīra* for the earlier Prakrit stage of Kaśmīri. Of this form we have in *Kaspeira* (pronounced Kaspīra) as close a rendering as Greek writing permitted.[2]

The Sanskrit form of the name, *Kaśmīra*, has, as far as we can go back, been always the one in official use. By it the country has been, and is still to this day, generally known abroad (Hindi *Kaśmīr*, Persian *Kashmīr*.) The preservation of the popular Prakrit **Kaśvīra* by Ptolemy deserves hence attention with regard to the original source from which this particular item of information was obtained.

Kaspeiroi of Dionysios and Nonnos.

6. It is very probable that we have also to connect with Kaśmīr a curious notice which Stephen of Byzance has preserved from the *Bassarika*, a lost poem of Dionysios of Samos. The passage, first apparently noticed by D'Anville, mentions the KASPEIROI as a tribe famous among all Indians for their fast feet.[3] We do not know the

is really meant) is not greater than that which can plainly be proved in the case of his entry for *Barbarei*, the port at the mouth of the Indus.

[1] I cannot refrain from quoting here in full the very just remarks of SIR HENRY YULE, *Cathay and the Way Thither*, p. cli, which ought ever to be remembered by those who have to deal with Ptolemy on Indian soil. "We see here how Ptolemy's Asiatic Geography was compiled. It is evident that he first drew his maps embodying all information that he had procured, however vague and rough it might be. From these maps he then educed his tables of latitudes and longitudes and his systematic topography. The result is that everything assumes an appearance of exact definition; and indications on the map which meant no more than (somewhere hereabouts is said to be such a country), became translated into a precision fit for an Act of Parliament."

[2] Thus the tribal name *Aspasioi* of Arrian (iv. 23) reproduces the Sanskrit *Aśvaka*; comp. MCCRINDLE, *Invasion of India*, p. 333.

[3] The text of the passage is reproduced by TROYER, ii. p. 307. Another short quotation from the same text mentions the *Ariénoi* along with the Κασπεῖροι.

time of this Dionysios. Nor is there any indication as to the source from which he may have taken the reference. That the Kaśmīrīs had abroad the reputation of being good pedestrians may be concluded from a remark of Albērūnī.[1] It is clear that the natural conditions of an alpine valley enclosed by difficult mountain ranges are likely to develop the marching powers of its inhabitants. The Rājataraṅgiṇī gives us in fact several instances of very respectable marching performances. It shows at the same time the scant use made of riding animals in the mountains.[2] There is thus more than the mere name to justify us in referring the notice of Dionysios of Samos to Kaśmir.

We meet with the name of the *Kaspeiroi* also in the Dionysiaka of Nonnos. There they are mentioned among the Indian tribes rising in arms against Bacchos.[3] As Nonnos' list names in the same passage also the Ariênoi whose name we see coupled with that of Kaspeiroi in the fragment of the *Bassarika*, it is probable that Nonnos has taken his reference either from the latter work or from some common source.

Kaspatyros of Herodotos.

7. We should, indeed, have a far earlier reference to Kaśmīr in classical literature, and one by no less an authority than the 'Father of history,' if the opinion of those scholars could be accepted who have thought to recognize the name of the Valley in the KASPATYROS of Herodotos. The facts are briefly the following. Herodotos mentions the city of Kaspatyros as the place at which the expedition under Scylax of Koryanda, sent by Darius to explore the course of the Indus, embarked.[4] He distinctly places this city in the Paktyan land (Πακτυϊκὴ γῆ). This is described as being to the north of the other Indians and apparently bordering on the Baktrian territory. The place meant by Herodotos is evidently the same that Hekataios knew before him by the name of KASPAPYROS and as a city of the Gandarians.[5]

The notice of Hekataios (circ. 549–486 B.C.) makes it clear that Kaspatyros or Kaspapyros, whichever form may be more accurate, must have been situated in that territory where the Indus first becomes navigable, *i.e.*, in the ancient Gandhāra, the present Peshawar District. That the designation *Paktyikē* used by Herodotus refers to the same

[1] *India*, transl. Sachau, i. p. 206.

[2] Compare *Rājat.* vii. 140, 1301; viii. 192, 379, 1588, 1796, 1887, 2673 *sq.*

[3] See *Dionysiaka*, xxvi. 165 *sqq.* I take this reference from TROYER, ii. p. 308.

[4] See iv. 44, also iii. 102. The points bearing on the interpretation of the passage have been fully discussed by SIR E. H. BUNBURY, *History of Ancient Geography*, i. pp. 228, 256.

[5] See Stephanos Byzant., s.v. ΓΑΝΔΑΡΙΚΗ; also Müller's *Fragmenta historic. graec.*, i. p. 12.

territory and represents the earliest mention of the ethnic name *Pakhtūn* or the modern Indian *Paṭhān*, seems also probable.[1] The exact site of Kaspatyros has not been identified. Considering the great changes which local nomenclature in Gandhāra has undergone, it perhaps never will be.[2]

WILSON was the first who distinctly attempted to connect the name of Kaspatyros with Kaśmīr.[3] But the idea seems to have occurred earlier. For D'Anville thought it necessary to refer to it and to refute it. Wilson saw clearly enough that the city of Scylax must have been situated close to the Indus and hence far away from Kaśmīr. If notwithstanding this important fact he yet proposed to identify its name with that of Kaśmīr, on the assumption that the borders of the latter kingdom extended as far as the Indus, the mistake must be traced to a fanciful etymology of the latter name.

Wilson assumed that the name Kaśmīr was derived from * *Kaśyapapura*, a name which he supposed to have been given to the country owing to its colonization by the Ṛṣi Kaśyapa. He supported this strange derivation by a reference to the uniform assertion of 'Oriental writers.'[4] But it is difficult to believe that he could have meant any

1 This identification seems to have been first made simultaneously by DORN and LASSEN; compare V. DE ST. MARTIN, *E'tude sur la géographie grecque de l'Inde*, Mém. de l'Acad. des Inscriptions, Sav. E'trang., 1re Série, V., p. 17 *sqq*. His note on Kaspatyros, *ib*. pp. 81–86, contains a judicious review of the whole question from the geographical point of view and a detailed account of earlier opinions. For a more recent résumé compare DARMESTETER, *Chants Populaires des Afghans*, pp. clxxx *sqq*.

2 Proper navigation begins now at Jahāngira, a place situated on the left bank of the Kābul River, some six miles above the confluence of the latter with the Indus at Attock. The lower part of the Kābul River's course lies in a well-defined single bed which, in view of the natural configuration of the banks, cannot have changed materially in historical times. Above Jahāngira the current becomes too strong for safe navigation.

I doubt very much whether the Indus immediately above Attock can ever have been suitable for proper navigation. The river is cut up there into many, often very shallow, channels and obstructed by continually shifting sandbanks. On the eastern bank spreads the low plain of Chach, which must have always left a wide scope to the vagaries of the great river. Taking into account these circumstances I should not be surprised if Scylax's expedition had chosen some place near Jahāngīra for the start on their voyage. There are many ruined sites near the latter place, and near Alladhēr closeby on the Indus.

3 See *Essay*, p. 117; for a reproduction of the argument, also, *Ariana Antiqua*, p. 136 *sq*.

4 "This (the name of Cashmir) was derived, it is uniformly asserted by the Oriental writers, from the colonization of the country by Casyapa, the first settlement or city being named after him Casyapapur, converted in ordinary pronuncia-

better authorities than the Persian Tārīkhs of Kaśmīr, of the 17th and 18th century, which he had occasion to consult in connection with his above-quoted Essay. They, indeed, indulge in whimsical etymologies like Kashmīr, *i.e.*, *Kashap* (Kaśyapa) + *mar* (maṭha), etc. But neither these etymologies nor the name **Kaśyapapura* are in any way known to our genuine sources.

Wilson would scarcely have chosen to put forth such a derivation, had the whole of the Chronicle or the other Kaśmīrian texts been at the time accessible to him. Extensive as this literature is, it does not furnish any evidence whatever for *Kaśyapapura or a similar name having ever been used as a designation of the country. This fact is all the more significant as allusions to the legendary origin of the country are otherwise so frequent. The philological impossibility of deriving Kaśmīra from *Kaśyapapura need scarcely be specially indicated at the present day.[1] A reference to the theory was, however, here necessary, as it has found its way into works of authorities like Ritter, Lassen and Humboldt, and has hence been reproduced even by recent writers.[2]

SECTION II.—CHINESE RECORDS.

Earliest Chinese notice.

8. If classical literature has thus nothing to tell us of Kaśmīr but the bare name, it is very different with the Chinese records. Buddhist pilgrims from China on their way to the sacred sites of the Indian plains visited Kaśmīr and chose it as a resting place. Their itineraries as well as the records of the political relations established with Kaśmīr during a period of Chinese extension to the west, furnish us with a series of interesting data for the old geography of Kaśmīr.

It seems difficult to ascertain from the materials at present accessible in translations or notices of European scholars, which is to be considered the earliest Chinese reference to Kaśmīr. The difficulty is connected with the use of the geographical term *Ki-pin*. This name

tion into Cashappur or Caspapur, the latter of which forms is the proper reading of the Greek text;" *Essay*, p. 117.

[1] It is curious to note that Kāśyapapura was, according to an Indian authority quoted by Albērūnī, *India*, transl. Sachau, i. p. 298, one of the old names of Multān.

[2] See RITTER, *Erdkunde*, ii. p. 1087; LASSEN, *Ind. Alt.*, ii. p. 635 (where for *Kaśyapapura > Kaśmīra an equally unfounded derivation from *Kaśyapamīra is substituted); HUMBOLDT, *Asie Centrale*, i. p. 102; for modern works, *e.g.*, MCCRINDLE, *Ancient India*, p. 108; Beal, *Si-yu-ki*, i. p. 148.

originally and properly designated the Upper Kābul Valley.[1] It appears, however, at a period when Chinese knowledge of India was less developed, to have been used in a vague and general fashion for a variety of territories on the northern confines of India, among them also Kaśmīr. However this may be, our loss seems scarcely to be great, as these notices of the Chinese Annalists regarding Ki-pin do not seem to give characteristic local details.[2]

The first clear reference to Kaśmīr which I can trace at present, is contained in a record dating from 541 A.D. It is taken from the account of an Indian envoy who reached China during the early part of the reign of the T'ang dynasty.[3] The name of Kaśmīr is not mentioned. Yet it is evident that M. PAUTHIER who published the extract, was right in referring to Kaśmīr the description given of the northern portion of India as a country "situated at the foot of the snowy mountains and enveloped by them on all sides like a precious jewel. In the south there is a valley which leads up to it and serves as the gate of the kingdom." The points noticed here are exactly those with which we meet in all Chinese accounts of Kaśmīr.

Visit of Hiuen Tsiang.

9. Ninety years after the date of this notice Kaśmīr was visited by HIUEN TSIANG. He reached the Valley from Uraśā in the west and resided in it as an honoured guest for fully two years. The records of the great Chinese pilgrim contain by far the fullest and most accurate description of Kaśmīr that has come down to us from a foreign pen during the period with which we are here concerned.[4]

Hiuen Tsiang must have entered Kaśmīr by the valley of the Vitastā as he describes his route as leading to the south-east of Uraśā, the present Hazāra District. After 'crossing over mountains and treading along precipices' he arrived at the 'stone gate which is the western entrance of the kingdom.' We shall see below that this gate known also to Ou-k'ong and Albērūnī, was the frontier watch-station or *Dvāra* in the gorge of Bārāmūla (Varāhamūla). He passed the first night on Kaśmīr soil at *Huṣkapura*, the modern Uṣkür, opposite Bārāmūla. Thence he proceeded to the capital which he describes

[1] Compare the explanations of Messrs. Lévi and Chavannes in their paper '*L'Itinéraire d'Ou-k'ong*, Journal asiatique, 1895, vi. pp. 371 *sqq.*, together with the supplementary and modifying statements, *ib.*, 1896, vii. pp. 161 *sq.*

[2] These notices are enumerated by Messrs. Lévi and Chavannes, *Journal asiat.*, 1895, vi. pp. 378 *sq.*

[3] G. PAUTHIER, *Examen méthodique des faits qui concernent le Thian-Tchou ou l'Inde*, Paris, 1839, p. 40.

[4] See *Si-yu-ki*, transl. Beal, i. pp. 148 *sqq.*; *Life of Hiuen Tsiang*, transl. Beal, pp. 68 *sqq.*

exactly in the position of the present S'rinagar. There he was lodged in the convent known as the *Jayendravihāra* which is named also in the Rājataraṅgiṇī.[1] A two years' stay, though chiefly passed in the study of 'the Sūtras and S'āstras', must have enabled Hiuen Tsiang to acquaint himself thoroughly with the Valley.

✓His description of the kingdom *Kia-shi-mi-lo* shows clearly that the geographical application of the term Kaśmīr must have been then, exactly as now, restricted to the great basin of the Vitastā and the side valleys drained by its tributaries above the Bārāmūla defile. He notices that the country is enclosed on all sides by mountains which are very high. "Although the mountains have passes through them, these are narrow and contracted." These natural bulwarks protected the country from neighbouring states 'which had never succeeded in subduing it.' Though the climate is cold and the snow plentiful, the soil is fertile and abounds with fruits and flowers. The inhabitants seem to have changed as little as the soil since Hiuen Tsiang's days. It is still easy to recognize in them the people whom he describes as "light and frivolous, and of a weak, pusillanimous disposition. The people are handsome in appearance, but they are given to cunning. They love learning and are well-instructed."

"Since centuries learning had been held in great respect in this kingdom." Hiuen Tsiang dwells with evident pleasure on the recollection of the learned conferences he had with the Kaśmīr doctors of the sacred law.[2] Kaśmīr had in earlier times played a great part in the traditions of the Buddhist church. Hiuen Tsiang relates at length the legends how the Arhat Madhyāntika had first spread the law of Buddha in the land; how in the time of Aśoka the five hundred Arhats had taken up their abode there; and how finally under the great Kaniṣka, king of Gandhāra, Kaśmīr had been the scene of the universal Council which fixed and expounded the Sacred Canon. Yet he observes that in his own time the kingdom as a whole was "not much given to the faith, and that the temples of the heretics were their sole thought."[3]

It is probably owing to this not very flourishing condition of contemporary Buddhism that Hiuen Tsiang mentions only a comparatively small number of Vihāras and Stūpas in the Valley. Among the Stūpas there were four ascribed to Aśoka. Beneath another Kaniṣka was believed to have deposited the canonical texts as fixed by his Council, engraved on sheets of copper. None of these structures have yet been

[1] Compare note iii. 355.

[2] See *Life*, p. 71 *sq*.

[3] See *Si-yu-ki*, i. p. 158.

identified with any certainty. But in their description the pilgrim furnishes us incidentally with a valuable topographical indication.

Speaking of the convent which prided itself on the possession of a miraculous tooth of Buddha, he indicates its site as being about 10 *li* (circ. 2 miles) to the south-east of the new city and to the north of the old city.[1] This proves that the capital of Hiuen Tsiang's time which corresponds to the present Śrīnagar, was then a comparatively new foundation, exactly as the Chronicle's account has it. At the same time the reference to the 'old city' enables us to fix with absolute certainty the earlier capital of Śrīnagarī at the present *Pāndrēṭhan*, the *Purāṇādhiṣṭhāna* of Kalhaṇa.[2]

√The two full years which Hiuen Tsiang, according to his own statement spent in Kaśmir,[3] represent a longer halt than any which the pious traveller allowed himself during his sixteen year's wanderings through the whole of India and Central Asia.[4] With all due respect for the spiritual fervour of the pilgrim and the excellence of his Kaśmīrian preceptors, it is difficult to suppress the surmise that the material attractions of the Valley had something to do with his long stay. The cool air of Kaśmīr, the northern aspect of its scenery and products, have at all times exercised their powerful charm over those visitors who themselves born in colder climes have come to the Valley from the heat and dust of the Indian plains. Just as these advantages attract in yearly increasing numbers European visitors from India Proper, so the modern Turkī pilgrims from Kashgar, Yarkand and other parts of Central Asia, whether on the way to Mecca or on their return, never fail to make a long stay in Kaśmīr.√

We should undoubtedly find the example of the modern Ḥājis followed also by Buddhist pilgrims if there were still any from those northern regions to take their way through Kaśmir to the holy places of India. It would be an interesting task to examine to what extent the fame of Kaśmīr as the 'paradis terrestre des Indes,' is the creation of the Valley's northern visitors, both European and Asiatic. Here it may suffice to add that Hiuen Tsiang before he reached Kaśmīr, must have had already his experience of the torrid heat and the other amenities of a Panjāb summer.[5] We shall also see that the example of the other Chinese pilgrim whom we are able to follow on his visit to Kaśmir, points exactly to the same conclusion.

1 *Si-yu-ki*, i. p. 158.

2 See below §§ 88, 89.

3 See *Life*, p. 72.

4 Compare the table of dates for Hiuen Tsiang's itinerary, CUNNINGHAM, *Ancient Geography*, pp. 563 *sqq*.

5 See CUNNINGHAM, *Ancient Geography*, p. 563 *sq*.

Hiuen Tsiang's narrative tells us that he left the Valley going in a south-westerly direction. He reached *Pun-nu-tso*, the Parṇotsa of the Chronicle and the modern Prūnts, after crossing mountains and passing precipices.[1] As the Tōṣamaidān route is the direct and most frequented route to that territory, it is very probable that Hiuen Tsiang also followed it. Parṇotsa as well as Rājapurī (Ho-lo-she-pu-lo) to which the pilgrim subsequently proceeded, had at the time of his visit no independent ruler, but were subject to Kaśmīr.

T'ang Annals.

10. The next Chinese notice of Kaśmīr, and one which is of considerable historical interest, is contained in the Annals of the T'ang dynasty.[2] They inform us that the first embassy from Kaśmīr arrived at the imperial court in or shortly after A.D. 713. In the year 720 *Tchen-t'o-lo-pi-li*, ruler of Kaśmīr, the Candrāpīḍa of the Chronicle, was accorded by imperial decree the title of king.

His brother and successor *Mou-to-pi* in whom Kalhaṇa's Muktāpīḍa or Lalitāditya has long ago been recognised, sent after the first Chinese expedition against *Po-liu* or Baltistān (between 736 and 747) an envoy called *Ou-li-to* to the Chinese court. He was to report the alleged victories of his master over the Tibetans but at the same time also to solicit the establishment of a camp of Chinese troops by the banks of the lake *Mo-ho-to-mo-loung* (the Mahāpadma Nāga or Volūr lake). The Kaśmīr king offered to provide all necessary supplies for an auxiliary force of 200,000 men. But the 'Divine Khān' found it more convenient to content himself with issuing decrees for the sumptuous entertainment of the ambassador and for the registration of Muktāpīḍa with the title of king. Since that time the relations of Kaśmīr with the celestial empire and the receipts of tribute from the former are said to have continued without interruption.

The description of Kaśmīr which is coupled with this record of the T'ang Annals, appears to be in the main copied from Hiuen Tsiang's *Si-yu-ki*. But in addition it furnishes us with an exact statement as to the Kaśmīr capital at that time. In my *Notes on Ou-k'ong's Account of*

1 *Si-yu-ki*, i. p. 162 *Life* p. 72.

2 The notice was first made known by A. RÉMUSAT's translation of the corresponding extract in Matuanlin's encyclopædia; see *Nouveaux Mélanges asiatiques*, Paris, 1829, i. pp. 196 *sqq.* An abstract of the same notice, but from the original text of the Annals, where the names are more correctly rendered, will be found in Messrs. LÉVI and CHAVANNES' *L'Itinéraire d'Ou-k'ong, Journal asiat.*, 1895, vi. pp. 354 *sqq.*

From REINAUD, *Mémoire sur l'Inde*, pp. 189 *sq.* it would appear that the names of Kaśmīr kings in this Chinese record and that of the Mahāpadma lake were first correctly identified by KLAPROTH, *Mémoires relatifs à l'Asie*, ii. pp. 275 *sq.* This work is at present not accessible to me.

Kaśmīr[1] I have shown that the *Po-lo-ou-lo-po-lo* of the Annals is a correct reproduction of *Pravarapura*, the old and official name of Śrīnagara. In the same way the name *Mi-na-si-to* given to the great river which flows to the west of the capital, represents a correct enough transcription of *Vitastā*. Both the names are recorded in the form which they bore in the official Sanskit, and are, therefore, evidently taken from the information given by the Kaśmīr envoys.

Ou-k'ong.

11. Not many years after Muktāpīḍa's embassy Kaśmīr was visited by another Chinese pilgrim, OU-K'ONG. Though greatly inferior to Hiuen Tsiang in learning and power of observation, he has yet left us information regarding the country which is of interest and value. The itinerary of Ou-k'ong the discovery and recent publication of which we owe to Messrs. Lévi and Chavannes,[2] contains the reminiscences of forty years' wanderings, taken down after the pilgrim's return to China and in a form regrettably brief. But whether it be due to Ou-k'ong's long stay in Kaśmīr or to other causes, his account is fortunately far more detailed in the case of Kaśmīr than in that of any other territory visited by him. His description of the Valley and the several sites mentioned by him have been fully discussed by me in the separate paper already quoted.[3] I need hence indicate here only the main results of this analysis.

Ou-k'ong reached Kaśmīr in the year 759 from Gandhāra, presumably by the same route as Hiuen Tsiang had followed. He took there the final vows of a Buddhist monk and spent there fully four years engaged, as his itinerary tells us, in pilgrimages to holy sites and in the study of Sanskrit.[4] Though he is said to have studied from day-break till night-fall, his diligence does not seem to have brought him much literary culture. This is curiously shown by the popular Apabhraṁśa forms in which our pilgrim records the names of the monasteries he specially singles out for notice. Four of these I have been able to identify with Vihāras mentioned in the Chronicle,[5] and two of them have left their names to villages which survive to the present day.

1 See pp. 26 *sqq.* in the above-quoted paper, published in the "Proceedings" of the Imperial Academy, Vienna (Philos.-histor. Class), 1896, vol. cxxxv.

2 See *L' Itinéraire d'Ou-k'ong*, Journal asiat., 1895, vi. pp. 341 *sqq.*

3 See *Notes on Ou-k'ong's account of Kaśmīr, loc. cit.*

4 See *L' Itinéraire d'Ou-k'ong*, p. 356.

5 Thus the monastery of *Ngo-mi-t'o-p'o-wan* (**Amitabhavana*) corresponds to the *Amṛtabhavana* Vihāra of Rājat. iii. 9, which has given its name to the present *Ântᵃbavan* near Śrīnagar. The 'monastère du mont *Ki-tché*, (**Kicā* < Skr. *kṛtyā*) is no other than the *Kṛtyāśrama Vihāra*, at the modern village *Kiṭsᵃhōm*, the legend of which is related at length by Kalhaṇa, i. 131 *sqq.* The Vihāra of the great king *Moung-ti* (*Mutti) was one of Muktāpīḍa's foundations, probably the *Mukta-

While Hiuen Tsiang mentions only about one hundred convents in the country, Ou-k'ong found more than three hundred and speaks in addition of the number of Stūpas and sacred images as considerable. We may conclude from this that there had been a rise in the popularity of Buddhism in the century intervening between the visits of the two pilgrims.

✓ Ou-k'ong describes the kingdom of Kaśmīr correctly enough as enclosed on all sides by mountains which form its natural ramparts. Only three roads have been opened through them, and these again are secured by gates. In the east a road leads to *T'ou-fan* or Tibet; in the north there is a road which reaches into *Poliu* or Baltistān; the road which starts from 'the western gate' goes to *K'ien-t'o-lo* or Gandhāra.[1]

We have here a clear enough description of the great routes through the mountains which since ancient times have formed the main lines of communication between the Valley and the outer world. The road to *T'ou-fan* corresponds undoubtedly to the present route over the *Zoji-Lā* to Ladākh and hence to Tibet. The road to *Po-liu* is represented by the present "Gilgit Road," leading into the Upper Kiṣangaṅgā Valley and thence to Skardo or Astōr on the Indus. The third road can be no other than the route which leaves the Valley by the gorge of Bārāmūla and follows the Vitastā in its course to the west. We have seen already that Hiuen Tsiang followed it when he entered Kaśmīr by 'the stone gate, the western entrance of the kingdom.' There can be doubt that in the gates (*fermetures*) closing these roads we have a reference to the ancient frontier watch-stations of which we find so frequent mention in our Kaśmīrian records.

Besides these three roads Ou-k'ong knew yet a fourth. "This, however, is always closed and opens only when an imperial army honours it with a visit." It is probable that this curious notice must be referred to one of the roads leading over the Pīr Pantsāl range to the south. Owing possibly to political causes these routes may have been closed to ordinary traffic at the time of Ou-k'ong's visit.[2]

The political relations between China and the northern kingdoms of India seem to have ceased soon after the time of Ou-k'ong. This was probably due to the Chinese power under the later T'ang gradually losing ground in Central Asia before the Uigurs and the Tibetans. The

vihāra at Huṣkapura: Uṣkür, iv. 188. In the 'monastère du général (*tsiang-kiun*)' it is easy to recognize the Vihāra of the Turk (Tuḥkhāra) *Caṅkuṇa* who was one of Muktāpīḍa's ministers. He is reported to have founded two monasteries called after his own name (iv. 211, 215).

1 See *L' Itinéraire d'Ou-k'ong*, p. 356.

2 See *Notes on Ou-k'ong*, p. 24 *sq.*

pilgrimages, however, of Chinese Buddhists to India continued during the next two centuries, and of one at least of these pilgrim parties it is recorded that it took the route through Kaśmīr.[1] But no detailed account bearing on Kaśmīr has yet come to light of these later pilgrimages.

Section III.—Muhammadan notices.

Kaśmīr closed to Arab geographers.

12. After the Greeks and the Chinese the early Muhammadan writers are our next foreign informants regarding the historical geography of India. If with one very remarkable exception they have nothing to tell us of Kaśmīr topography, the explanation is not far to seek. The first rush of Arab invasion in the Indus Valley during the eighth century had carried the Muhammadan arms at times close enough to the confines of Kaśmīr.[2] No permanent conquest, however, had been effected even in the plains of the Northern Panjāb. Protected in the West by the unbroken resistance of the S'āhis of Kābul and in the South by a belt of war-like Hindu hill-states, Kaśmīr had never been seriously threatened. Even when Islām at last after a long struggle victoriously over-spread the whole of Northern India, Kaśmīr behind its mountain ramparts remained safe for centuries longer.

Conquest and trade were the factors which brought so large a part of the ancient world within the ken of the early Muhammadan travellers and geographers. Both failed them equally in the case of Kaśmīr. For a classical witness shows us that a system of seclusion,—ever easy to maintain in a country so well guarded by nature as Kaśmīr,—hermetically sealed at that time the Valley to all foreigners without exception.

Even the well-informed Al-Mas'ūdī who had personally visited the Indus Valley, is unable to tell us more about Kaśmīr than that it is a kingdom with many towns and villages enclosed by very high and inaccessible mountains, through which leads a single passage closed by a gate.[3] The notices we find in the works of Al-Qazwīnī and Al-Idrīsī are practically restricted to the same brief statement. The references in other geographical works are even more succinct and vague.[4]

1 Compare Yule, *Cathay*, p. lxxi., and Julien, *Journal asiat.*, 1847, p. 43.

2 See Reinaud, *Mémoire sur l'Inde*, pp. 195 *sq.*; Alberūnī, *India*, i. p. 21.

3 See *Al-Mas'ūdī's* "Meadows of Gold," transl. Sprenger, i. p. 382.

4 The silence of the early Muhammadan geographers as regards Kaśmīr was duly noticed by Ritter, *Asia*, ii. p. 1115.—For Al-Qazwīnī, see Gildemeister, *De rebus Indicis*, p 210; for Al-Idrīsī, Elliot, *History of India*, i. pp. 90. *sq.*

For the notices of other Arab geographers, see *Bibliotheca geographorum*

13. Notwithstanding the circumstances above indicated, Arabic literature furnishes us with a very accurate and valuable account of old Kaśmīr. We owe it to the research and critical penetration of

Albērūnī's interest in Kaśmīr.

ALBĒRŪNĪ of whom indeed it might be said as of an early British explorer of Afghānistān,[1] that he could look through the mountains. The great Muhammadan scholar had evidently utilized every opportunity during his long stay at Ghazna and in the Panjāb, (A.D. 1017-30) for collecting information on Kaśmīr.

His interest in the distant alpine valley is easily understood. He, himself, tells us in the first chapter of his great work on India, how Hindu sciences when the victories of Maḥmūd had made the Hindus 'like atoms of dust scattered in all directions,' had retired far away from the conquered parts of the country. They "fled to places which our hand cannot yet reach, to Kaśmīr, Benares and other places."[2] In another passage he speaks again of Benares and Kaśmīr as the high schools of Hindu sciences.[3] He repeatedly refers to Kaśmīrian authors, and from the notices shown below it is evident that among his informants, if not among his actual teachers, there were Kaśmīrian scholars.[4]

The curious fact that Albērūnī himself composed some Sanskrit treatises for circulation among 'the people of Kaśmīr,'[5] proves beyond all

arabicorum, ed. De Goeje, i. p. 4; ii. pp. 9, 445; v. p. 364; vi. pp. 5, 18, 68; vii. pp. 89, 687; also *Abū-l-Fidā*, ed. Reinaud, pp. 361, 506.

1 Mountstuart Elphinstone.

2 ALBĒRŪNĪ's *India*, transl. Sachau, i. p. 22.

3 *India*, i. p. 173.

4 Albērunī, ii. 181, refers particularly to Kaśmīrian informants with whom he conversed regarding the miracle of the '*Kūdaishahr*,' *i.e.*, the *Kapaṭeśvara* Tīrtha (see below § 112). The way in which the pilgrimage to this spot was described to Albērūnī, makes it quite certain that his informants were personally familiar with the Tīrtha. The same must be said of his note on the pilgrimage to the temple of Śāradā (i. 117; see below § 127). The details regarding a local Kaśmīr festival (ii. p. 178), the anecdote about the propagation of the *Śiṣyahitāvṛtti* in Kaśmīr (i. 135), are such as could not well have reached Albērūnī otherwise but by verbal communication.

Writing himself in A.D. 1030 he refers to a statement contained in the almanac for the Śaka year 951 (A.D. 1029-30) 'which had came from Kashmīr' (i. p. 391). He could scarcely have secured such an almanac except through Kaśmīrian Paṇḍits who even at the present day, wherever they may be, make it a point to provide themselves from home with their local *nakṣatrapattrikā*.

For references to Kaśmīrian authors or texts specially connected with Kaśmīr, see i. pp. 126, 157, 298, 334, i. p. 54 (Viṣṇudharma), etc. Compare also the very detailed account of the calendar reckoning current in Kaśmīr and the conterminous territories, ii. p. 8.

5 See *India*, Prof. Sachau's preface, p. xxiv., and the introduction to his edition of the text, p. xx.

doubt the existence of special relations between the great *Mleccha* scholar and that jealously guarded country. These relations seem strange considering what Albērūnī himself tells us so graphically about the rigid isolation of Kaśmīr. We can scarcely explain them otherwise than by personal intercourse with Kaśmīrian Pandits.

In view of these indications we can hardly go wrong in attributing a great portion of Albērūnī's detailed knowledge of Kaśmīr topography to these learned informants. But we also know that the chances of war had given him an opportunity of supplementing this knowledge in part by personal observation. Albērūnī refers in two places to his personal acquaintance with the fortress *Lauhūr* (or Lahūr) on the confines of Kaśmīr. In an extract from my commentary on the Rājataraṅgiṇī already published,[1] I have proved that Albērūnī's Lauhūr is identical with the castle of *Lohara*, so frequently mentioned in the Chronicle. Its position is marked by the present Lohᵊrin on the southern slope of the Pīr Pants̱āl range.

'Loharakoṭṭa' is undoubtedly the same as the Fort of Lōh-kōt which according to the uniform report of the Muhammadan historians brought Maḥmūd's attempt at an invasion of Kaśmīr to a standstill. It is hence certain that Albērūnī had accompanied this unsuccessful expedition. It probably took place in A.D. 1021. Though it failed to reach Kaśmīr, it must have given Albērūnī ample opportunity to collect local information and to acquaint himself with the topography of those mountain regions which formed Kaśmīr's strongest bulwark to the south. The result is yet clearly traceable in the accuracy with which he describes the relative position of the most prominent points of this territory.

Is it too much to suppose that Albērūnī had at one time or the other Kaśmīrian Paṇḍits in his employ? We know that in preparing the vast materials digested in his book he worked largely with the help of indigenous scholars. Judging from his own description of the state of Hindu sciences in the conquered territories and the bitter enmity prevailing there against the dominant Mlecchas, it is doubtful whether he could have secured there such assistance as he required.

Albērūnī himself, when describing the difficulties in the way of his Indian studies, tells us (i. p. 24): "I do not spare either trouble or money in collecting Sanskrit books from places where I supposed they were likely to be found, and in procuring for myself, even from very remote places, Hindu scholars who understand them and are able to teach me."

Kaśmīr has always been distinguished by an over-production of learning. Its Paṇḍits have been as ready in old days as at present to leave their homes for distant places wherever their learning secured for them a livelihood (compare BÜHLER, Introd. to the *Vikramāṅkadevacarita*, p. xvii; also *Indische Palæographie*, p. 56).

[1] See my note on the '*Castle of Lohara*,' *Indian Antiquary*, 1897, pp. 225 *sqq.*, or Note *E*, on Rājat. iv. 177, §§ 12, 13.

Albērūnī's account of Kaśmīr.

14. Albērūnī's main account of Kaśmīr is contained in Chapter xviii. which gives 'various notes on the countries of the Hindus, their rivers and their ocean.'[1] Compared with the description of the rest of India, it is disproportionately detailed. Albērūnī first sketches in broad but correct outlines the political division of the mountain region which lies between the great Central Asian watershed and the Panjāb plain. He then refers to the pedestrian habits of the Kaśmīrians and notes the use by the nobles of palankins carried on the shoulders of men, a custom fully illustrated by the Chronicle and accounted for by the nature of the communications in the mountains.[2]

What follows deserves full quotation. "They are particularly anxious about the natural strength of their country, and therefore take always much care to keep a strong hold upon the entrances and roads leading into it. In consequence it is very difficult to have any commerce with them. In former times they used to allow one or two foreigners to enter their country, particularly Jews, but at present they do not allow any Hindu whom they do not know personally to enter, much less other people."

We have here a full and clear statement of that system of guarding all frontier-passes which we have found alluded to already in the Chinese records. It explains the great part which is played in the Kaśmīr Chronicles by the frontier watch-stations, the *Dvāras* and *Draṅgas*. It is of all the more interest as the last traces of the system, in the form of *rāhdārī*, have disappeared in Kaśmīr only within quite recent memory.[3]

Albērūnī then proceeds to describe the 'best known entrance to Kashmīr.' Though the starting point of his itinerary cannot be identified with absolute certainty, it is clear that he means the route which ascends the Jehlam Valley. From "the town *Babrahān*, half way between the rivers Sindh (Indus) and Jailam, 8 farsakh are counted to the bridge over the river where the water of the *Kusnārī* is joined by that of the *Mahwī*, both of which come from the mountains of *Shamīlān* and fall into the Jailam." Though there seems to be here some slight confusion, I have little doubt that the point meant by 'the bridge over the river' corresponds to the present Muzaffarābād, at the confluence

1 See *India*, i. pp. 206 *sqq*.

2 Compare e.g. *Rājat* iv. 407; v. 33, 219; vii. 478; viii. 2298, 2636, 2674, 3165, etc.

The word *katt* which Albērūnī gives as the indigenous term of the palankin, is perhaps a corrupted Apabhraṁśa form of *karṇīratha*, often named in the Rājat.

3 Compare my *Notes on the Ancient Topography of the Pīr Pantsāl Route*, *J. A. S. B.*, 1895, pp. 382 *sqq*; also below § 40.

of the Jehlam and Kiṣangaṅgā. The easiest route to Kaśmīr from the west leads through the open central portion of Hazāra (Uraśā) to Mansahra; hence across the Kunhār and Kiṣangaṅgā rivers to Muẓaffarābād, and then up by the right side of the Jehlam Valley to Bārāmūla.[1] In *Kusnārī* it is easy to recognize with Prof. Sachau the present Kunhār River which falls into the Jehlam a few miles below its great bend at Muẓaffarābād.[2] The Mahwī is evidently meant to designate the Kiṣangaṅgā.[3] If thus interpreted the only error in Albērūnī's description is that it makes the Kunhār join the Kiṣangangā whereas in reality it falls into the Jehlam after the latter's junction with the Kiṣangaṅgā.

I have shown in my note on Rājat. v. 215 that the route here indicated, which was a favorite one until the modern "Jehlam Valley Tonga Road" was constructed, is distinctly referred to already in Kalhaṇa's account of S'aṁkaravarman's march to and from Uraśā. The distance of 8 farsakh corresponds according to Albērūnī's reckoning to about 39 English miles.[4] Referring to the map and the modern route measurements[5] this distance carries us to a point between Mansahra and the next stage Abbottabad, *i.e.*, exactly into the neighbourhood where according to the evidence given in the above-quoted note the old capital of Uraśā must be located. 'Babrahān' which cannot be identified at present, is perhaps intended to represent the name of this old town which could fairly be described as situated midway between the Indus and Jehlam.

From Muẓaffarābād onwards,—where there is still a bridge over the Kiṣangaṅgā just as at the time (1783) when Forster crossed here on his way from Kaśmīr to Attock,[6] and as, if our explanation is right, in the time of Albērūnī,—we can follow the route quite plainly. Albērūnī counts five days of march "to the beginning of the ravine whence the

1 This route is described, *e.g.*, by Drew, *Jummoo*, p. 528, 'as the easiest route from the Panjāb to Kaśmīr.'

2 *Kunhār* represents the regular phonetic derivative of a Skr. **Kuśnārī*, medial *ś* becoming always *h* under a phonetic law common to Kaśmīrī and the related dialects; for the change *hn* > *nh* compare Grierson, *Phonology of Indo-Aryan Vernaculars, Z. D. M. G.*, 1896, p. 33.

3 I am unable to account for the name *Mahwī*. Could it be the corruption of an Apabhraṁśa derivative of *Madhumatī*? This name, though properly applied to an affluent of the Kiṣangaṅgā, is used in a Māhātmya also for the latter river itself; see Note *B*, Rājat. i. 37, § 16.

4 Compare Prof. Sachau's note, *India*, ii. p. 316. Albērūnī values his *farsakh* at 4 Arabian miles or approximately 4 × 2186 yards. Hence 1 *farsakh* = $4\frac{1704}{1760}$ English miles.

5 See Drew, *loc. cit.*

6 See G. Forster, *Journey from Bengal to England*, 1808, ii. p. 46.

river Jailam comes,' that is, of the gorge through which the river flows immediately below Bārāmūla. This estimate agrees closely with the actual road distance between Muzaffarābād and Bārāmūla which is given by Drew as 84 miles.[1] At the other or Kaśmīr end of the ravine Alberūnī places quite correctly 'the watch-station *Dvār*' (Skr. *Dvāra*) the position of which, as we shall see below, is marked to this day by the site of the old gate known as *Drang*.

Alberūnī's description of the Valley.

"Thence leaving the ravine you enter the plain, and reach in two more days *Addishtān*, the capital of Kashmīr, passing on the road the village *Ushkārā*." All this is perfectly accurate. Adhiṣṭhāna 'the capital' is, of course, meant for Śrīnagara[2] and Ushkārā for *Uṣkür*, opposite Bārāmūla, the ancient Huṣkapura already mentioned by Hiuen Tsiang.[3] Alberūnī's mention of Uṣkür which is on the left river bank, shows that then as now the ordinary road from the 'Gate of Varāhamūla' to Śrīnagara passed on the left or southern side of the Valley. Two marches are still counted for this part of the journey.

The capital is correctly described as "being built along both banks of the river Jailam which are connected with each other by bridges and ferry boats." It is said to cover 'a space of four *farsakh*.' This if interpreted to mean 'a space of four Farsakh in circumference,' would not be too far from the truth, assuming that all suburban areas around the city are included in the estimate. The course of the river above and below the capital is traced rightly enough as far as the Valley is concerned. "When the Jailam has left the mountains and has flowed two days' journey, it passes through Addishtān. Four Farsakh farther on it enters a swamp of one square Farsakh." Here, of course, the Volur lake (Mahāpadma) is meant. "The people have their plantations on the borders of this swamp, and on such parts of it as they manage to

1 See *loc. cit.* According to Drew's table six marches are counted, but one of them is very short. On the modern route following the opposite side of the river five marches are now reckoned from Domēl, opposite to Muzaffarābād, to Bārāmūla.

2 *Adhiṣṭhāna*, used again ii. p. 181, is a term which indicates that Alberūnī's informant was a Sanskrit-speaking person. The common designation of the capital was *Śrīnagara* or simply *Nagara*; see § 91 below.

3 The text as rendered by Prof. Sachau, speaks of "*Ushkārā* which lies on both sides of the Valley, in the same manner as *Barāmūlā*." There is either some corruption in the text here or Alberūnī's informant had not made himself sufficiently clear. What he must have meant, is that Ushkārā lay on the opposite side of the river in the same manner as Barāmūlā, that is at the entrance of the ravine. Barāmūlā as the text spells the name, reproduces an earlier form of the Kaśmīrī *Varahmul*, from Skr. *Varāhamūla*.

reclaim. Leaving this swamp, the Jailam passes the town of Ūshkārā, and then enters the above-mentioned ravine."

The only mistake and this one easily explained is contained in the account of the river's origin. It is described as rising "in the mountains *Haramakōt* where also the Ganges rises; cold, impenetrable regions where the snow never melts nor disappears." It is easy to recognize here the reference to Mount *Haramukuṭa* and the sacred Gaṅgā-lake at the foot of its glacier in which Kaśmīrian tradition places the source of the Sindhu river.[1] The latter is the greatest tributary of the Vitastā within Kaśmīr and is traditionally identified with the Gaṅgā, as on the other hand the Vitastā with the Yamunā.[2] The special sanctity of the Sindu ('Uttaragaṅgā') and the popularity of its supposed source as a pilgrimage place sufficiently account for the substitution in Albērūnī's notice.

Entering the open plain of the Kaśmīr Valley by the Bārāmūla gorge "you have for a march of two more days, on your left the mountains of Bolor and Shamīlān, Turkish tribes who are called *Bhattavaryān*. Their king has the title of *Bhatta-Shāh*." It is clear that Albērūnī's informant here means the mountain ranges to the north and north-west of the Valley which form its borders towards the Dard country and Baltistān. The latter has been known by the name of Bolor for many centuries.[3] I am unable to trace in Kaśmīrian or other sources the names of the 'Shamīlān' and 'Bhatta.'[4] But as a subsequent remark mentions '*Gilgit*, *Aswīra*, and *Shiltās*,' that is the modern Gilgit, Hasōr (Astōr) and Cilās as their chief places, there can be no doubt that the inhabitants of the Dard territory to the north-west of Kaśmīr are meant together with the Baltis.

Description of Pīr Pantsāl.

"Marching on the right side [of the river], you pass through villages, one close to the other, south of the capital and thence you reach the mountain *Kulārjak*, which is like a cupola, similar to the

1 See below, § 57, and Rājat. note i. 57.

2 See *Rājat.* note i. 57. In *Haracar.* iv. 54 the Vitastā itself is designated as the 'Gaṅgā of the north' (Uttaragaṅgā). This renders the location of its source in the lake of Haramukuṭa still more intelligible from a traditional point of view.

3 Compare YULE, *Marco Polo*, i. pp. 187, sq.; CUNNINGHAM, *Anc. Geogr.*, p. 83.

4 Albērūnī's *Bhatta* may possibly represent the term *Bhuṭṭa* or *Bhauṭṭa* (the modern Kś. *Buṭ*[a]) which is applied in the Sanskrit Chronicles to the population of Tibetan descent generally, from Ladākh to Baltistān. (See *Rājat.* note i. 312). Albērūnī calls their language Turkish, but it must be remembered that he has spoken previously (i. p. 206) of 'the Turks of Tibet' as holding the country to the east of Kaśmīr. There the Tibetans in Ladākh and adjacent districts are clearly intended.

mountain *Dunbāwand* (Damāwand). The snow there never melts. It is always visible from the region of Tākēshar and Lauhāwar (Lahore)."

I have already elsewhere shown that the mountain here described is the *Taṭakūṭī* peak (33° 45′ lat. 74° 33′ long.).[1] It rises to a height of 15,500 feet in the central part of the Pīr Pantsāl range and is the loftiest as well as the most conspicuous point of the mountain chain to the south of Kaśmīr. It has the shape described by Albērūnī, is surrounded by extensive snow-fields and can be seen through the greatest part of the year from the Panjāb districts of Siālkōt and Gujrānwāla corresponding to the old Tākēshar (Ṭakkadeśa). Albērūnī puts the distance between this peak and the Kaśmīr plain at two farsakh. This estimate is somewhat too low, inasmuch as the direct distance on the map between the peak and the nearest point of the open Valley is about 15 miles.

He is, however, quite exact in placing the fortress *Lauhūr* to the west of it as we have already seen that this stronghold is identical with the *Loharakoṭṭa* of the Chronicle, the present Lohᵃrin. The entrance to the Lohᵃrin Valley lies almost due west of Taṭakūṭī. To the south of the peak he places 'the fortress *Rājagiri*' which is also mentioned by Kalhaṇa, vii. 1270, and must be looked for somewhere in the Upper Sūran Valley. Albērūnī speaks of these two hill fortresses as "the strongest places" he had ever seen.

He had personally had an opportunity of judging of their strength when accompanying Maḥmūd's expedition against Kaśmīr. On that occasion he had made the observation of the latitude of Lauhūr (Lohara) to which he refers in another chapter of his work.[2] The result of this observation, 33° 40′ lat. as shown in the author's Canon Masudicus, very closely approaches the real one, which is 33° 48′ according to the Survey map. It is very probable that he obtained at the same occasion the very accurate information regarding the distance from Lauhūr to the Kaśmīr capital. He gives it as 56 miles, "half the way being rugged country, the other half plain." Albērūnī's measurement according to the previously stated valuation represents about 69 English miles. This is but little in excess of the actual road distance viâ the Tōṣᵃmaidan pass as estimated by me on the tour referred to in the above-quoted paper. The description of the road, too, corresponds closely to the actual character of the route.

Albērūnī closes his account of Kaśmīr geography with a reference to the town of *Rājawarī* which is the *Rājapurī* of the Chronicles, the

1 See my paper '*The Castle of Lohara*,' *Ind. Ant.*, 1897, § 12.

2 See *India*, i. p. 317, with Prof. Sachau's note ii. p. 341. In the same passage he quotes the latitude of S'rīnagar as 34° 9′ from the *Karaṇasāra*.

modern *Rajauri.* In Hindu times it was the capital of a small hill-state situated immediately to the south of the Pīr Pantsāl range and often tributary to Kaśmīr. Albērūnī distinctly names it as the farthest place to which Muhammadan merchants of his time traded and beyond which they never passed. We have already seen what the connection was which enabled him to collect reliable and detailed information of the region beyond that barrier. As another proof of the accurate knowledge thus acquired, we may finally mention his description of the Kaśmīr climate which is far more exact than any account available to us previous to the second quarter of this century.[1]

Section IV.—Indian notices.

Deficiency of non-Kaśmīrian texts.

15. Nothing, perhaps, can illustrate better the lamentable lack of exact geographical information in general Sanskrit literature than to turn from the accounts of the Chinese pilgrims and Albērūnī to what Indian authors, not Kaśmīrians themselves, can tell us of the Valley.

Were we to judge merely from the extreme scantiness of the data to be gleaned from their extant works, we might easily be led to assume that Kaśmīr was to them a country foreign and remote in every way. However, we observe the same vagueness and insufficiency of local references in the case of territories immediately adjoining the old centres of literary activity. It is hence evident that the conspicuous absence of useful information on Kaśmīr may equally well be attributed to the general character of that literature.

The name *Kaśmīra,* with its derivative *Kāśmīra,* as the designation of the country and its inhabitants, respectively, is found already in the Gaṇas to Pāṇini's grammar and in Patañjali's comments thereon.[2] The Mahābhārata too refers in several passages to the *Kāśmīras* and their rulers, but in a fashion so general and vague that nothing more but the situation of the country in the hill region to the north can be concluded therefrom.[3]

The Purāṇas enumerate the *Kāśmīras* accordingly in their lists of northern nations. But none of the tribal names, partly semi-mythical,

[1] See *India*, i. p. 211, and below, § 77.

[2] See the references in the Thesaurus of Böhtlingk-Roth, s. v. *Kāśmira*, and in supplement V., p. 1273. The references to other texts in this paragraph have also been taken from that work except where otherwise specified.

[3] Compare in particular *Mahābh.* II. xxvii. 17.

which are mentioned along with them in the Purāṇas examined by me, indicate any more distinct location of the country.[1]

Varāhamihira (circ. 500 A.D.) in his *Bṛhatsaṁhitā* includes the Kāśmīras curiously enough in the north-eastern division. Among the regions and peoples named under the same heading there are a number of purely legendary character like 'the kingdom of the dead' (*naṣṭa-rājya*), the 'gold region,' 'the one-footed people,' etc. But besides these names and others of a different type which cannot be clearly identified, we recognize the names of tribes which undoubtedly must be located in the immediate neighbourhood of Kaśmīr. Thus we have the *Abhisāras, Daradas, Dārvas, Khaśas, Kīras*, and somewhat more distant the country of *Kulūta* (Kulu) and the *Kauṇindas* or *Kaulindras* (Ptolemy's Κυλινδρίνη).[2]

Perhaps the most specific piece of information regarding Kaśmīr that Sanskrit literature outside the Valley can convey to us, is contained in the term *Kāśmīra* or *Kāśmīraja* which designates the saffron and according to the lexicographers also the root of the *kuṣṭha* or *costus speciosus*. Both the saffron and the Kuṣṭha have since early times been famous products of Kaśmīr.[3]

SECTION V.—THE KAS'MĪR CHRONICLES.

Abundance of Kaśmīrian sources.

16. The want of detailed and exact geographical information just noticed in old Indian literature generally stands in striking contrast to the abundance of data supplied for our knowledge of old Kaśmīr by the indigenous sources. The explanation is surely not to be found in the mere fact that Kaśmīrian authors naturally knew more of their own country than others for whom that alpine territory was a distant, more or less inaccessible region. For were it so, we might reasonably expect to find ourselves equally well informed about the early topography of other

1 Compare *Vāyupur.* xlv. 120; xlii. 45; *Padmapur.* I. vi. 48, 62; *Bhāgavatapur.* XII. i. 39; *Viṣṇupur.* IV. xxiv. 18.

2 See *Bṛhatsaṁhitā*, xiv. 29 *sqq.*, and *Ind. Ant.*, 1893, pp. 172, 181; also ALBĒRŪNĪ, *India*, i. p. 303.

3 Regarding the saffron cultivation of Kaśmīr, compare LAWRENCE, *Valley*, p. 342, and below, § 78.

The *kuṣṭha*, now known in Kaśmīr by the name of *kuṭh*, is the aromatic root of the Saussurea Lappa which grows in abundance on the mountains of Kaśmīr; see LAWRENCE, p. 77. The *kuṭh* is still largely exported to China and might be hence one of the medicinal plants which Hiuen Tsiang particularly notices among Kaśmīr products; see *Si-yu-ki*, i. p. 148.

parts of India which have furnished their contingent to the phalanx of Sanskrit authors. Yet unfortunately this is by no means the case.

The advantageous position we enjoy in Kaśmīr is due to a combination of causes of which the most important ones may at once be here indicated. In the first place we owe it to the preservation of connected historical records from a comparatively early date which acquaint us with a large number of particular localities and permit us to trace their connection with the country's history.

Another important advantage results from the fact that Kaśmīr, thanks chiefly to its geographical position and the isolation resulting from it, has escaped those great ethnic and political changes which have from time to time swept over the largest portion of India. Local tradition has thus remained undisturbed and still clings to all prominent sites with that tenacity which is characteristic of alpine tracts all over the world. The information preserved by this local tradition in Kaśmīr has often proved for our written records a most welcome supplement and commentary.

Finally it must be remembered that in a small mountain country like Kaśmīr, where the natural topographical features are so strongly marked and so permanent, the changes possible in historical times as regards routes of communication, sites for important settlements, cultivated area, etc., are necessarily restricted. The clear and detailed evidence which the facts of the country's actual topography thus furnish, enables us to elucidate and to utilize our earlier data, even where they are scanty, with far greater certainty and accuracy than would be possible on another ground. The observations here briefly indicated will be in part illustrated by the review of our Kaśmirian sources.

Kalhaṇa's Rājataraṅgiṇī.

17. Epigraphical records on stone or copper such as elsewhere in India form the safest basis for the study of local topography, have not yet come to light in Kaśmīr. The few fragmentary inscriptions hitherto found are all of a late date and do not furnish any topographical information. In their absence Kalhaṇa's Rājataraṅgiṇī is not only the amplest but also the most authentic of our sources for the historical geography of Kaśmīr. The questions connected with the historical value of the work, its scope and sources, have been fully discussed in the introduction to my translation. Here we have only to consider its character as our chief source of information on the old topography of Kaśmīr.

KALHAṆA's work, composed in the years 1148-49 A.D., is our oldest record of the history of the various dynasties which ruled Kaśmīr from the earliest period to the time of the author. The earlier Chronicles which Kalhaṇa has used and quoted, have all been lost. We are hence unable to judge what he took from each, and how he worked up their contents. Largely legendary in the first three Books, his narrative reaches firm historical ground with the Kārkoṭa dynasty in the Fourth Book. From Avantivarman's reign (A.D. 855–883) onwards which opens the Fifth Taraṅga, the Chronicle may be considered an accurate and reliable historical record. As the author approaches his own time, his narrative grows more and more detailed.

In illustration of the latter fact it may be mentioned that of the whole work comprising nearly eight thousand S'lokas, more than one-half is devoted to the relation of the reigns which fill the century and a half immediately preceding the date of composition. We have certainly no reason to regret the fulness with which Books vii. and viii. relate the events of the author's own time and of the period that lay near it. From a historical point of view, Kalhaṇa's detailed account of contemporary history and the near past must always retain its value. We can appreciate its advantages also with special regard to the elucidation of the old topography of the country. This will become at once clear by a brief analysis of the topographical information contained in the Chronicle.

It is doubtful whether Kalhaṇa writing for readers of his own country and time, would have deemed it necessary to give us a connected and matter-of-fact description of the land, even if the literature which he knew and which was his guide, had furnished him with a model or suggestion for such a description. The nearest approach to it is contained in a brief passage of his introduction, i. 25–38. This acquaints us in a poetical form with the legends concerning the creation of Kaśmīr and its sacred river, the Vitastā, and enumerates besides the most famous of the many Tīrthas of which Kaśmīr has ever boasted in abundance. The few panegyric remarks which are added in praise of the land's spiritual and material comforts, i. 39–43, do credit to the author's love of his native soil. But they can scarcely be held to raise the above to a real description of the country.

Kalhaṇa's notices of Tīrthas.

18. Notwithstanding the absence of such a description Kalhaṇa's Chronicle yet proves by far our richest source of information for the historical geography of Kaśmīr. This is due to the mass of incidental notices of topographical interest which are spread through the whole length of the narrative. They group themselves conveniently under three main heads.

Considering the great attention which the worship of holy places has at all times claimed in Kaśmīr, we may well speak first of the notices which appertain to the *Topographia sacra* of the Valley. Kaśmīr has from early times to the present day been a land abundantly endowed with holy sites and objects of pilgrimages. Kalhaṇa duly emphasizes this fact when he speaks, in the above-quoted introductory passage, of Kaśmīr as a country 'where there is not a space as large as a grain of sesamum without a Tīrtha.'[1]

Time and even the conversion to Islām of the great majority of the population has changed but little in this respect. For besides the great Tīrthas which still retain a fair share of their former renown and popularity, there is scarcely a village which has not its sacred spring or grove for the Hindu and its Ziārat for the Muhammadan. Established as the latter shrines almost invariably are, by the side of the Hindu places of worship and often with the very stones taken from them, they plainly attest the abiding nature of local worship in Kaśmīr.

This cannot be the place to examine in detail the origin and character of these Tīrthas and their importance for the religious history of the country. It will be enough to note that the most frequent objects of such ancient local worship are the springs or *Nāgas*, the sacred streams and rivers, and finally the so-called *svayaṁbhū* or 'self-created' images of gods which are recognized by the eye of the pious in various natural formations. These several classes of Tīrthas can be traced throughout India wherever Hindu religious notions prevail, and particularly in the sub-Himalayan regions (Nepāl, Kumaon, Kāngra, Udyāna or Swāt). Still there can be no doubt that Kaśmīr has from old times claimed an exceptionally large share in such manifestations of divine favour.

Nature has indeed endowed the Valley and the neighbouring mountains with an abundance of fine springs. As each of these has its tutelary deity in the form of a *Nāga*,[2] we can easily realize why popular tradition looks upon Kaśmīr as the favourite residence of these deities.[3] Hiuen Tsiang already had ascribed the superiority of Kaśmīr over other countries to the protection it received from a Nāga.[4] Kalhaṇa, too, in his introduction gives due prominence to the distinction which the land

[1] i. 38.

[2] Compare my note i. 30 on the Nāgas and their worship.

[3] The *Nīlamatapurāṇa*, 900–972, gives a long list of Kaśmīr Nāgas and puts their number at thousands, nay *Arbudas* (see 971).

[4] *Si-yu-ki*, i. p. 148. Hiuen Tsiang, like other Chinese pilgrims, calls the Nāgas by the term of 'dragon;' no doubt because the popular conception represents them under the form of snakes living in the water of the springs or lakes they protect.

enjoys as the dwelling-place of *Nīla*, king of Nāgas, and of many other of his tribe.[1]

Kalhaṇa's frequent references to sacred springs and other Tīrthas are of topographical interest, because they enable us to trace with certainty the earlier history of most of the popular pilgrimage places still visited to the present day. The list already mentioned acquaints us with the miraculous springs of *Pāpasūdana* and *Tri-Saṁdhyā*, *Sarasvatī's* lake on the *Bheḍa* hill, the 'Self-created Fire' (*Svayaṁbhū*), and the holy sites of *Nandikṣetra*, *Śāradā*, *Cakradhara* and *Vijayeśa*. It shows which were the Tīrthas most famous in Kalhaṇa's time. The legends connected with the early semi-mythical kings give the chronicler frequent occasion in the first three Books to speak in detail of particular sacred sites. Almost each one of the stories furnishes evidence for the safe location of the latter.[2] But also in the subsequent and purely historical portions of the work we read often of pilgrimages to such sacred places or of events which occurred at them.

Kalhaṇa shows more than once so accurate a knowledge of the topography of particular Tīrthas that his personal visits to them may be assumed with great probability. This presumption is particularly strong in the case of *Nandikṣetra* which his father Caṇpaka is said to have often visited as a pilgrim and to have richly endowed, and of the neighbouring shrine of *Bhūteśvara*.[3] Also the distant Tīrtha of Śāradā in the Kiṣangaṅgā Valley seems to have been known personally to the Chronicler.[4] Considering the popularity which pilgrimages to sacred sites have always enjoyed among Kaśmīrians, the conclusion seems justified that Kalhaṇa owed perhaps no small part of his practical acquaintance with his country's topography, to the tours he had made as a pilgrim.

Kalhaṇa's references to foundations.

19. A second fruitful source of valuable topographical notices is contained in those very numerous references which Kalhaṇa makes to the foundation of towns, villages, estates, shrines, and buildings by particular kings. If we leave aside the curious list, i. 86–100, taken by

[1] *Rājat.* i. 28-31. The Nāgas are supposed to have come to Kaśmīr when Kaśyapa, their father, had drained 'the lake of Satī,' and to have found there a refuge from Garuḍa; comp. *Nīlamata*, 59 *sqq.*

[2] Compare the legends of the *Sodara* spring, i. 123 *sqq.*; of the *Kṛtyāśrama* Vihāra, i. 131 *sqq.*; of the Jyeṣṭharudra at *Nandikṣetra* and *Śrīnagarī*, i. 113, 124; the story of the *Suśravas* Nāga, i. 203 *sqq.*; the description of the pilgrimage to the *Takṣaka* Nāga, i. 220 *sqq.*; the story of the *Īśeśvara* temple, ii. 134; of *Raṇasvāmin*, iii. 459 *sqq.*, etc.

[3] See vii. 954; viii. 2365 and note v. 55 *sqq.* Compare also below, § 57.

[4] See Note L, viii. 2492, § 4.

Kalhaṇa from Padmamihira in which certain local names are by fanciful etymologies connected with seven of the 'lost kings,'[1] it may be safely assumed that these attributions are based either on historical fact or at least on genuine local tradition. Kalhaṇa specially informs us in his introduction[2] that among the documents he had consulted for his work, there were 'the inscriptions recording the consecration of temples and grants [of land] by former kings.' Such records no doubt supplied a great portion of the numerous notices above referred to. Often such notices may have been taken from less authentic sources. But we may always claim for them the merit of acquainting us with the names of the respective localities and buildings, as used in the official language of Kalhaṇa's time, and with the traditions then current regarding their origin and date.

The system of nomenclature which was regularly followed in Kaśmīr in naming new foundations, must have helped to preserve a genuine tradition regarding the founder. In the vast majority of cases the names of new towns and villages are formed by the addition of *-pura* to the name of the founder, either in its full or abbreviated form.[3] Similarly the names of temples, monasteries, Maṭhas and other religious structures show the name of their builder followed by terms indicating the deity or the religious objects to which the building was dedicated.[4] Many of

[1] See regarding this unhistorical list note i. 86. The local names, like *Khonamuṣa*, *Godharā*, *Samāṅgāsā*, etc., are all genuine enough. What Padmamihira did was to evolve fictitious names of kings out of these by means of popular etymology.

[2] i. 15.

[3] Thus we have, *e.g.*, the well-known localities of *Huṣkapura*, *Kaniṣkapura*, *Juṣkapura* (which retain the memory of their Indo-Scythian founders); *Pravarapura* (for Pravarasenapura), the old official designation of the present capital; *Padmapura*, *Avantipura*, *Jayapura* (for Jayāpīḍapura) and a host of others. The custom of naming new localities in this fashion, or of renaming earlier ones in honour of the actual ruler, can be traced through successive periods of Muhammadan and Sikh rule down to the present day; comp. *e.g.*, *Zainᵃpōr* (named after Zainu-l-'ābidīn); *Shahābuddīnpūr* (now Shādipūr); *Muḥammadpūr*; *Raṇbīrsinghpūr* (intended to replace Shāhābād), etc.

[4] Thus in the case of Śiva-temples *-īśa* or *-īśvara* is invariably added (comp., *e.g.*, Pravareśvara, Amṛteśvara, etc.), as in that of Viṣṇu-shrines with equal regularity *-svāmin* (*-keśava*); comp. *e.g.*, *Muktasvāmin* (built by Muktāpīḍa), *Avantisvāmin*, *Bhīmakeśava* (erected by Bhīmapāla Sāhi), etc.

Buddhist monasteries receive the name of their founder with the addition of *-vihāra* or *-bhavana*; comp. *Jayendravihāra*, *Caṅkuṇavihāra*, *Amṛtabhavana* (founded by Queen Amṛtaprabhā, the present Ântᵃbavan), *Skandabhavana* (for Skandaguptabhavana), and many more, as shown in my *Notes on Ou-k'ong*, p. 4.

For Maṭhas compare e. g. *Diddāmaṭha* (Didᵃmar); *Subhaṭāmaṭha*, *Nandāmaṭha*, *Loṭhikāmaṭha*, *Cakramaṭha*, etc.

these religious structures left their names to the sites at which they were erected. They can thus be traced to the present day in the designations of villages or city quarters.[1]

The topographical interest which Kalhaṇa's notices of town-foundations possess is considerably enhanced by the fact that in more than one case they are accompanied by accurate descriptions of the site chosen and the buildings connected with them. Thus Kalhaṇa's detailed accounts of the foundation of *Pravarapura*, iii. 336–363, is curiously instructive even in its legendary particulars. It enables us to trace with great precision the original position and limits of the city which was destined to remain thereafter the capital of Kaśmīr.[2] Similarly the description given of *Parihāsapura* and its great shrines has made it possible for me to fix with accuracy the site of the town which Lalitāditya's fancy elevated for a short time to the rank of a capital, and to identify the remains of the great buildings which once adorned it.[3] Not less valuable from an antiquarian point of view is the account given to us of the twin towns *Jayapura* and *Dvāravatī* which King Jayāpīḍa founded as his royal residence near the marshes of Andᵊrkōṭh.[4] We shall see below to what extent the correct identification of the extant ruins of Kaśmīr has been facilitated by these and similar accounts of the Rājataraṅgiṇī.

Topographical data in historical narrative.

20. Valuable as the data are which we gather from the two groups of notices just discussed, it may yet be doubted whether by themselves, that is, unsupported by other information, they can throw as much light on the old topography of Kaśmīr as the notices which we have yet to consider. I mean the whole mass of incidental references to topographical points which we find interwoven with the historical narrative of the Chronicle.

It is evident that where localities are mentioned in the course of a connected relation of events, the context if studied with due regard to the facts of the actual topography, must help us towards a correct identification of the places meant. In the case of the previous notices the Chronicler has but rarely occasion to give us distinct indications as to the position of the sites or shrines he intended. In our

1 The name of the *Amṛtabhavana*, iii. 9, survives in the present Ântᵃbavan; *Diddāmaṭha* and *Skandabhavana* in the Didᵃmar and Khandᵃbavan quarters of S'rinagar; similarly Lalitāditya's great temple of *Mārtāṇḍa* left its name to the village and district of Maṭan.

2 See note iii. 339–349 and below, § 92.

3 Compare Note F, iv. 194–204, and below, § 121.

4 See note iv. 506–511; also below, § 122.

attempts to identify the latter we have therefore only too often to depend either on the accidental fact of other texts furnishing the required evidence, or to fall back solely on the comparison of the old with modern local names. That the latter course if not guided and controlled by other evidence, is likely to lead us into mistakes, is a fact which requires no demonstration for the critical student.

It is different with the notices the consideration of which we have left to the last. Here the narrative itself, in the great majority of cases, becomes our guide and either directly points out to us the real locality meant or at least restricts to very narrow limits the area within which our search must proceed. The final identification can then be safely effected with the help of local tradition, by tracing the modern derivative of the old local name, or by other additional evidence of this kind.

For the purpose of such a systematic search it is, of course, a very great advantage if the narrative is closely connected and detailed. And it is on this account that, as already stated above (§ 17), Kalhaṇa's lengthy relation of what was to him recent history, in Books vii. and viii., is for us so valuable. An examination of the topographical notes in my commentary on the Chronicle will show that the correct identification of many of the localities mentioned in the detached notices of the first six Books has become possible only by means of the evidence furnished by the more detailed narrative of the last two.

In this respect the accounts of the endless rebellions and other internal troubles which fill the greater portion of the reigns of the Lohara dynasty, have proved particularly useful. The description of the many campaigns, frontier-expeditions and sieges connected with these risings supplies us with a great amount of topographical details mutually illustrating each other. By following up these operations on the map,—or better still on the actual ground, as I was often able to do,—it is possible to fix with precision the site of many old localities which would otherwise never have emerged from the haze of doubt and conjecture.

In order to illustrate those general remarks it will be sufficient to refer to a few typical examples among the many identifications thus arrived at. As the corresponding notes of my commentary fully indicate the evidence on which these identifications are based, as well as the process of reasoning by which they were arrived at, it will not be necessary here to go into details. A very characteristic example is furnished by the important stronghold and territory of LOHARA, which was formerly supposed to be Lahore. Its correct location at the present *Lohᵃrin* and the identification of the several places and routes mentioned in the same neighbourhood became possible only, as Note *E*, iv. 177, shows,[1] through the indications contained in Kalhaṇa's description of the several sieges which this mountain fastness underwent in his own time. Similar instances are the identifications of the Gopâdri hill (the present Takht-i Sulaimān), and of the streams Mahāsarit and Kṣiptikā (Mār and Kutᵊkul). Though prominent features in the topography of the capital itself, they could not have been correctly located but for the evidence supplied by the narrative of the last Book.[2] The same is the case, *e.g.*, with the name of the district Holaḍā (Vular) and the important ethnic designation of *Khaśa*.[3]

Accuracy of Kalhaṇa's topograhy.

21. It is impossible to read attentively Kalhaṇa's Chronicle and in particular those portions which give fuller occasion for the notice of localities, without being struck with the exactness of his statements regarding the latter and with, what I may call, his eye for matters topographical.

We must appreciate these qualities all the more if we compare Kalhaṇa's local references with that vague and loose treatment which topographical points receive at the hands of Sanskrit authors generally.[4] If it has been possible to trace with accuracy the great majority of localities mentioned in the Chronicle, this is largely due to the precision which Kalhaṇa displays in his topographical terminology. It is evident that he had taken care to acquaint himself with the localities which formed the scene of the events he described. Here too I may refer for more detailed evidence to my translation of the work and the notes which accompany it. A few characteristic points may, however, be specified as examples.

Striking evidence for the care with which Kalhaṇa indicates topo-

1 Compare also my paper on the 'Castle of Lohara,' *Ind Ant.* 1897, p. 225 *sqq.* below, § 49.

2 Compare for *Gopādri*, notes i. 341; viii. 1104-10; for the *Mahāsarit*, note iii. 339-349; for the *Kṣiptikā*, note viii. 732.

3 See notes i. 306 and i. 317.

4 Nor should we forget the difficulty which Kalhaṇa had to face by writing in metrical form. True indeed it is what Albērūnī says of this form as adopted by Hindu scientific writers: "Now it is well-known that in all metrical compositions there is much misty and constrained phraseology merely intended to fill up the metre and serving as a kind of patchwork, and this necessitates a certain kind of verbosity. This is also one of the reasons why a word has sometimes one meaning and sometimes another" (*India*, i. p. 19).

Fortunately Kalhaṇa has managed to escape these dangers as far as the topographical notices of his work are concerned. We find in his local terminology neither that mistiness nor multiplicity of meaning Albērūnī so justly complains of.

graphical details, is furnished by his description of the great operations which were carried out under Avantivarman with a view to regulating the course of the Vitastā and draining the Valley.[1] Thanks to the exactness with which the relative position of the old and new confluence of the Vitastā and Sindhu is described, before and after the regulation, respectively, it has been possible even after so many centuries to trace in detail the objects and results of an important change in the hydrography of the Valley.[2]

Equal attention to the topographical details we find in numerous accounts of military operations. Of these it will suffice to quote here the descriptions of the several sieges of S'rīnagar, under Sussala;[3] the battle on the *Gopādri* hill in the same reign;[4] the blockade of *Lohara*, with the disastrous retreat through the mountains that followed,[5] and, last but not least, the siege of the *Śiraḥśilā* castle. The topographical accuracy of the latter account as proved in Note *L*, viii. 2492, almost presupposes on Kalhaṇa's part a personal examination of the site. It is all the more noteworthy, because the scene of the events there recorded was a region outside Kaśmīr proper, distant and difficult of access.

There are also smaller points that help to raise our estimate of Kalhaṇa's reliability in topographical matters. Of such I may mention for example the close agreement we can trace everywhere between Kalhaṇa's statements regarding distances, whether given in road or time-measure, and the actual facts. The number of marches reckoned by him is thus always easily verified by a reference to the stages observed on the corresponding modern routes.[6] Not less gratifying is it to find how careful Kalhaṇa is to distinguish between homonymous localities.[7] In addition we must give credit to our author for the just observation of many characteristic features in the climate, ethnography, and economical condition of Kaśmīr and the neighbouring regions.[8] All these notices help to invest with additional interest the data furnished for the old topography of the country.

1 Compare v. 84–121.

2 Compare Note *I*, v. 97–100, on the *Vitastāsindhusaṁgama*, and below, §§ 69–72.

3 See viii. 729 *sqq*; 1060 *sqq*.

4 Compare viii. 1099–1115.

5 See viii. 1842-80 and Note *E*, iv. 177, § 10.

6 Compare for distance measurements note i. 264; v. 103; vii. 393; for the reckoning of marches on the Vitastā Valley route, v. 225; on the Tōṣ̱maidān pass, vii. 140; on the route to the Pīr Pantsāl Pass, vii. 558; on the way to Mārtāṇḍa, vii. 715, etc.

7 Compare notes i. 113; i. 124; v. 123 on the several *Jyeṣṭharudras* and the way in which Kalhaṇa specifies them.

8 Compare below, §§ 77–79.

If the advantages thus accorded to us are duly weighed there seems every reason to congratulate ourselves on the fact that the earliest and fullest record of Kaśmīr history that has come down to us was written by a scholar of Kalhaṇa's type. Whatever the shortcomings of his work from a historical point of view may be, we may well claim for him the merit that he has provided us with a sound and ample basis for the study of the historical geography of his country.

Sanskrit form of local names.

22. Another point still remains to be considered here in connection with Kalhaṇa's Chronicle, *viz.*, to what extent can we accept the Sanskrit forms found in his text as the genuine local names of the period. This question deserves attention, because the popular language actually spoken in Kaśmīr in Kalhaṇa's time and for many centuries earlier, was not Sanskrit but undoubtedly an Apabhraṁśa dialect derived from it, which has gradually developed into the modern Kaśmīrī.

Notwithstanding this circumstance I think that Kalhaṇa's local names can on the whole safely be taken as the genuine designations of the localities, *i.e.*, those originally given to them. My grounds for this belief are the following.

We have ample evidence to show that Sanskrit was the official and sole literary language of the country, not only in Kalhaṇa's own time but also in those earlier periods from which the records used by him may have dated. This official use of Sanskrit we know to have continued in Kaśmīr even into Muhammadan times. It assures us at once that the vast majority of village and town names must from the beginning have been given in Sanskrit. A detailed examination of Kalhaṇa's local names will easily demonstrate, on the one hand that these names are of genuinely Sanskrit formation, and on the other, that their modern Kaśmīrī representatives are derived from them by a regular process of phonetic conversion. We look in vain among this class of old local names for any which would show a foreign, *i.e.*, non-Aryan origin and might be suspected of having only subsequently been pressed into a Sanskritic garb.

As Sanskrit was used as the language of all official records for many centuries previous to Kalhaṇa's time, the Sanskrit names originally intended for the great mass of inhabited places could be preserved, in official documents anyhow, without any difficulty or break of tradition. And from such documents most of Kalhaṇa's notices of places were undoubtedly derived, directly or indirectly.

Only in rare cases can we suppose that the original form of a local name of this kind had been lost sight of, and that accordingly the Chronicler, or his authority, had to fall back on the expedient of sanskritizing in its stead the Apabhraṁśa or Kaśmīrī form, as well as he could. There are in fact a few instances in which we have indications of such a metamorphosis. Thus we find the same local name spelt either *Bhaleraka* or *Baleraka* in the Chronicle, and a village which Kalhaṇa calls *Ghoramūlaka*, referred to by Abhinanda, the author of the Kādambarīkathāsāra (first half of 9th century), as *Gauramūlaka*.[1] It is difficult to avoid the conclusion that we have here varying attempts to reproduce in a Sanskritic garb original Apabhraṁśa names. But these cases are very rare indeed, and even in them other explanations of the different spellings are possible.

These observations apply with nearly the same force also to other local names recorded in the Chronicle, such as those of mountains, streams, passes, etc. The great majority of these names must have very early found their place in official documents or, as we shall see below, in the Sanskrit legendaries or Māhātmyas of the numerous Tīrthas. If any of them are in reality adaptations of Prakrit or Apabhraṁśa forms, their quasi-official use is yet likely to have originated a long time before the date of Kalhaṇa.

Even to the present day the local nomenclature of Kaśmīr, whether in the Valley or in the mountains, shows throughout an unmistakeably Sanskritic character. This is most clearly illustrated by the constant recurrence of such terms as *-pūr* or *pōr* (< pura), *-mar* (< maṭha), *-ᵃśhōm* (< āśrama), *-kōṭh* (< koṭṭa), *-gām* or *gōm* (< grāma), *-kuṇḍᵃl* (< kuṇḍala), *-vōr* (< vāṭa), in village names; of *-sar* (< saras), *-nambal* (< naḍvalā), *nāg* (< nāga) in names of lakes, marshes, etc.; of *-van* (< vana), *-nār*, (< nāḍa), *-marg* (< maṭhikā), *-gul* (< galikā), *brār* (< bhaṭṭārikā), *-vath* (< patha) in designations of alpine localities, peaks, passes, etc.; *-kul* (< kulyā), *-khan* (< khani) in names of streams and canals.

The Sanskrit etymology of the specific names preceding these terms, is even in their modern phonetic form very often equally transparent. At an earlier stage of the language the Apabhraṁśa names must have approached the corresponding Sanskrit forms much more closely. The reproduction of the popular names in a Sanskrit form could have then but rarely been attended with much difficulty or doubt. We may hence safely assume that the Sanskrit forms recorded by Kalhaṇa represent in most cases correctly the original local names, and in the remainder cannot differ much from them.

Later Sanskrit Chronicles.

23. The later Sanskrit Chronicles which were composed with the distinct object of continuing Kalhaṇa's work, furnish valuable supplements to the topographical information contained in the latter.

[1] Compare notes viii. 1861, and vii. 1239; viii. 2410.

These Chronicles are the *Rājataraṅgiṇī* of Jonarāja who continued the narrative down to the reign of Sultān Zainu-l-'ābidin and died over his work, A.D. 1459;[1] the *Jaina-Rājataraṅgiṇī* composed by Jonarāja's pupil S'rīvara which deals in four Books with the period A.D. 1459–86;[2] and finally, the Fourth Chronicle which was begun under the name *Rājāvalipatākā* by Prājyabhaṭṭa and completed by his pupil S'uka some years after the annexation of Kaśmīr by Akbar, A.D. 1586.[3]

It will be seen from the above dates that the narrative of the last two works falls entirely beyond the period of Hindu rule to which our enquiry is limited, and which may be considered to close finally with the usurpation of Shāh Mīr, A.D. 1339. The same holds good of the greater portion of Jonarāja's Chronicle. The reigns of the late Hindu rulers, from Jayasiṁha to Queen Koṭā, are there disposed of with a brevity corresponding more to their own insignificance than to the intrinsic historical interest of the epoch.[4] Notwithstanding this difference in date the materials supplied by these later Chronicles have often proved of great use in clearing up points of the old topography of Kaśmīr. For the mass of localities mentioned in them goes back to the Hindu period, and the names by which they are referred to, are also still mostly the old ones.

Yet on the whole the inferiority of these later Chronicles when compared with Kalhaṇa's work, is as marked in the matter of topographical information as it is in other respects. In the first place it must be noted that the whole text of these three distinct works does not amount to more than about one-half of Kalhaṇa's work. For references to sacred sites and buildings and other places of religious interest the account of Muhammadan reigns offers naturally but little opportunity. The incidental notices of other localities are also in proportion less numerous and instructive. For these later authors allow considerably more room to episodic descriptions and do by no means show that care for accuracy in topographical statements which we have noticed in Kalhaṇa.

It is curious to note how the gradual decline of Hindu learning in Kaśmīr during the period of troubles and oppression which lasted with short interruptions for two and a half centuries previous to Akbar's conquest, is marked also in the character and contents of these later

[1] See *S'rīv.* i. 6.

[2] See Fourth Chron. 6.

[3] Compare Fourth Chron. 8 *sqq.* Prājyabhaṭṭa's composition ended with the year A.D. 1513-14 and the reign of Fataḥ Shāh (verses 14-64).

[4] The narrative of the period 1149–1339 A.D. fills only 305 verses in Jonarāja's Chronicle (347 according to the Bombay edition).

Chronicles. JONARĀJA was a scholar of considerable attainments, but apparently without any originality. He shows himself yet well-acquainted with the old local nomenclature of the Valley, though outside it he too commits himself to forms like *Puruṣavīra* (for Peshawar, recte Puruṣapura), etc.

ŚRĪVARA is a slavish imitator of Kalhaṇa, not above reproducing whole verses of his predecessor. His text looks often more like a *cento* from the Rājataraṅgiṇī than an original composition. Notwithstanding the thorough study of Kalhaṇa's work which this kind of exploitation presupposes, we find Śrīvara more than once betraying ignorance of the old names for well-known Kaśmīr localities. Thus we have the name of the *Mahāsarit* stream transformed into *Mārī*, an evident adaptation of the modern Mār;[1] *Siddhapatha*, the modern Sidau, represented as *Siddhādeśa*;[2] the Tīrtha of Mārtāṇḍa regularly referred to by its modern name *Bhavana* (Bavan), etc.[3]

The work of PRĀJYABHAṬṬA and ŚUKA is inferior in composition even to Śrīvara's Chronicle, and by the increased number of modern local names proves its authors' scant familiarity with the old topography of Kaśmīr. Thus the ancient *Kṛtyāśrama*, the scene of Kalhaṇa's Buddhist legend, i. 131 *sqq.*, figures repeatedly in their narrative as *Kīcāśrama*, *i.e.*, by its modern name Kiṭṭ^{a}hōm.[4] Even the well-known *Rājapurī* is metamorphosed into *Rājavīra* (!), a queer reproduction of the modern *Rajaurī*.[5] The old castle of *Lohara* reappears as *Luhara*, an evident approach to the present Lōh^{a}rin;[6] the ancient site of *Cakradhara* is turned into *Cakrādhāra*, etc.[7]

It is evident that when Sanskrit ceased to be the language used for official purposes, the knowledge of the ancient names of localities and of the traditions connected with the latter must have become gradually more and more restricted. In view of this decrease of traditional knowledge we have to exercise some caution when utilizing the evidence of the later historical texts for the elucidation of the old topographical data. At the same time it is easy to realize that their help is often of considerable value when connecting links have to be traced between those earlier data and the facts of modern topography.

1 See *Śrīv.* i. 440; iii. 278; comp. note on *Rājat.* iii. 339.

2 *Śrīv.* iii. 354; iv. 203, 661.

3 *Śrīv.* i. 376; iii. 372.

4 See Fourth Chron. 234, 240, 384; compare also note on *Rājat.* i. 147.

5 Fourth Chron. 542, *sqq.*

6 *Ib.*, 134, 143, *sqq.*

7 *Ib.*, 330.

24. It is convenient to refer here briefly to the Persian Tārīkhs of Kaśmīr which to some extent may be looked upon as continuing the works of Kalhaṇa and his Paṇḍit successors. Unfortunately they furnish no material assistance for the study of the old topography of the country.

Persian Tārīkhs.

All these works give in their initial portion an account of the Hindu dynasties which pretends to be translated from the Rājataraṅgiṇī. Yet the abstract so given is in each case very brief and chiefly devoted to a reproduction of the legendary and anecdotal parts of Kalhaṇa's narrative. We thus look in vain in these abstracts for the modern equivalents of those local names, the identification of which is attended with any difficulty.

In illustration of this it may be mentioned that even the Tārīkh of Ḥaidar Malik Cādura (Tsādᵘr),[1] which is the earliest work of this class accessible to me and the fullest in its account of the Hindu period, compresses the narrative of Jayasiṁha's reign, filling about two thousand verses in the Rājataraṅgiṇī, into two quarto pages. Of the localities mentioned in the original account of this reign not a single one is indicated by the Muhammadan Chronicler.

The later works which all belong to the 18th or the present century, are still more reticent on the Hindu period and seem to have largely copied Ḥaidar Malik's abstract. Taking into account the endless corruptions to which local names written in Persian characters are exposed, it will be readily understood why reference to these texts on points of topographical interest yields only in the rarest cases some tangible result.

25. It is a fortunate circumstance that several of the older Kaśmīr poets whose works have been preserved for us, have had the good sense to let us know something about their own persons and homes. The topographical details which can be gleaned from these authors, though comparatively few in number, are yet of distinct value. They enable us to check by independent evidence Kalhaṇa's local nomenclature, and in some instances acquaint us with localities of which we find no notice in the Chronicles.

Kaśmīr poets.

The first and most helpful of these Kaśmīrian authors is the well-known polyhistor KṢEMENDRA. His works, composed in the second and third quarter of the 11th century, form important landmarks in various fields of Indian literature. Kṣemendra seems to have felt a genuine

[1] Written A.H. 1027, *i.e.*, A.D. 1617, in the twelfth year of Jahāngīr's reign. Ḥaidar Malik takes his epithet *Cādura*, recte *Tsādᵘr*, from the Kaśmīr village of that name situated in the Nāgām Pargaṇa, some 10 miles south of Srīnagar, close to the village of Vahᵉtōr.

interest, rare enough among Indian scholars, for the realities of his country and the life around him. He does not content himself with informing us of his family, the date of his works and the places where he wrote them.[1]

In the *Samayamātṛkā*, one of his most original poems, which is intended to describe the snares of courtezans, he gives among other stories an amusing account of the wanderings of his chief heroine, Kaṅkālī, through the length and breadth of Kaśmīr.[2] The numerous places which form the scene of her exploits, can all easily enough be traced on the map. More than once curious touches of true local colour impart additional interest to these references. To Kṣemendra's poem we owe, *e.g.*, the earliest mention of the Pīr Pantsāl Pass (*Pañcāladhārā*) and its hospice (*maṭha*).[3] There too we get a glimpse of the ancient salt trade which still follows that route with preference. Elsewhere we see the heroine smuggling herself as a Buddhist nun into the ancient Vihāra of *Kṛtyāśrama*, etc.[4]

A different sketch of topographical interest we owe to the poet Bilhaṇa. He left his native land early in the reign of King Kalaśa (1063-89 A.D.), and after long wanderings became famous as the court poet of the Cālukya king Tribhuvanamalla Parmāḍi in the Dekhan. In the last canto of his historical poem, the *Vikramāṅkadevacarita*, Bilhaṇa gives us a glowing picture of the beauties of the Kaśmīr capital. Notwithstanding its panegyrical character, this account is laudably exact in its local details.[5] In another passage the poet describes to us his rural home and its surroundings at the village of *Khonamuṣa*, south-east of Śrīnagar. His touching verses attest as much his yearning for his distant home as the faithfulness of his local recollections.[6]

1 Compare the colophons of the various works first discovered and noticed by Prof. Bühler, *Report*, pp. 45 *sqq.* and Appendix.

2 This humorous peregrination fills the ii. Samaya of the work; see *Kāvyamālā* edition, pp. 6-16. The abundance of curious local details makes a commentated translation of the little Kāvya very desirable, notwithstanding the risky nature of part of its contents. A personal knowledge of Kaśmīr would certainly be required for the task.

3 See *Samayam.* ii. 90 *sqq.* The *maṭha* on the pass corresponds to the present *'Aliābād Sarai*, a short distance below the top of the pass on the Kaśmīr side; see below, § 44.

4 *Samayam.* ii. 61 *sqq.*

5 Prof. Bühler to whom we owe the discovery of Bilhaṇa's chief work, has given in his Introduction an admirable analysis of the contents of Sarga xviii. as illustrating the poet's biography. For his description of contemporary Śrīnagara, see pp. 7 *sqq.*

6 See *Vikram.* xviii. 70 *sqq.* Prof. Bühler during his Kaśmīr tour, 1875, had the satisfaction of visiting the poet's native place, the present village of *Khunamoh.*

Similar in character though less ample in detail, is the description of Kaśmīr and its capital Pravarapura which Maṅkha, Kalhaṇa's contemporary, inserts in the iii. Canto of his Kāvya *Śrīkaṇṭhacarita.*[1] Here we have the advantages of a commentary written by Jonarāja, the Chronicler, which duly notices and explains the points of local interest.

The Lokaprakāśa.

26. To complete our review of those Kaśmīrian texts of topographical interest which may be distinguished as secular, we must refer briefly to the curious glossary and manual which goes by the name of *Kṣemendra's Lokaprakāśa.* Professor A. Weber has recently published valuable extracts from this text.[2] I myself have had occasion to refer to it frequently in the notes on the Rājataraṅgiṇī.[3] The work represents a strange mixture of the usual Kośa and a practical handbook dealing with various topics of administration and private life in Kaśmīr.

A great deal of the information contained in it is decidedly old, and probably from the hand of our well-known Kṣemendra. But there are unmistakeable proofs, both in the form and contents of the book, showing that it has undergone considerable alterations and additions down even to the 17th century. This is exactly what we must expect in a work which had remained in the practical use of the Kaśmīrian 'Kārkuns' long after the time when Sanskrit had ceased to be the official language of the country.

The Lokaprakāśa supplies us with the earliest list of Kaśmīr Parganas. It gives besides the names of numerous localities inserted in the forms for bonds, 'Huṇḍīs,' contracts, official reports, and the like which form the bulk of Prakāśas ii. and iv. The Pargaṇa list as well as these forms exhibit local names of undoubtedly ancient date side by side with comparatively modern ones. Some of the latter belong to places which were only founded during the Muhammadan rule.[4]

He could thus verify on the spot every point of the description which Bilhaṇa gives of that "coquettish embellishment of the bosom of Mount Himālaya;" see *Report*, pp. 4 *sqq.*

1 See *Śrīkaṇṭhac.* iii. 10–24, 68 *sqq.*

2 See *Zu Kṣemendra's Lokaprakāśa*, in *Indische Studien*, xviii. pp. 289–412.

3 See particularly Note *H* (iv. 495), on the Kaśmīr monetary system, § 10.

4 Compare, *e.g.*, in Prakāśa ii. *Jainanagara*, founded by Zainu-l-'ābidīn (see *Jonar.* 1153); *Alābhadenapura* (*Śrīv.* iv. 318), etc.

SECTION VI.—THE NĪLAMATA AND MĀHĀTMYAS.

The Nīlamata-purāṇa.

27. We have already above drawn attention to the fact that Kaśmīr has since early times been pre-eminently a country of holy sites and places of pilgrimage of all kinds. These objects of ancient local worship have always played an important part in the historical topography of the Valley and the adjacent mountain regions. It is hence no small advantage that there are abundant materials at our disposal for the special study of this *Topographia sacra* of Kaśmīr.

The oldest extant text which deals in detail with Kaśmīrian Tīrthas, is the *Nīlamatapurāṇa*. This work which Kalhaṇa used as one of his sources,[1] claims to give the sacred legends regarding the origin of the country and the special ordinances which Nīla, the lord of Kaśmīr Nāgas, had revealed for the worship and rites to be observed in it.[2]

It is unnecessary to refer here to the legends which are related at the commencement of work, and to 'the rites proclaimed by Nila' which together with the former occupy about two-thirds of the extant text.[3] These parts have been fully discussed by Prof. Bühler in his lucid analysis of the Nilamata.[4] The remaining portions, however, deserve here special notice as forming,—to use Prof. Bühler's words—"a real mine of information, regarding the sacred places of Kaśmīr and their legends."

In the first place we find there a list of the principal Nāgas or sacred springs of Kaśmīr (vv. 900–975). This is followed by the interesting legend regarding the Mahāpadma lake, the present Volur, which is supposed to occupy the place of the submerged city of *Candrapura* (vv. 976–1008).[5] The Purāṇa then proceeds to an enumeration of miscellaneous Tirthas chiefly connected with Śiva's worship (vv. 1009-48). To this is attached a very detailed account, designated as *Bhūteśvaramāhātmya*, of the legends connected with the sacred lakes and sites on Mount Haramukuṭa (vv. 1049-1148).[6] Of a similar Māhātmya relating to the Kapaṭeśvara Tīrtha, the present Kōṭhēr,[7] only a fragment is found in our extant text (vv. 1149-68). The list of

[1] See *Rājat.* i. 14.

[2] Compare *Rājat.* i. 178–184.

[3] *Nīlamata*, vv. 1-366, contain the legends, v. 367–899 the rites above referred to.

[4] See *Report*, pp 38 *sqq*.

[5] Compare below, § 74, and *Report*, p. 10.

[6] Compare below, § 57, and *Rājat.* notes i, 36, 107, 113.

[7] See below, § 112, and *Rājat.* i. 32 note.

Viṣṇu-Tīrthas which succeeds it (vv. 1169–1248), is comparatively short, as indeed the position of this god is a secondary one in the popular worship of Kaśmīr.

After a miscellaneous list of sacred Saṁgamas or river-confluences, Nāgas and lakes (vv. 1249-78) we are treated to a somewhat more detailed synopsis of the chief Tīrthas of Kaśmīr (vv. 1271–1371). This is of special interest, because an attempt is made here to describe the Tīrthas in something like topographical order, and to group with them such localities as are visited on the same pilgrimage. It is thus possible to determine, with more certainty than in the case of other Tīrtha lists, the particular holy sites intended by the author.

This synopsis starts in the east with the fountain of the Nilanāga (Vērnāg), and follows with more or less accuracy the course of the Vitastā and its affluents down to the gorge of Varāhamūla. A short *Vitastāmāhātmya*, describing the origin and miraculous powers of this the holiest of Kaśmīr rivers (vv. 1371–1404), closes the text of Nīlamata, such as it is found in our Manuscripts.

This text is unfortunately in a very bad condition owing to numerous lacunæ and textual corruptions of all kinds. Prof. Bühler held that the Nīlamata in its present form could not be older than the 6th or 7th century of our era.[1] It appears to me by no means improbable that the text has undergone changes and possibly additions at later periods. On the whole, however, the local names found in it bear an ancient look and agree closely with the forms used by Kalhaṇa. The difference in this respect between the Nīlamata and the Māhātmyas, in their extant recensions, is very marked and helps to prove the comparatively late date of most of the latter. On the other hand it deserves to be noted that without the more systematic and detailed accounts of the various Tīrthas as found in the Māhātmyas, the identification of many of the sacred places referred to in the Nīlamata would probably have been impossible.

The fact of all extant copies of the work showing practically the same defective text, seems to indicate that the changes and additions to which I alluded above, cannot be quite recent. If such a revision had been made at a time comparatively near to the date of our oldest MS. we could, after the analogy of other instances, expect an outwardly far more correct, *i.e.* 'cooked,' text. The operation here suggested was actually performed some thirty years ago by the late Paṇḍit Sāhibrām. Receiving the orders of Mahārāja Raṇbīr Singh to

[1] Compare *Report*, p. 40. The oldest and best MS. of the Nīlamata which I was able to secure and collate, is dated in the Laukika year 81. This date judging from the appearance of the MS. probably corresponds to A.D. 1705–6.

prepare the text of the Nīlamata for edition, he 'revised' the work with scant respect for its sacred character by filling up the lacunæ, expanding obscure passages, removing ungrammatical forms, etc.[1] Fortunately Prof. Bühler reached Kaśmīr early enough to learn the origin of this 'cooked' text, and to give due warning as to its true character.

The Nīlamata seems thus to have escaped in recent times that process of continual adaptation which, as we shall see, must be assumed to have greatly affected all extant Māhātmyas. The reason probably is that it could never have been used, like the latter, as a practical pilgrims' manual and itinerary by the Purohitas of the various Tīrthas.

The Haracarita-cintāmaṇi.

28. Among the texts dealing specially with the sacred sites of Kaśmīr the *Haracaritacintāmaṇi* can be placed, perhaps, nearest in date to the Nīlamata-purāṇa. It is not like the latter and the Māhātmyas, an anonymous composition, claiming recognition in the wide folds of canonical Purāṇa literature. It owns as its author the poet *Jayadratha*, of the Kaśmīrian family of the Rājānakas, and a brother of Jayaratha. The pedigree of the family as given in Jayaratha's *Tantrālokaviveka*, a S'aiva treatise, shows that Jayadratha must have lived about the end of the 12th or beginning of the 13th century.[2]

His work which is written in a simple Kāvya style, relates in thirty-two Cantos as many legends concerning S'iva and his various Avatāras.[3] Eight of these legends are localized at well-known Kaśmīrian Tīrthas. They give the author ample opportunity of mentioning other sacred sites of Kaśmīr directly or indirectly connected with the former.[4]

Jayadratha's detailed exposition helps to fix clearly the form which the legends regarding some of the most popular of Kaśmīrian Tīrthas had assumed in the time immediately following Kalhaṇa. The local names as recorded by Jayadratha, agree closely with those of the Rājataraṅgiṇī.[5] They prove clearly that the forms employed by Kalhaṇa must have been those generally current in the Sanskrit usage of the period. For the interpretation of Nīlamata's brief notices the Hara-

1 See *Report*, pp. 33, 38.

2 Compare BÜHLER, *Report*, pp. 61, 81, cliii.

3 The *Haracaritacintāmaṇi* has recently been printed as No. 61 of the *Kāvyamālā* Series, Bombay, (1897), chiefly from the text as contained in my MS. No. 206.

4 The cantos containing these legends are i. Jvālāliṅgāvatāra, iv. Nandirudrāvatāra, vii. Cakrapradāna; x.-xiv. Vijayeśvara-, Piṅgaleśvara-, Vitastā-, Svayaṁbhunātha-, Kapaṭeśvara Avatāras.

5 An index of the Kaśmīr local names in the Haracaritacintāmaṇi, with explanatory notes, has been prepared under my supervision by P. Govind Kaul and printed as an Appendix to the Kāvyamālā edition.

caritacintāmaṇi is of great value. Its plain and authentic narrative enables us often to trace the numerous modifications which the various local legends as well as the names of the localities connected with them have undergone in the extant Māhātmyas.

29. Reference has already been made above to the numerous texts known as *Māhātmyas* which we possess of all the more important Tīrthas of Kaśmīr. They claim with few exceptions to be extracted from Purāṇas or Purāṇic collections (*Saṁhitās*).[1] Ordinarily they set forth in detail the legends relating to the particular pilgrimage place, the spiritual and other benefits to be derived from its visit, and the special rites to be gone through by the pilgrims at the various stages of the itinerary. The abstract given of the S'āradāmāhātmya in Note *B*, on Rājat. i. 37, may serve to indicate the manner in which these subjects are usually treated in the average texts of this class.

The Māhātmyas.

Prof. Bühler was the first to recognize the value of the Māhātmyas for a systematic study of the old topography of Kaśmīr. Among the Sanskrit Manuscripts which he acquired during his tour in Kaśmīr, there are sixteen distinct texts of this kind.[2] My own search in this direction, facilitated by successive visits to the various Tīrthas themselves, has enabled me to collect altogether fifty-one separate Māhātmya texts. The list of my collection which has been given in a supplementary Note,[3] may be considered fairly to exhaust the present range of this literature.

In extent the Māhātmyas vary greatly. By the side of texts like the *Vitastāmāhātmya* with its fifteen hundred S'lokas, we have legendaries of more modest dimensions amounting only to a few dozens of verses. Equally marked differences in the matter of age become apparent on closer examination.

Unmistakeable indications prove that many of the Māhātmyas now in actual use are of late composition or redaction. Among the texts so characterized, the Māhātmyas of some of the most popular pilgrimage places, like the Haramukuṭa lakes, the cave of Amaranātha, Īśeśvara (Iśᵉbar), are particularly conspicuous. The indications here referred to are furnished chiefly by the local names which in their very form often betray a modern origin. This may conveniently be illustrated by a

[1] Most of the Kaśmīr Māhātmyas allege to be portions of the *Bhṛṅgīśasaṁhitā*. Others claim special authority by representing themselves as parts of the Ādi, Brahma, Brahmavaivarta, Varāha and Bhaviṣyat Purāṇas.

[2] See *Report*, pp. iv. *sqq*. Nos. 48, 51, 52, 55, 62, 75, 82, 84, 99, 100 there quoted as separate texts are only chapters of the *Amaranāthamāhātmya*.

[3] See Supplementary Note *AA*.

brief analysis of the most instructive of such names found in the *Vitastāmāhātmya.*

This text claims to furnish an account of all the Tīrthas along the course of the holy river and is designated as a portion of the *Bhṛṅgīśasaṁhitā.* Notwithstanding this pretended antiquity we find the famous Nīlanāga introduced to us by the name of *Viranāga* (i. 58; ii. 33). This form is wholly unknown to the Nīlamata, Rājataraṅgiṇī or any old text. It is nothing but a clumsy rendering of the modern name of the village *Vērnāg* near which this fine spring is situated.[1] The ancient site of *Jayavana,* mentioned by Bilhaṇa and Kalhaṇa, the present *Zevan,* is metamorphosed into *Yavanī* (vi. 4).[2] The village of Pāndrēṭhan which derives its name from *Purāṇādhiṣṭhāna,*[3] 'the old capital,' and bears the latter designation even in S'rīvara's Chronicle, figures as *Pādudṛṣṭika* (!), xii. 24. That *Mākṣikasvāmin* (Māy[9]sum)[4] and the *Mahāsarit* (Mār)[5] appear as *Māyāsīmā* and *Mārī,* can after this specimen of fancy nomenclature scarcely surprise us.

But we must all the same feel somewhat startled when we find that this text which claims to be revealed by S'iva, refers repeatedly to the modern village of *Shād[i]pūr,* at the confluence of the Vitastā and Sind, by the name of *S'āradāpura. Shād[i]pūr,* an abbreviation for *Shahābuddīnpūr,* was, as Jonarāja's Chronicle shows, founded only in the 14th century by Sultān Shahābu-d-dīn.[6] Quite on a level with the knowledge of old topography here displayed are many other references to localities, *e.g.,* the mention of the modern garden *Shālimār,* a creation of the Mughals (S'ālamāra), xxi. 39; of the ancient Huṣkapura as *Uṣaḥkaraṇa*[7] (for Uṣkür !), xxix. 103, etc.

In several cases these fancy renderings of modern local names are explained by whimsical etymologies which again in due turn give rise to new-fangled legends quite in the style of the old *nidānakathās.*

Similar proofs of modern origin can be traced in several other popular Māhātmyas, though perhaps not with equal frequency. Thus we find in the *Haramukuṭagaṅgāmāhātmya* the name of the sacred mountain itself transformed from *Haramukuṭa* into *Haramukha* (the

1 The name *Vērnāg* is probably derived from the name of the Pargaṇa *Vēr,* mentioned by Abū-l-Faẓl, ii. p. 370.

2 See below, § 105.

3 See *Rājat.* iii. 99 note and below, § 89; also *S'rīv.* iv. 290.

4 See *Rājat.* iv. 88 note and below, § 99.

5 Compare *Rājat.* iii. 339-349 note and below, § 65.

6 See *Jonar.* 409. A popular etymology accepted in good faith by more than one European writer, sees in Shād[i]pūr the 'village of the marriage,' scil. between the Vitastā and Sind Rivers!

7 Compare *Rājat.* i. 168 note and below, § 124.

present Haramukh),[1] the ancient site of *Bhūteśvara* (Buthʻsēr) so well-known to the Rājataraṅgiṇī and all old texts, turned into *Bodheśvara*, etc. In the *Amaranāthamāhātmya* of which there is a comparatively old copy in the Poona collection, we are also treated to *Padṛṣṭi* as the Sanskrit name of Pāndrēṭhan, to *Suśramanāga* (for Kś. *Suśramnāg*) as the name of the lake where the Nāga *Suśravas* of the old legend took up his abode,[2] and the like. Examples of local names similarly perverted in other Māhātmyas will have to be mentioned *passim* in our account below.

It is important to note that by the side of texts like those just mentioned, there are others which on the whole show close conformity with our genuine old sources both in matter of legend and local names.[3] And even in the Māhātmyas which in their present form we have every reason to consider as recent compositions, there is often abundant evidence of the use of earlier materials and traditions.[4] It will be easier to understand the singular discrepancies in the value and character of these texts on examining the peculiar conditions under which they have originated.

Origin and purpose of Māhātmyas.

30. The Māhātmyas are in the first place hand-books for the Purohitas of the particular Tīrthas who have the privilege of taking charge of the pilgrims. They serve the priests as chief authorities for the claims they put forth on behalf of the holiness of their Tīrtha, and for the rewards they promise for its visit. They are also intended to support their directions as to the rites to be observed by the pilgrim, and the route to be taken by him on the journey. It is usual for the Purohitas to recite the Māhātmya for the benefit of their clients in the course of the pilgrimage tour. At the same time its contents are expounded to them by a free verbal rendering in Kaśmīrī.

1 See below, § 57. The kh at the end of the modern name is due to a phonetic law of Kaśmīrī which requires the aspiration of every final tenuis; see *J. A. S. B.*, 1897, p. 183.

2 Compare *Rājat.* i. 267 note. The modern Kś. form *Suśramnāg* is the regular phonetic derivative of *Suśravanāga* by which name the lake is designated in the Nīlamata, Haracaritacintāmaṇi, etc.

3 Among such the Māhātmya collection known as the *Sarvāvatāra* (No. 213 in my list of MSS.), the *Mārtāṇḍamāhātmya* (No. 219), the *Vijayeśvaramāhātmya* (No. 220), may be particularly mentioned. None of these, however, are now known to the local Purohitas, more recent and inferior texts having taken their place.

4 Thus *e.g.*, the Māhātmya of the present *Iśᵉbạr* (*Īśeśvara*; see Rājat. ii. 134) shows plainly its very recent origin by calling the Tīrtha *Īśavihāra* (a garbled reproduction of Iśᵉbrōr < Iśeśvara), and by similar blunders. Yet it knows correctly the sacred spring of *Śatadhārā* already mentioned by Kṣemendra.

As but very few of the priests have enough knowledge of Sanskrit to follow the text intelligently, these translations are more or less learned by heart. Often as my manuscripts show, interlinear Kaśmīrī glosses are resorted to in order to assist the reader's memory.

These local priests known now in Kaśmīr as *thān^a^paṭ^i* (Skr. *sthānapati*), are as a rule quite as ignorant and grasping as their confrères, the Pujāris, Bhōjkis, etc., of India proper. They are held deservedly in very low estimation by the rest of the Brahman community. That their condition was more or less the same in earlier times too, though their influence and numbers may have been greater, can be safely concluded from more than one ironical allusion of Kalhaṇa.[1] These are the people to whose keeping the Māhātmya texts have always been entrusted. Their peculiar position and calling explain, I think, most of the curious changes which the latter have undergone.

Tenacious as local worship is, there is the evidence of concrete cases to show that not only the route of pilgrimage, but the very site of a Tīrtha has sometimes been changed in comparatively recent times. In proof of this it will suffice to refer to the detailed account I have given of the transfers that have taken place in the case of the ancient Tīrthas of *Bheḍā* and *Śāradā*.[2] Minor modifications must naturally have been yet far more frequent. The visit of a principal Tīrtha is regularly coupled with bathings, Śrāddhas and other sacrificial functions at a series of other sacred spots. The choice of these subsidiary places of worship must from the beginning have depended on local considerations. As these changed in the course of time, variations in the pilgrimage route must have unavoidably followed.

To bring the text of the Māhātmya into accord with these successive changes was a task which devolved upon the local Purohitas. The texts we have discussed above bear, in fact, only too manifestly the traces of their handiwork. Sound knowledge of Sanskrit and literary culture are likely to have been always as foreign to this class of men as they are at present. When it became necessary for them to introduce the names of new localities into the text of the Māhātmya there was every risk of these names being shown not in their genuine old forms, but in hybrid adaptations of their modern Kaśmīrī equivalents. This risk naturally increased when Sanskrit ceased to be the official language of Kaśmīr, and the knowledge of the old local names was gradually lost even among those maintaining scholarly traditions in the country.

[1] Compare *Rājat.* ii. 132 note and v. 465 *sqq.*; vii. 13 *sqq.*; viii. 709, 900 *sqq.*, 939.
[2] Compare Notes *A* (Rājat. i. 35) and *B* (Rājat. i. 37).

Popular etymology in local names of Māhātmyas.

31. Another potent cause seems to have co-operated in this vitiation of the local nomenclature of the Māhātmyas. I mean 'popular etymology.' We have already referred to the tendency displayed throughout these tracts of making the names of localities, rivers, springs, etc., the starting-point for legendary anecdotes. For men of such very scant knowledge of Sanskrit as the *thān*^a*pat*^i*s* invariably are, it was naturally far easier to explain such etymological stories when they were based on the modern local names.

It is undoubtedly this reason which has, *e.g.*, led the compiler of the present Haramukuṭagaṅgāmāhātmya to substitude the name *Karaṅkanadī* for the old *Kanakavāhinī*. By the latter name the stream coming from the Haramukuṭa lakes is designated in all our old texts, as explained in my note on Rājat. i. 149–150. By turning Kāṅk^anai, the modern derivative of this old name, into *Karaṅkanadī*, 'the skeleton-stream,' the compiler of the Māhātmya gets an occasion to treat his readers to a legend likely to appeal to their imagination. The river is supposed to have received this appellation, because Garuḍa had dropped at its Saṁgama with the Sindhu the skeleton (*karaṅka*) of the Ṛṣi Dadhīci which Indra before had used as his weapon, etc.[1] This story, it is true, is wholly unknown to the Nīlamata or any other old text. But, on the other hand, it has got the great merit of being easily explained and proved to any Kaśmīrī pilgrim. He cannot fail to realize the manifest connection between *Karaṅka* and his familiar *k*^a*ranz*, 'skeleton.'

An exactly similar case of 'popular etymology' has been noticed in the analysis of the Śāradāmāhātmya as contained in my Note *B* (i. 37). There the name of the village *Sun*^o*-Drang* is reproduced as *Suvarṇārdhāṅgaka* and explained by a legend, how the Muni Śāṇḍilya had at that spot half his body (*ardhāṅgaka*) turned into gold (*suvarṇa*), etc. In reality the village name is derived from the old term *Draṅga*, 'watch-station,' by which the place is mentioned by Kalhaṇa.[2] The distinguishing prefix *Sun*^o-, meaning 'gold' in Kaśmīrī, was given to it, because it lay on the route to the old gold-washing settlements in the Kiṣangaṅgā Valley.[3]

1 The story is spun out at great length in Paṭala iii. of the *Haramukuṭagaṅgāmāhātmya*, MS. No. 221.

2 See viii. 2507, 2702.

3 For other examples of local names in Māhātmyas metamorphosed for the above reason, compare my notes Rājat. vi. 177 (*Bhīmadvīpa* in the Mārtāṇḍamāh., for Bum^ozu); i. 267 (*Śeṣanāga* in the Amareśvaramāh., for the older *Suśramanāga*, recte *Suśravonāga*); Note *C*, i. 124 (*Jyeṣṭheśvara*, the present Jyēṭhēr, turned into a site of Jyeṣṭhā), etc.

It would be easy to multiply examples showing the strange vicissitudes to which old topographical names are exposed at the hands of the local Purohita. But the explanations already given will suffice to prove that the topographical data found in Māhātmyas can only then be used safely when they are critically sifted and supported by our more reliable sources.

A critical examination of these data is, however, much impeded by the difficulty we experience in fixing the exact age of particular Māhātmyas and their component portions.[1] Even in the case of apparently old texts modern additions and changes may be suspected, while again the most recent concoctions may preserve fragments of genuine tradition.[2] In view of these considerations I have not thought it safe to crowd my maps with hundreds of names of petty Tīrthas as found in the Māhātmyas, but have marked only those pilgrimage sites the ancient names of which can be established with certainty.

[1] The difficulty here indicated is increased by the fact that no really old manuscripts of Māhātmyas seem to be preserved in Kaśmīr. MSS. written on birch-bark, *i.e.*, earlier than the 17th century, are quite unknown at present. Of the numerous paper MSS. I have examined, none seem to me older than two centuries at the utmost. It is probable that this absence of older copies is due to the rough usage to which Māhātmya MSS. are exposed when carried about on the pilgrimage tours.

[2] I am glad that chance gave me an opportunity of gaining some personal experience of the manner in which Māhātmyas are occasionally produced. Some ten years ago the Purohitas or Bāchbaṭṭas of the Ganᵃpatyār quarter in S'rīnagar recovered an ancient Liṅga from a Mosque and began to erect a small shrine for it near the river Ghāṭ of Malᵃyār. Guided by a local tradition which, as far as I can judge, may be genuine, they believed this to have been the site of the shrine of S'iva *Vardhamāneśa* mentioned already in the Rājataraṅgiṇī (see note ii. 123). The Liṅga was re-consecrated accordingly by this name.

In 1891, when examining old sites in this part of the city, I also visited the temple of Vardhamāneśa then under construction. The interest I showed in the old Liṅga and in the tradition regarding it, coupled with an appropriate Dakṣiṇā, soon secured me the confidence of the head-Purohita of the little shrine. 'Paṇḍit' T.R., a man more intelligent than the average of his fraternity, was not slow to confess to me that the Māhātmya of the Tīrtha *in spé* was as yet under preparation. Some weeks later when in camp near S'rīnagar, I received the visit of my Purohita from Vardhamāneśa's shrine. He brought me the draft of the new Māhātmya and asked my assistance in revising it.

I found it to consist chiefly of extracts from the Vitastāmāhātmya. The passages dealing with Vardhamāneśa and the neighbouring Tīrthas within the city had been suitably amplified with laudatory verses in the usual Māhātmya style culled from other texts. The vested interests of other local shrines had received due recognition by being included in the *Yātrā* of Vardhamāneśa. I did what I could to indicate the genuine names of these localities. This quasi-antiquarian co-operation does not seem to have detracted from the popularity of the new Māhātmya among the Bāchbaṭṭas of Ganᵃpatyār.

Abū-l-Fazl's account of Tīrthas.

32. It is a curious fact that among our authorities for the *Topographia sacra* of Kaśmīr we must allow a conspicuous place to a Muhammadan writer. It is Abū-l-Fazl, the minister of Akbar, who in the chapter of his Āīn-i Akbarī dealing with the 'Sarkār of Kashmīr' has left us a very accurate account of many of the holy places in the Valley.[1] Abū-l-Fazl's detailed description of Kaśmīr is valuable in many respects to the historical student. But it is particularly in connection with our topographical search that we must feel grateful to the author for having like his great master "caught some of the enthusiasm of the Valley" (Rennell).

Abū-l-Fazl tells us that "the whole country is regarded as holy ground by the Hindu sages." He also refers in general terms to the numerous shrines dedicated to the various deities and to the popular worship of 'snakes,' *i.e.*, the Nāgas, "of whom wonderful stories are told." He then proceeds to describe in detail the most notable sites, giving among these particular prominence to what Dr. Bernier aptly called 'les merveilles' of the country.

This account of Abū-l-Fazl represents for us an authentic survey of all the Kaśmīrian Tīrthas that were well-known and popular at the end of the 16th century. It serves as a most useful link between our older texts dealing with these pilgrimage places and the modern tradition. It helps us to check the data of the Māhātmyas in many particulars of topographical interest. Abū-l-Fazl's notes have enabled me to trace in more than one instance the position of ancient Tīrthas or particular features regarding them which have since his time been wholly forgotten.[2] It cannot be doubted that Abū-l-Fazl's list of sacred sites to which we have to refer so frequently in our subsequent notes, was supplied by competent Brahman informants just as his abstract of the Sanskrit Chronicles.

[1] Vol. i. pp. 564–570 in Prof. Blochmann's edition of the *Āīn-i Akbarī*; vol. ii. pp. 354–366 in the Bibliotheca Indica translation of the work (Col. H. S. Jarrett). Abū-l-Fazl's account of Kaśmīr would well deserve a fuller commentary than the one which the translator, in the absence of special local studies, was able to give. The account of Mīrzā Ḥaidar (in the Tārīkh-i Rāshidī) and Bernier's notes could conveniently be discussed on the same occasion.

[2] Compare my notes on *Bheḍagiri* (i. 35), the *Sāradātīrtha* (i. 37), the *Takṣakanāga* (i. 220); also supplementary note to i. 107.

Section VII.—Local tradition.

Local tradition of the learned.

33. It now remains for us only to indicate briefly what help surviving tradition offers for the study of the ancient topography of Kaśmīr. The tradition with which we are here concerned, presents itself in two forms. One is the tradition of the 'learned,' regarding the ancient sites of the country in general, kept up more or less in connection with written records. The other is that genuine local tradition which is strictly confined in its limits but is kept up equally among literate and illiterate of particular places.

Among those who represent in Kaśmīr learned tradition of the former type there must again be distinguished the few Paṇḍit families of Śrīnagar in which the serious study of Sanskrit Śāstras has been maintained, and the great host of 'Bāchbaṭṭas.' With the latter class we have already become partially acquainted in the course of our examination of the Māhātmyas. We have had occasion to note the conspicuous absence of genuine knowledge as regards the ancient topography of the country in those texts which form the characteristic products of this class' literary activity.

The Purohitas' knowledge of Sanskrit is ordinarily of the scantiest kind, and their 'reading' confined to Māhātmyas and devotional texts learned by heart without proper comprehension. We can hence scarcely expect them to have preserved genuine traditions regarding those historically interesting localities which are mentioned only in the Chronicles. It is only in the matter of those sacred sites, pilgrimage routes and the like which form as it were, their own particular professional domains, that their testimony can claim special attention. Yet even in this limited field the Purohitas' traditions are, as we have seen, often of a very modern growth. Their statements, therefore, require under all circumstances to be tested with critical caution.

Sāhibrām's Tīrthasaṅgraha.

34. 'Learned' tradition as represented by the Śrīnagar Paṇḍits of modern times, is best guaged by an examination of what the late Paṇḍit Sāhibrām († 1872) has specially recorded on the subject of ancient sites.

P. Sāhibrām who was undoubtedly the foremost among Kaśmīrian Sanskrit scholars of the last few generations, had been commissioned by the late Mahārāja Raṇbīr Singh to prepare a descriptive survey of all ancient Tīrthas of Kaśmīr. For this purpose a staff of Paṇḍits was placed at his disposal whose business it was to collect the necessary materials in the various parts of the country. The large work which was to be prepared on the basis of these materials, was never completed, and of the latter themselves I was able to recover only small portions.[1] But some time before his death Paṇḍit Sāhibrām had drawn up abstracts of the information he had collected under the title of *Kāśmīratīrthasaṁgraha*, and of these I have been also able to obtain copies. The most detailed and apparently latest recension of this Tīrthasaṁgraha is the one contained in No. 61 of Prof. Bühler's collection of MSS. now at Poona.

This little work gives a list of numerous Tīrthas with brief indications of their special features and position, arranged in the topographical order of Parganas. It is useful enough as a comprehensive synopsis of such sacred sites as were known at the time to local worship. The references to many obscure little shrines, Nāgas, etc., show that the enquiries of Paṇḍit Sāhibrām's assistants had been extensive. But the work proves at the same time how little help traditional learning in Kaśmīr could offer in our days for the serious study of the old topography of the Valley.

Paṇḍit Sāhibrām's plan is to indicate each Tīrtha's position by mentioning the territorial division in which it is situated, as well as the nearest village or other well-known locality. It was undoubtedly the learned author's desire to give all local names in their old Sanskrit forms as far as they were known to him. Accordingly we find a number of localities correctly mentioned by their genuine old designations. But unfortunately the number of the latter is truly insignificant when compared with those local names which are plainly recognizable as new fabrications, as worthless as those already mentioned in connections with the topography of the modern Māhātmyas.

In consideration of the fact that P. Sāhibrām deserves to be looked upon as the best representative of modern Kaśmīrian scholarship,[2] it is only just to illustrate the above remarks by a few examples. I take them only from among those local names the genuine forms of which can be easily ascertained from the Rājataraṅgiṇī. The lake of the Nāga *Suśravas*,[3] the present Suśram Nāg, is named *Suśramanāga* in one

[1] The papers acquired by me refer to some of the north-eastern Parganas and contain descriptions (in Sanskrit) of the various Nāgas, Liṅgas, etc., the miraculous stories relating to them, together with the devotional texts which are supposed to be used at their worship. Quaint illustrations and maps accompany the text. The whole forms a large-sized folio. The critical value of these records is very slight.

[2] See Prof. BÜHLER's *Report*, pp. 4, 38.

[3] See *Rājat.* i. 267 note, and below, § 59.

recension and *Suṣumṇanāga* (!) in the other. The old Parganas of *Holaḍā, Laulāha, Khūyāśrama* are turned on account of their modern names Vular, Lōlau, Khuy[a]hōm, into the 'Rāṣṭras' of *Volara, Lalava, Khoyahāma.* Bān[a]hāl, the old *Bāṇaśālā*,[1] figures as *Bhānuśālā*; Khruv, the ancient *Khaḍūvī*,[2] known correctly even to so late a text as the Lokaprakāśa, as *Khrāva.* The well-known Khonamuṣa (Khun[a]moh) appears as *Kṣuṣṇamoṣagrāma* (!) The name of the ancient village *Jayavana*[3] which fares badly too, as we have seen, in the Māhātmyas, is metamorphosed into *Jīvana*; *Raṇyil*, the old *Hiraṇyapura*,[4] is with a flight of historical fancy turned into a foundation of king Raṇāditya (!).

Even the sacred Tīrtha of *Tūlamūlya* (Tul[a]mul) does not escape a renaming as *Sthūlamūla*, though in this case the local Māhātmya, with its *Tūlamūla*, keeps close enough to the old name.[5] After this, village names like *Uṣkara, Rāmāśrama, Kīcakāśrama*, as designations of the old *Huṣkapura, Rāmuṣa, Kṛtyāśrama* can scarcely surprise us.[6] The number of districts, towns, villages, streams, lakes and other topographical features (exclusive of Tīrthas) mentioned by Paṇḍit Sāhibrām amounts to nearly three hundred. But scarcely two dozens of the names given for them are in accord with our old authorities.

Paṇḍit Sāhibrām was one of the few modern Kaśmīrian scholars who have seriously occupied themselves with the Rājataraṅgiṇī and the later Chronicles. This is shown by the elaborate abstracts he had prepared of these works.[7] Hence the indifferent knowledge of ancient topography as displayed in his Tīrthasaṁgraha, must appear all the more striking. Yet in reality it is easily enough accounted for.

What knowledge learned tradition in Kaśmīr has retained of ancient sites as distinct from Tīrthas and the like, is confined to a few prominent localities which, for one reason or the other, were of special interest to the Paṇḍits. Thus the capital *Pravarapura-Śrīnagara* with several of its quarters, *Vijayeśvara, Suyyapura, Varāhamūla, Padmapura*, and some other places of importance in the Valley have continued to be known by their ancient names. This was probably because these names never ceased to be employed in colophons of Sanskrit manuscripts, in horoscopes, and similar records. In the case of a

1 See note viii. 1665, and below, § 41.

2 See note viii. 733; also § 105 below.

3 Compare note vii. 607, and § 105 below.

4 See note i. 287, and § 104 below.

5 Compare note iv. 638.

6 See notes i. 168; ii. 55; i. 147.

7 These abstracts, called *Rājataraṅginīsaṁgraha*, were acquired by Prof. BÜHLER; see Nos. 176–8 of the Poona collection. It deserves to be noted that in them no attempt whatever is made to explain points of topographical interest.

few other localities again like *Jayapura*, *Dāmodara's Uḍar*, *Cakradhara*, there were well-known popular legends which plainly indicated their identity with sites mentioned in the Rājataraṅgiṇī. But for the great mass of ancient places there were no special reasons of this kind to assure a recollection of their old names. It is hence only natural that all genuine knowledge of their identity and earlier history has gradually disappeared from the Paṇḍits' tradition.

Nothing but systematic enquiry on the lines of modern historical research could help towards a recovery of the knowledge thus lost. But such an enquiry could not be expected either from P. Sāhibrām or any other indigenous scholar uninfluenced by Western critical methods.

Popular local tradition.

35. Popular local tradition has fortunately in Kaśmīr proved far more tenacious than the tradition of the learned. I have often derived from it valuable aid in my local search for particular sites. My antiquarian tours have given me ample opportunity to convince myself that when collected with caution and critically sifted, such local traditions can safely be accepted as supplements to the topographical information of our written records. In illustration of this statement I may refer to the evidence gathered from local tradition in reference to the sites of *Lohara*,[1] *Hastivañja*,[2] *Kramavarta*,[3] *Jayapura*,[4] *Skandabhavana*,[5] etc.

In more than one instance it can be shown that local legends which Kalhaṇa heard, still cling unchanged to the same sites. As striking examples may be mentioned here the legends concerning *Dāmodara's Uḍar*,[6] the burned city of King *Nara*,[7] the temple of *Pravareśa*.[8]

It cannot be doubted that this tenacity of local tradition in Kaśmīr is due largely to the isolation secured for the country by its alpine position. Nothing is more instructive in this respect than a comparison with the territories of ancient Gandhāra and Udyāna, or with the Panjāb plains. These regions so rich in ancient Hindu sites are particularly devoid of local traditions connected with them. This fact is easily understood if we think of the many and great ethnic changes which

1 See Rājat. Note *E* (iv. 177), § 15.

2 See Rājat. note i. 302, and *J. A. S. B.*, 1895, pp. 379 *sq.*

3 Compare Note *D* (iii. 227); *J. A. S. B.*, 1895, pp. 384 *sq*; also below, § 43.

4 See note iv. 506 *sqq.*, and below, § 122.

5 See Note *K* (vi. 137).

6 See note i. 156; below, § 119.

7 See note i. 202; below, § 108.

8 See note iii. 350; below, § 96.

have passed over the land. Kaśmīr, fortunately for antiquarian research, throughout its known history has escaped such great convulsions and the breaks of tradition usually connected with them.

The influence of the geographical position of Kaśmīr can be traced here also in another direction. Mountainous surroundings and consequent isolation tend everywhere in alpine countries to develop and foster conservative habits of life and thought. We find these habits most strongly marked in the population of the valley, and may safely ascribe to them a great share in the preservation of local traditions.

CHAPTER III.

GENERAL GEOGRAPHY.

SECTION I.—POSITION AND CONFIGURATION OF KAŚMĪR VALLEY.

The name Kaśmīra.

36. Nature itself when creating the great Valley of Kaśmīr and its enclosing wall of mountains, seems to have assured to this territory not only a distinct geographical character but also a historical existence of marked individuality. We see both these facts illustrated by the clearly defined and constant use of the name which the territory has borne from the earliest accessible period.

This name, KAŚMĪRA in its original Sanskrit form, has been used as the sole designation of the country throughout its known history. It has uniformly been applied both by the inhabitants and by foreigners. We can trace back its continued use through an unbroken chain of documents for more than twenty-three centuries, while the name itself undoubtedly is far more ancient. Yet notwithstanding this long history the current form of the name down to the present day has changed but slightly in the country itself and scarcely at all outside it.

The Sanskrit *Kaśmīra* still lives as *Kaśmīr* (in Persian spelling *Kashmir*) all through India and wherever to the West the fame of the Valley has spread. In the language of the inhabitants themselves the name is now pronounced as *Kaśīr*.[1] This form is the direct phonetic derivative of *Kaśmīr*, with regular loss of the final vowel and assimila-

[1] The adjective *Kạ'śur* 'Kaśmīrian' corresponds to Skr. *Kāśmīra*. The *u* of the last syllable is probably due to the *v* of an intermediate form * Kāśvīra; see below.

tion of *m* to the preceding sibilant. With reference to a phonetic rule, prevalent through all Indo-Aryan Vernaculars, which favours the change of medial Skr. *m* into *v*,[1] we are led to assume an intermediate Prakrit form **Kaśvīr*[*a*]. In support of this we may point to the striking analogy of the Kaśmīr local name *Sāngas* which, as shown in my note on Rājat. i. 100, goes back through an older recorded form *Svāngas* to **Smāṅgāsā*, the *Samāṅgāsā* of the Chronicle. It has already been shown above that we have to recognize in this **Kaśvīra* the original Prakrit form which Ptolemy's Κάσπειρα, Κασπειρία (pronounced Kaspīra, Kaspīria) are intended to transcribe.[2]

Etymologies of name.

Linguistic science can furnish no clue to the origin of the name *Kaśmīra*, nor even analyze its formation.[3] This fact, however, has not saved the name from being subjected to various etymological guesses which for curiosity's sake may receive here a passing notice. It must be held to the credit of Kaśmīrian Sanskrit authors that their extant writings are wholly innocent of this display of etymological fancy.

No less illustrious a person than the Emperor Bābar opens the list. His suggestion was that the name may be derived from the hill-tribe '*Kās*' living in the neighbourhood of Kaśmír.[4] We easily recognize here the reference to the *Khaśas* of the lower hills. Their name, however, in its true form has, of course, no connection with Kaśmīr. Another etymology, first traceable in the Ḥaidar Malik's Chronicle and hence reproduced by other Muhammadan writers,[5] derives the first part of the name from '*Kas͟hap*,' *i.e.*, Kaśyapa, and the second either from

[1] Compare DR. GRIERSON's remarks, *Z. D. M. G.*, l. p. 16.

[2] See above, § 5.

[3] If the Uṇādisūtra, 472, *Kaśer muṭ ca* is to be applied to the word *Kaśmīra*, the latter would have to be dissolved into *kaś-m-īra* according to the traditional grammatical system.

[4] See *Memoirs of Baber, transl. by Leyden and Erskine*, p. 313. A Persian MS.: of the text adds that *mīr* signifies mountain. ERSKINE, *Introduction*, p. xxvii., improves upon this etymology by extending it to Kashgar, the Casia regio and Casii Montes of Ptolemy. RITTER, *Erdkunde*, ii. p. 1127, from whom I take this reference, not unjustly queries why the learned editor should have stopped short of the *Caspium mare* and other equally manifest affinities.

Babar's conjecture figures still seriously in a note of the latest translation of the Aīn-i Akbarī, ii. p. 381.

Regarding the name and habitation of the *Khaśas*, compare *Rājat.* i. 317 note.

[5] It was first introduced to the European reader by TIEFFENTHALER's extract from Ḥaidar Malik's Chronicle compare *Description historique et géographique de l' Inde*, ed. Bernouilli (1786), i. p. 79 (also p. 89 as to source). Compare also WILSON, *Essay*, p. 94, for a similar note from the *Wāqi'āt-i Kas͟hmīr* of Muḥammad 'Aẓīm; here کشف سر is a clerical error for کشف میر.

mar, *i.e.*, Skr. *maṭha* 'habitation,' or a word *mīr*, supposed to mean 'untain.'[1]

It was, perhaps, a belief that this whimsical etymology represented some local tradition, which induced even so great a scholar as Burnouf to risk the conjectural explanation of Kaśmīra as * *Kaśyapamīra*, *i.e.*, 'the sea of Kaśyapa.'[2] There is neither linguistic nor any other evidence to support this conjecture. It would hence scarcely have been necessary to refer to it had it not on the authority of a great name found its way also into numerous works of a more general character.[3]

Extent and position of Kaśmīr.

37. Just as the name Kaśmīr has practically remained unchanged through the course of so many centuries, so also has the territorial extent of the country which it designated. This has always been confined to the great valley drained by the headwaters of the Vitastā and to the inner slopes of the ring of mountains that surround it.

The natural limits of the territory here indicated are so sharply marked that we have no difficulty in tracing them through all our historical records, whether indigenous or foreign. Hiuen Tsiang, Ou-k'ong and Albērūnī's accounts, as we have seen, show them clearly enough. Kalhaṇa's and his successors' Chronicles prove still more in detail that the Kaśmīr of Kaśmīrian tradition never extended materially beyond the summit-ridges of those great ranges which encircle and protect the Valley.

A detailed description of the geographical position of Kaśmīr does not come within the scope of this paper. Nor is it needed since there is an abundant modern literature dealing with the various aspects of the geography of the country. For an accurate and comprehensive account I may refer to the corresponding portion of Mr. Drew's work and to the graphic chapter which Mr. Lawrence devotes to the description of the Valley.[4] It will, however, be useful to allude here briefly to some of the characteristic features in the configuration of the country which have an important bearing on its ancient topography.

Kaśmīr owes its historical unity and isolation to the same facts which give to its geographical position a distinct and in some respects

[1] The Kś. word *mar* < Skr. *maṭha*, is in common use in the country as the designation of Sarais, shelter-huts on passes, etc. *Mīr* might have been connected by Ḥaidar Malik's Paṇḍit informants with the name of Mount *Meru* or with *mīra*, meaning according to a Kośa *parvataikadeśa*, see *B. R.*, s. v.

[2] Compare his note in Humboldt, *L'Asie centrale*, i. p. 92.

[3] See, *e.g.*, Lassen, *Ind. Alt.*, i. p. 54 note; McCrindle, *Ancient India as described by Ptolemy*, p. 108; V. de St. Martin, *Mém. de l' Acad. des Inscript., Sav. E'trang.*, v., ii. p. 83; Kiepert, *Alte Geographie*, 1878, p. 36.

[4] See F. Drew, *The Jummoo and Kashmir Territories*, 1875, Chapters viii.–x.; W. Lawrence, *The Valley of Kasmir*, 1895, pp. 12–39.

almost unique character. We have here a fertile plain embedded am high mountain ranges, a single valley large enough to form a king for itself and capable of supporting a highly developed civilizat n. Its height above the sea, nowhere less than 5000 feet, and its peculiar position assure to it a climate equally free from the heat of India and the rigours of cold, peculiar to the higher mountain regions in the north and east.

The form of the country has been justly likened to a great irregular oval, consisting of a similarly shaped level vale in the centre and a ring of mountains around it. The low and more or less flat part of the country measures about 84 miles in length, from south-east to north-west, while its width varies from 20 to 25 miles. The area comprised in this part has been estimated at 1800 or 1900 square miles.[1] Around this great plain rise mountain ranges which enclose it in an almost unbroken ring. Their summit lines are everywhere but for a short distance at the southernmost point of the oval, more than 10,000 feet above the sea. For the greatest part they rise above 13,000 feet, while the peaks crowning them tower up to altitudes close on 18,000 feet. Reckoned from the summit lines of these ranges, the length of the irregular oval enclosed by them is about 116 miles, with a varying width from 40 to 75 miles. The whole area within these mountain boundaries may be estimated at about 3,900 square miles.

The slopes of the mountains descending towards the central plain are drained by numerous rivers and streams all of which join the Vitastā within the Kaśmīr plain. The side-valleys in which these tributaries flow, add much ground to the cultivated area of the country several of them being of considerable length and width. But even the higher zones of the mountain-slopes where cultivation ceases, add their share to the economical wealth of the country. They are clothed with a belt of magnificent forests, and above this extend rich alpine pastures, close up to the line of perpetual snow.

In the great mountain-chain which encircles the country, there is but one narrow gap left, near to the north-west end of the Valley. There the Vitastā after uniting the whole drainage of Kaśmīr flows out by the gorge of Bārāmūla (Varāhamūla) on its course towards the sea. For a distance of nearly 200 miles further this course lies through a very contracted valley which forms a sort of natural gate to Kaśmīr. It is here that we find the old political frontier of Kaśmīr extending beyond the mountain-barriers already described. For about 50 miles below the Varāhamūla gorge the narrow valley of the Vitastā was held in Hindu times as an outlying frontier tract of Kaśmīr.[2]

1 Compare DREW, *Jummoo*, p. 162, for this and subsequent statements.

2 See below § 53.

Legend of Satīsaras.

38. The general configuration of the country here indicated in its broadest outlines may be held to account for the ancient legend which represents Kaśmīr to have been originally a lake. This legend is mentioned by Kalhaṇa in the Introduction of his Chronicle and is related at great length in the Nīlamata.[1]

According to this earliest traditional account the lake called *Satīsaras*, 'the lake of Satī (Durgā),' occupied the place of Kaśmīr from the beginning of the Kalpa. In the period of the seventh Manu the demon Jalodbhava ('water-born') who resided in this lake, caused great distress to all neighbouring countries by his devastations. The Muni Kaśyapa, the father of all Nāgas, while engaged in a pilgrimage to the Tīrthas in the north of India, heard of the cause of this distress from his son Nīla, the king of the Kaśmīr Nāgas. The sage thereupon promised to punish the evil-doer and proceeded to the seat of Brahman to implore his and the other gods' help for the purpose. His prayer was granted. The whole host of gods by Brahman's command started for Satīsaras and took up their position on the lofty peaks of the *Naubandhana Tīrtha* above the lake Kramasaras (Kōns^a^r Nāg). The demon who was invincible in his own element, refused to come forth from the lake. Viṣṇu thereupon called upon his brother Balabhadra to drain the lake. This he effected by piercing the mountains with his weapon, the ploughshare. When the lake had become dry, Jalodbhava was attacked by Viṣṇu and after a fierce combat slain with the god's war-disc.

Kaśyapa then settled the land of Kaśmīr which had thus been produced. The gods took up their abodes in it as well as the Nāgas, while the various goddesses adorned the land in the shape of rivers. At first men dwelt in it for six months only in the year. This was owing to a curse of Kaśyapa, who angered by the Nāgas had condemned them to dwell for the other six months together with the Piśācas. Accordingly men left Kaśmīr for the six months of winter and returned annually in Caitra when the Piśācas withdrew. Ultimately after four Yugas had passed, the Brahman Candradeva through the Nīlanāga's favour acquired a number of rites which freed the country from the Piśācas and excessive cold. Henceforth Kaśmīr became inhabitable throughout the year.

The legend of the desiccation of the lake is alluded to also by Hiuen Tsiang, though in another, Buddhistic form.[2] Its main features as related in the Nīlamata, live to this day in popular tradition. They

[1] See *Rājat.* i. 25-27; *Nīlamata*, vv. 26-237. A detailed extract of the Nīlamata's story has been given by Prof. BÜHLER, *Report*, p. 39.

[2] See *Si-yu-ki*, transl. Beal, i. p. 149.

are also reproduced in all Muhammadan abstracts of the Chronicle.[1] From Ḥaidar Malik's Tārīkh the legend became known to Dr. Bernier who prefaces with it his description of the 'Paradis terrestre des Indes.'[2] It has since found its way into almost every European account of Kaśmīr.

Lacustrine features of Valley.

It is probable that this legend had much to do with drawing from the first the attention of European travellers to certain physical facts apparently supporting the belief that Kaśmīr was in comparatively late geological times wholly or in great part occupied by a vast lake. But few seem to have recognized so clearly as the late Mr. Drew, the true relation between the legend and the above facts. I cannot put his view which from a critical point of view appears to be self-evident, more clearly than by quoting his words: "The traditions of the natives—traditions that can be historically traced as having existed for ages—tend in the same direction, [*viz.*, of the Vale having been occupied by a lake,] and these have usually been considered to corroborate the conclusions drawn from the observed phenomena. Agreeing, as I do, with the conclusion, I cannot count the traditions as perceptibly strengthening it; I have little doubt that they themselves originated in the same physical evidence that later travellers have examined."[3]

The geological observations upon which modern scientific enquirers like Mr. Drew and Colonel Godwin Austin, have based their belief as to the former existence of a great lake, are mainly concerned with the undoubted 'lacustrine deposits' found in the so-called Uḍars or Karēwa plateaus to be noticed below. But it seems to me very doubtful whether we can reasonably credit the early Kaśmīrians with a correct scientific interpretation of such geological records. It appears far more probable that the legend was suggested by an observation of the general form of the valley and by a kind of natural inference from the historical changes in the country's hydrography.

We shall see below that great drainage operations took place at various periods of the country's history which extended the cultivated ground and reduced the area covered by lakes and marshes. To any one, however ignorant of geology, but acquainted with the latter fact, the picture of a vast lake originally covering the whole Valley might naturally suggest itself. It would be enough for him to stand on a hill-side somewhere near the Volur, to look down on the great lake and the adjoining marshes, and to glance then beyond towards that narrow gorge

1 Compare, *e.g.*, *Āīn-i Akb.*, ii. p. 380; Wilson, *Essay*, p. 93.

2 See Bernier, *Travels in the Mogul Empire*, ed. Constable, p. 393.

3 See *Jummoo*, p. 207.

of Bārāmūla where the mountains scarcely seem to leave an opening. It is necessary to bear in mind here the singular flights of Hindu imagination as displayed in the Purāṇas, Māhātmyas and similar texts. Those acquainted with them, will, I think, be ready to allow that the fact of that remarkable gorge being the single exit for the drainage of the country, might alone have sufficed as a starting-point for the legend.

In respect of the geological theory above referred to it may yet be mentioned that in the opinion of a recent authority "even the presence of true lacustrine deposits does not prove that the whole of the Kaśmīr lake basin was ever occupied by a lake."[1] At the present day true lacustrine deposits are still being formed in the hollows of the rock basin represented by the lakes of the north-west portion of the Valley. It is held probable "that the conditions have been much the same as at present, throughout the geological history of the Kaśmīr Valley," only a minor area of the latter having at various periods been occupied by lakes.

Whatever view may ultimately recommend itself to geologists, it is certain that the lacustrine deposits of Kaśmīr, though of no remote date, speaking by a geological standard, are far older than any monuments of man that have yet been discovered.[2] Mr. Drew was undoubtedly right in denying the existence of lacustrine deposits round any known ancient buildings or other works of man in the Valley.

Kaśmīr defended by its mountains.

39. None of the natural features of Kaśmīr geography have had a more direct bearing on the history of the country than the great mountain-barriers that surround it. They may hence rightly claim our first consideration.

The importance of the mountains as the country's great protecting wall has at all times been duly recognized both by the inhabitants and foreign observers. Since an early time Kaśmīrians have been wont to pride themselves on their country's immunity from foreign invasion, a feeling justified only by the strength of these natural defences. We find it alluded to by Kalhaṇa who speaks of Kaśmīr as unconquerable by the force of soldiers and of the protection afforded by its mountain walls.[3] The feeling is very clearly reflected in all foreign records. We have already seen what special notice is taken by Hiuen Tsiang and Ou-k'ong of the mountains enclosing the kingdom and of the difficulty of the passes leading through them.[4] The statements of the early Arab

[1] See OLDHAM'S *Manual of Indian Geology* (1893), quoted by MR. LAWRENCE, *Valley*, p. 50.

[2] See DREW, *Jummoo*, pp. 207 sq.

[3] See *Rājat.* i. 31, 39.

[4] Compare above, §§ 9, 11.

geographers brief as they are, lay due stress on the inaccessible character of the mountains. Albērūnī does the same and shows us besides the anxious care taken in old days to maintain this natural strength of the country by keeping strict watch over the passes.[1]

Even when Kaśmīr had suffered a partial conquest from the north and had become Muhammadanized, the belief in the invincibility of its bulwarks continued as strong as before. Thus Sharīfu-d-dīn, the historian of Tīmūr, writing apparently from materials collected during the great conqueror's passage through the Panjāb Kōhistān (circ. A.D. 1397), says of Kaśmīr: "This country is protected naturally by its mountains on every side, so that the inhabitants, without the trouble of fortifying themselves, are safe from the attacks of enemies." The subsequent account of the routes into Kaśmīr and other exact details suggest that the author of the *Ẓafarnāma* had access to genuine Kāśmīrian information.[2]

Watch-stations on mountain routes.

40. It is this defensive character of the mountain ranges to which we owe most of our detailed information regarding their ancient topography. We have already in connection with the accounts of Albērūnī and the Chinese pilgrims had occasion to note the system of frontier watch-stations by which a careful guard was kept on the passes leading through the mountains. These fortified posts and the passes they guarded, play an important part in the narrative of Kalhaṇa and his successors. As most of the Chronicle's references to Kaśmīr orography are directly connected with these watch-stations it will be useful to premise here a few general remarks regarding their character and purpose.[3]

The small forts which since ancient times closed all regularly used passes leading into the Valley, are designated in the Chronicles by the word *dvāra* 'gate' or by the more specific terms *draṅga* or *ḍhakka*. Numerous passages show that they served at the same time the purposes of defence, customs and police administration. They were garrisoned by troops under special commanders, designated as *draṅgeśa* or *draṅgādhipa*. The control over all these frontier stations and the command of the 'Marches' generally was vested in Hindu times in one high state officer, known by the title of *dvārapati*, 'lord of the Gate,' or equivalent terms.[4]

[1] See above, §§ 12, 14.

[2] See the extract from Sharīfu-d-dīn's Ẓafarnāma in *Tārīkh-i-Rashīdī*, transl. by N. Elias and E. D. Ross, p. 432; compare also Ritter, *Asien*, ii. pp. 1122, *sq.*

[3] For detailed references regarding these stations see my notes, *J. A. S. B.*, 1895, pp. 382 *sqq.*; *Rājat.* i. 122; iii. 227 (*D*).

[4] Compare *Rājat.* note v. 214.

The organization of the system was somewhat changed in Muhammadan times when the guarding of the several routes through the mountains was entrusted to feudal chiefs known as Maliks (Skr. *mārgeśa*).[1] These held hereditary charge of specific passes and enjoyed certain privileges in return for this duty. In other respects the system underwent scarcely any change. The fortified posts with their small garrisons survived on all important routes almost to our own days being known as *rāhdārī* in the official Persian.[2]

It may be noted that apart from their character as military defences against foreign inroads the Draṅgas were also in another respect true 'gates' to the country. Nobody was allowed to pass outside them coming from the Valley without a special permit or pass. The system thus provided an important check on unauthorized emigration which was withdrawn only after the last Kaśmīr famine (1878).[3]

In order to appreciate fully the importance of these frontier watch-stations it should be remembered that the mountain regions immediately outside Kaśmīr were almost in every direction held by turbulent hill-tribes. To the hardy Dards (*Darad*) in the north and the restless Khakhas (*Khaśa*) in the south and west the rich Kaśmīr with its weak population has always appeared as a tempting prey. The last inroad of plundering Khakhas occurred not more than half a century ago and will not soon be forgotten.[4] At the same time it is certain that the valour of these hardy mountain clans on the confines of Kaśmīr has at all times contributed greatly to the natural strength of the mountain defences. Without this protective belt the latter themselves would scarcely have remained so long proof against foreign invasion.

[1] A detailed and interesting account of the *Maliks* and the routes held by them is given by Baron HÜGEL, *Kaschmir*, ii., pp. 167 *sqq.*; i., p. 347.

[2] See *J. A. S. B.*, 1895, p. 385; also below, § 49, 52.

[3] For an early reference to this system of passports at the *Dvāras*, see *Jonar.* 654. For a description of the cruel exactions often connected with 'Rāhdārī,' compare LAWRENCE, *Valley*, p. 215. I have never been able to visit the sites of the old watch-stations at the several passes without thinking of the scenes of human suffering they must have witnessed for centuries.

[4] Compare *Rājat.* i. 317 note.

SECTION II.—THE PĪR PANTSĀL RANGE.

Kaśmīr orography.

41. In order to understand correctly the data relating to the ancient topography of the mountains around Kaśmīr, it is necessary to acquaint ourselves with their actual configuration and character. In the following account it will be possible only to indicate the most prominent features of this mountain system, and those directly connected with the historical data under discussion. For detailed information on Kaśmīr orography a reference to the lucid and instructive account in MR. DREW's work may be specially recommended.[1]

The mountain ring enclosing Kaśmīr is divided into three main ranges. One of these, usually designated as the *Pīr Pantsāl* Range, forms the boundary of the Kaśmīr Valley to the south and southwest. It may be considered to begin from the southernmost part of the Valley where the Bānᵃhāl Pass, 9200 feet above the sea, marks the lowest depression in the chain of mountains. After running for about 35 miles from east to west the range turns to the north-northwest. In this direction it continues for about fifty miles more, and after attaining its greatest elevation in the Taṭakūṭi Peak (15,524 feet above the sea), gradually descends towards the Valley of the Vitastā. All important old routes towards the Panjāb cross this great mountain barrier, and this circumstance enables us to trace some interesting information regarding its ancient topography.

Eastern portion of Pīr Pantsāl Range.

The Bānᵃhāl Pass at the eastern extremity of the range must owing to its small elevation have always been a convenient route of communication towards the Upper Cināb Valley and the eastern of the Panjāb hill-states. It takes its modern name from a village at the south foot of the pass which itself is mentioned in Kalhaṇa's Chronicle by the name of BĀṆAŚĀLĀ.[2] The castle of Bāṇaśālā was in Kalhaṇa's own time the scene of a memorable siege (A.D. 1130) in which the pretender Bhikṣācara was captured and killed. Coming from the Cināb Valley he had entered *Viṣalāṭā*,[3] the hill district immediately south of the Bānᵃhāl Pass with the view to an invasion of Kaśmīr. As his move-

[1] See *Jummoo*, pp. 192–206.

[2] See *Rājat.* viii. 1665 *sqq.* and note. Bānᵃhāl is the direct phonetic derivative of Skr. *Bāṇaśālā*, medial Skr. *ś* being regularly changed into *h* in Kaśmīrī.

[3] See *Rājat.* viii. 177. The name of Viṣalāṭā is probably preserved in that of the river *Bichlārī*. Viṣalāṭā more than once served as a safe retreat for Kaśmīrian refugees; comp. *Rājat.* viii. 177, 697, 1074.

ment fell in the commencement of the winter, he could not have selected a more convenient route. The Bānᵃhāl Pass is the only one across the Pīr Pantsāl Range on which communication is never entirely stopped by snowfall. Kalhaṇa's narrative shows that the political and ethnographic frontier of Kaśmīr ran here as elsewhere on the watershed of the range. For the castle of Bāṇaśālā, though so near as to be visible already from the top of the pass (*saṁkaṭa*), was already held by a Khaśa chief.[1]

Proceeding westwards from Bānᵃhāl we come to a group of three snowy peaks reaching above 15,000 feet. With their bold pyramidal summits they form conspicuous objects in the panorama of the range as seen from the Valley.[2] Kaśmīr tradition locates on them the seats from which Viṣṇu, S'iva and Brahman, according to the legend already related, fought Jalodbhava and desiccated the Satīsaras. The westernmost and highest of these peaks (15,523 feet) forms the famous NAUBANDHANA Tīrtha. According to the legend related in the Nīlamata and other texts and connected with the Indian deluge story, Viṣṇu in his fish Avatāra had bound to this peak the ship (*nau*) into which Durgā had converted herself to save the seeds of the beings from destruction.[3] At the foot of this peak and to the northwest of it, lies a mountain lake over two miles long known now as *Kōnsᵃr Nāg*, the KRAMASARAS or *Kramasāra* of the Nīlamata and Māhātmyas.[4] It is supposed to mark a footstep (*krama*) of Viṣṇu, and is the proper object of the Naubandhana pilgrimage.

About 8 miles straight to the west of this lake, the range is crossed by a pass, over 14,000 feet high, known now by the name of *Sīdau* or *Būdil*. It lies on a route which in an almost straight line connects S'rīnagar with Akhnūr and Siālkōt in the Panjāb plain. Running up and down high ridges it is adapted only for foot traffic, but owing to its shortness was formerly a favourite route with Kaśmīrīs.[5] The name *Sīdau* is given to the pass from the first village reached by it on the

1 *Rājat.* viii. 1674, 1683. *Saṁkaṭa* is the regular term for 'pass.'

2 Marked on maps as 'Brama Sakal,' perhaps a corruption for *Brahmaśikhara* 'Brahman's peak.'

3 See *Nīlamata*, 33 *sqq.*; *Haracar.* iv. 27; *S'rīv.* i. 474 *sqq.*; *Sarvāvatāra* iii. 4, 12; v. 43, etc.

4 See *S'rīv.* i. 482 *sqq.* where a visit of Sulṭān Zainu-l-'ābidīn to this lake is related at length; *Nīlamata*, 121, 1272; *Naubandhanamāhātmya*, passim; *Sarvāvatāra* iii. 10; v. 174, etc.

5 According to DREW, *Jummoo*, p. 524, the distance from Jammu to S'rīnagar by the Sidau route is reckoned at 129 miles while *viâ* the Bānᵃhāl it is 177 miles.

The name Būdil is given to the pass from the hill-district adjoining it on the south; compare my note *Rājat.* vi. 318.

Kaśmīr side. It is by this name, in its original form SIDDHAPATHA, that the pass is mentioned in Kalhaṇa's Chronicle as the route chosen for a pretender's irruption in Sussala's reign.[1]

A snowy peak close to the west of the pass of Siddhapatha marks the point where the main range changes its direction towards north-northwest. From the same point there branches off in a westerly direction the lower Ratan Pīr Range to which we shall have to refer below. Beyond this lie the passes of Rūpri and Darhāl, both above 13,000 feet in height. They are not distinctly named in the Chronicles. But as they give most direct access to Rajauri, the ancient *Rājapurī*, and are crossed without much trouble during the summer months they are likely to have been used from an early time. Near the Darhāl Pass lies the *Nandan Sar*, one of the numerous tarns which along this portion of the chain mark the rock-ground beds of old glaciers. It is probably the *Nandana Nāga* of the Nīlamata.

Pīr Pantsāl Route.

42. About five miles due north of the Nandan Sar we reach the lowest dip in the central part of the whole range. It is marked by the pass known as *Pīr Pantsāl*, 11,400 feet high. The route which crosses it has from early days to the present time been the most frequented line of communication from Kaśmīr to the central part of the Panjāb. The frequent references which the Chronicles make to this route, permit us to follow it with accuracy from the point where it enters the mountains. This is in the valley of the Rembyār[a] River (*Ramaṇyāṭavī*), a little below the village of *Hür^apōr*.

This place, the ancient ŚŪRAPURA, is often referred to as the entrance station for those reaching Kaśmīr from Rājapurī and the neighbouring places, or *vice versâ* as the point of departure for those travelling in the opposite direction.[2] Śūrapura was founded by Śūra, the minister of Avantivarman, in the 9th century evidently with the intention of establishing a convenient emporium on this important trade-route.[3] He transferred to this locality the watch-station (*draṅga*) of the pass. Its site, as I have shown in my *Notes on the Ancient Topography of the Pīr Pantsāl Route*,[4] can still be traced at the place known as *Ilāhī Darwāza* ('the gate of God'), a short distance above the village. We find the

[1] See *Rājat.* viii. 557. In the Chronicles of Śrīvara and his successors the tract about Sidan is repeatedly referred to as *Siddhādeśa*, an evident adaptation of the Kś. form of the name.

[2] See *Rājat.* iii. 227, Note *D*, § 1.

[3] Compare *Rājat.* v. 39 note.

[4] See *J. A. S. B.*, 1895, p. 385. This paper should be compared for all details regarding the other sites along this route.

commanders of this frontier-station more than once engaged in military operations against intending invaders from the other side of the mountains.

Ascending the valley of the Rembyār[?] or Ramaṇyāṭavī for about 7 miles we reach the point where the streams coming from the Pīr Pantsāl and Rūprī Passes unite. In the angle formed by them rises a steep rocky hillock which bears on its top a small ruined fort known as *Kāmelankōṭh.* These ruins probably go back only to the time of 'Aṭā Muḥammad Khān,' the Afghān Governor of Kaśmīr, who, about 1812, fortified the Pīr Pantsāl Route against the Sikh invasion then threatening. But I have proved in the above-quoted paper that they mark the original position of the ancient watch-station on this route before its transfer to S'ūrapura.[1] Kalhaṇa, iii. 227, calls this site *Kramavarta.* This name is rendered by a glossator of the 17th century as *Kāmelanakoṭṭa* and still survives in the present *Kāmelankōṭh* (**Kramavartānāṁ koṭṭa*).

43. The old 'Imperial Road' constructed in early Mughal times then ascends the narrow valley, keeping on its left side high above the Pīr Pantsāl stream. At a distance of about four miles above Kāmelankōṭh and close to the Mughal Sarai of 'Alīābād, a high mountain-ridge slopes down from the south and falls off towards the valley in a wall of precipitous cliffs. The ridge is known as *Hastivañj.* This name and the surviving local tradition makes it quite certain that we have here the spot at which a curious legend told by Kalhaṇa was localized from early times.[2]

Hastivañja.

The Chronicle, i. 302 *sqq.* relates of King *Mihirakula* whose identity with the White Hun ruler of that name (circ. 515–550 A.D.) is not doubtful, that when on his return from a tour of conquest through India he reached the 'Gate of Kaśmīr,' he heard the death-cry of an elephant which had fallen over the precipice. The gruesome sound so delighted the cruel king that he had a hundred more elephants rolled down at the same spot. The old glossator on the passage informs us that "since that occurrence the route by which Mihirakula returned, is called *Hastivañja.*" The Persian Chroniclers too in reproducing the anecdote give *Hastivanj* as the name of the locality.

The local tradition of the neighbouring hill tracts still knows the story of a king's elephants having fallen down here into the gorge below. It also maintains that the old route to the Pass, in the times before the construction of the 'Imperial Road', crossed the *Hastivañj* ridge and followed throughout the right bank of the Pīr Pantsāl

[1] *J. A. S. B.*, 1895, pp. 384 *sq.*

[2] Compare *J. A. S. B.*, 1895, pp. 378 *sqq.*

stream. This is fully borne out by a statement of Abū-l-Fazl.[1] Describing the several routes available on the march from Bhimbhar to Kaśmīr, he clearly distinguishes "the route of Hastivanj (MSS. Hastivatar) which was the former route for the march of troops," from the 'Pīr Pantsāl route' which Akbar used on his visits to Kaśmīr.

The name Hastivanj contains in its first part undoubtedly *hasti*, the Kś. derivative of Skr. *hastin*, 'elephant.' The second part is connected by the Persian compilators with the root *vañj* meaning 'to go' in Western Panjābī. The close connection between the name and the local legend already heard by Kalhaṇa is evident enough. But whether the latter had any foundation in fact or merely arose from some 'popular etymology' of the name, cannot be decided.

The story helps in any case to make it quite clear that the ancient route from the Pīr Pantsāl Pass kept to the right or southern side of the valley. My enquiries on the spot showed that this route though neglected for many centuries is passable for laden animals and not unfrequently used by smugglers.[2]

Pañcāladhārāmaṭha.

44. 'Aliābād Sarai is a Mughal hospice erected for the shelter of travellers about half a mile above Hastivañj. It is about the highest point on the ascent to the pass where fuel can conveniently be obtained. I think it hence probable that the *Maṭha* or hospice which Kṣemendra mentions on the Pīr Pantsāl Pass, must have been situated somewhere in this neighbourhood.

[1] See *Āīn-i Akb.*, ii. pp. 347 *sq.* The form *Hastivatar* in the text is a clerical error for *Hastivanj*, easily explained in Persian characters.

[2] Dr. Bernier who in the summer of 1665 accompanied Aurangzeb's court to Kaśmīr, has left us, in his Ninth Letter to M. de Merveilles, an accurate and graphic account of the Pīr Pantsāl Route. While ascending the Pass from the Panjāb side he passed the spot where two days earlier an accident had happened curiously resembling Mihirakula's story. Fifteen of the elephants carrying ladies of the Imperial seraglio, owing to some confusion in the line of march, fell over the precipice and were lost; see *Bernier's Travels*, ed. Constable, p. 407. The curious Map of Kaśmīr given in the Amsterdam edition of 1672 shows accordingly the '*Pire Penjale*' mountain with a troop of elephants rolling in picturesque confusion over its side.

Former editions of Ince's '*Hand-book*' placed the scene of this accident at a spot called Lāl Ghulām just opposite Hastivañj on the 'Imperial Road.' It is evident that this wrong location was due to the original compiler having somehow confused Bernier's account and the local tradition referring to Hastivanj. The edition of 1888, p. 64, rectifies this mistake, but still indicates Lāl Ghulām as the site "of many a dreadful accident" before the causeway of the 'Imperial Road' was made. As a matter of fact, the left side of the valley was not used at all as a route before the construction of the 'Imperial Road' along its cliffs.

Of the accident on Aurangzeb's march no recollection survives.

Kṣemendra makes this interesting reference in that curious portion of the Samayamātṛkā already alluded to, which describes the wanderings of the courtezan Kaṅkālī.[1] The heroine of his story after effecting some petty thefts in Kaśmīr proceeds to *Sūrapura*. There she passes herself off as the wife of a load-carrier (*bhārika*) engaged on the 'salt road.'[2] By this term the Pīr Pantsāl route is quite correctly designated. It has remained to the present day the chief route by which the produce of the Panjāb salt-mines coming *viâ* Jehlam and Bhimbhar enters Kaśmīr.[3] She keeps up the disguise which is evidently intended to help her through the clutches of the officials at the frontier watch-station, by taking next morning a load on her head and starting with it towards the pass (*saṁkaṭa*). On the way she passes along high mountains by precipitous paths deeply covered with snow. By nightfall she reaches the PAÑCĀLADHĀRĀMAṬHA after having in the meantime assumed the guise of a respectable housewife and apparently disposed of her load. It being late in the season, she passes the night there shivering with cold. Thence she finds her way open to India where a career of successful adventures awaits her.

The name Pañcāla.

45. Kṣemendra's itinerary is of particular value because it supplies us with the only mention of the old name of the pass I can trace. It is certain that with him PAÑCĀLADHĀRĀ designates the highest portion of the route, *i.e.*, the Pass of the Pīr Pantsāl. It is equally obvious that *Pañcāla* is the original of the modern Kś. *Pantsāl* which is in fact identical with the earlier form except for the regular change of Skr. *c* into Kś. *ts*. In the Pahāṛī dialect of the population inhabiting the valleys to the south the name is still pronounced *Pañcāl*.[4]

[1] See *Samayam.* ii. 90 *sqq.*, and above, § 25.

[2] Professional load-carriers or Coolies are found to this day in numbers in Hür°pōr, Puṣiāna and other places near the Pīr Pantsāl Pass. Of Zainu-l-ʿābidīn it is specially reported that he settled a colony of load-carriers from *Abhisāra* (*i.e.*, the country about Bhimbhar) at the customs-station of Sūrapura; see *Śrīv.* i. 408. Coolies are the only means of transport on the Pīr Pantsāl and other passes when the snow lies to any depth.

[3] Salt is a considerable article of import into Kaśmīr where it is wholly wanting; see LAWRENCE, *Valley*, p. 393. I remember vividly the long strings of salt-laden bullocks which I used to meet daily when marching into Kaśmīr by the Pīr Pantsāl route.

[4] I am not certain of the origin of the pronunciation of the name as *Pīr Panjāl* now accepted by Anglo-Indian usage. It is known neither on the Kaśmīr nor on the Panjāb side of the range itself. It meets us first in Bernier's 'Pire Penjale.' Tieffenthaler, however writes more correctly *Pensal*; see *Description de l'Ind* 1786, pp. 87 *sq.*

The term *dhārā* which is added to Pañcāla, represents in all probability the equivalent of our 'pass.' Skr. *dhārā* means generally the sharp edge of some object. According to Wilson's Dictionary, as quoted by Böthlingk-Roth, the word also carries the specific meaning of 'edge of a mountain.' It is probable that this meaning was taken by Wilson's Paṇḍits from some Kośa. In any case it agrees closely with the use of the word *dhār* in the modern Pahāṛī dialects south of Kaśmīr. There it is well-known as the designation of any high mountain ridge above the region of alpine pasture.

We are tempted to see in *Pañcāla* a distinct local name, either of the Pass itself or of the whole mountain chain. But the use of the modern derivative *Panṭsāl* presents difficulties in the way of a certain conclusion. The word Panṭsāl is applied in Kaśmīr chiefly to the great mountain chain which forms the boundary of the country to the south, *i.e.*, the range to which conventional European usage gives the name of 'Pīr Panṭsāl.' Yet the meaning now conveyed to a Kaśmīrī by the term Panṭsāl, is scarcely more than that of 'high mountain range.'

The word is used in combination with specific names for the designation of subordinate branches of the great range towards the Panjāb. Thus the range crossed on the way from the Pīr Panṭsāl Pass to Rajaurī, is known as '*Ratan Panṭsāl*,' and the one crossed by the Hāji Pīr Pass between Ūrī and Prūnts (Pūnch) as '*Hāji Panṭsāl*.' Sometimes, but not so generally, the term is applied also to mountains wholly unconnected with the Pīr Panṭsāl system.

On the whole I am inclined to believe that *Pañcāla* > *Panṭsāl* had originally the character of a specific local name. It may have been applied either to the whole of the great southern chain of mountains or its central portion about the Pīr Panṭsāl Pass. Subsequent usage may then have extended the application of the term just as it has that of the name 'Alps' in Europe. Our materials, however, are not sufficient to enable us to trace the history of the word with certainty.[1]

Pīr, a term for pass.

46. In this connection it will be useful briefly to notice also the word *Pīr* which forms the first part of the modern designation of the Pass. This word is now used more or less frequently for 'Pass' both in Kaśmīr and the hill-tracts south of it. Mr. Drew who seems to have given more attention to local nomenclature in these hills than other travellers, in his explanation of the term starts from the well-known meaning of *Pīr* in Persian, an 'old man' and thence a 'saint or Faqīr.'[2]

[1] The main facts regarding the modern use of the word Panṭsāl have been quite correctly recognized already by Drew, *Jummoo*, p. 157.

[2] See *Jummoo*, p. 157 note.

He refers to the common practice of Faqīrs establishing themselves on Passes for the sake of refreshing travellers and of receiving their alms. "When any noted holy Faqīr died on a Pass, the place became sacred to his memory, and was often called after him, his title of Pīr being prefixed; at last it became so common for every important Pass to have a name beginning with Pīr that the word acquired the secondary meaning of Mountain Pass." MR. DREW refers to the fact that Dr. Bernier already found an aged hermit established on the Pass who had resided there since the time of Jahāngīr. He was supposed "to work miracles, cause strange thunders, and raise storms of wind, hail, snow and rain." From this 'Pīr,' Mr. Drew thinks, the Pass acquired the first part of its present name.

I agree with the above explanation as far as the use of the Persian word *Pīr* is concerned. But I suspect that the custom of connecting mountain passes with holy personages rests on a far older foundation. Superstitious belief has at all times and in all mountainous regions peopled the solitary summits and high ridges with spirits and other supernatural beings. To this day Kaśmīrian Brahmans fully believe in the presence of Devatās and 'Bhūtas' of all sorts on high mountain passes. In those parts of the Himālaya where Hinduism has survived among all classes, this superstition can, no doubt, be found still more fully developed.

On all Kaśmīr Passes, however rarely visited, stone-heaps are found marking the supposed graves of imaginary 'Pīrs.' Every pious Muhammadan on passing adds his stone to them. Yet these little cairns existed there in all probability long before Islām reached the country. Exactly the same custom is observed, *e.g.*, by the Hindu Pilgrims to Amaranātha on crossing the Vāv^{a}jan Pass above the lake of Suśravonāga, 'to please the Devas' as the Māhātmya says.[1]

We can show that almost all famous Ziārats in Kaśmīr, whether of real or imaginary Muhammadan saints, occupy sites which were sacred in earlier times to one or the other Hindu divinity. We can scarcely go far wrong in concluding by their analogy that the 'Pīrs' of the Muhammadan wayfarers have only taken the place of the older Hindu 'Devas.'

This surmise is strikingly corroborated by the only passage of the

[1] See *Amaranāthamāhātmya*, vii. 1 *sqq.* The stones placed are supposed to represent *maṭhikās*, 'shelter-huts', in which the gods can find refuge from the evil wind blowing on the pass (hence its alleged Sanskrit name *Vāyuvarjana*). The duty of making these Maṭhikās is enjoined in vii. 19. *Maṭhikāṁ ye na kurvanti tatraiva Vayuvarjane | dāruṇaṁ narakaṁ yānti śatakalpaṁ na saṁśayaḥ || kṛtvā tu maṭhikāṁ devi pūjayed vidhipūrvakam | arpayed devaprītyarthaṁ dakṣiṇābhiḥ samanvitam ||.*

Sanskrit Chronicles which mentions the Pīr Pantsāl Pass by its proper name. Śrīvara iii. 433, when relating the return of a Kaśmīr refugee 'by the route of Śūrapura' in the time of Ḥasan Shāh (circ. A.D. 1472–84), tells us of a fatal chill he caught "on the top of the *Pañcāladeva*." It is clear that the name here used corresponds exactly to the modern Pīr Pantsāl, 'Pīr' being the nearest Muhammadan equivalent for 'Deva.' Dr. Bernier's account has already shown us that popular superstition had not failed to transfer also the supernatural powers of the 'Deva' to the Pīr who acted as his representative on the Pass.

Pass of Pīr Pantsāl.

47. We may now return to the description of the old route where we left it at 'Aliābād Sarai and resume our journey towards the Pass. From the Mughal hospice the road ascends in a gently sloping valley westwards until at at a distance of about $4\frac{1}{2}$ miles the height of the Pass is reached. Close to the point where the descent towards the Panjāb begins, stands the hut of a Faqīr. He has inherited the post of Bernier's Pīr, but little of his spiritual powers and his emoluments. An octagonal watch-tower close by, occupied by a Sepoy post till a few years ago, may mark the site of an earlier outpost.

The descent is here as on all Passes of the range far steeper on the Panjāb side than towards Kaśmīr. *Puṣiāna*, the next stage, which is reached by zigzag paths along the rocky slope of the mountain, lies already more than 3000 feet below the Pass. The little village is an ancient place. It is undoubtedly the PUṢYĀṆANĀḌA of Kalhaṇa who mentions it repeatedly in connection with the civil wars of his own time.[1] Puṣyāṇanāḍa served often as a refuge for rebel leaders for whom Kaśmīr had become too hot. They could thence conveniently resume their inroads. We see here again clearly that the Kaśmīr frontier ran on the watershed of the range; for of Puṣyāṇanāḍa it is distinctly said that it belonged already to the territory of Rājapurī.

From Puṣiāna the road descends in a westerly direction along the bed of a stream which belongs to the headwaters of the Tauṣi (Tohī) of Prūnts. The next stage is the hill-village of Bahrāmgala, a considerable place which is mentioned already by Śrīvara under the name of BHAIRAVAGALA.[2] From Bahrāmgala the route turns to the south and crosses, by the Pass known as Ratan Pīr (8200 feet), the range which has already been mentioned as a branch from the Pīr Pantsāl chain. There the route enters the region of the middle mountains and descends in an open valley to Rajaurī, the ancient *Rājapurī*, where we may leave it.

[1] Compared *Rājat.* viii. 959 note. The ending *nāḍa* is identical with *nāla*, Anglo-Indicè 'Nullah,' *i.e.*, 'valley, ravine.'

[2] See *Śrīv.* iv. 529, 589.

Central part of Pīr Pantsāl.

48. Beyond the Pīr Pantsāl Pass the summit-line of the main range rises again considerably. The *Tangtala* Pass which is about five miles due north of the Pīr Pantsāl Pass and is mentioned by Abū-l-Fazl,[1] is already far higher. The track crossing it is scarcely practicable for animals.

The same is the case, as personal experience showed me, with the next two Passes, known by the Pahārī names of *Cittapānī* and *Cōṭī Galī*; they are both over 14,000 feet high. The first one was probably used on occasion of the inroad related by S'rīvara, iv. 589 sqq. We are told there of a rebel force which coming from Rajaurī evaded the troops of Sultān Muḥammad S͟hāh posted at S'ūrapura, by crossing the mountains in the direction of KĀCAGALA. This place, as shown on the map, corresponds undoubtedly to the alpine plateau or 'Marg' of *Kāc*ᵊ*gul* on the northern slope of the Pīr Pantsāl range.

A short distance to the northwest of the Cōṭī Galī Pass the range culminates in its greatest snowy peak, Mount *Taṭakūṭī*, which rises to a height of 15,524 feet. Owing to its bold shape and central position this peak is the most conspicuous object in the panorama of the whole range, whether seen from the Kaśmīr Valley or from the Panjāb plains. To the north it presents a precipitous face of unscaleable rocks. On the south it is surrounded by snowfields which on the occasion of an ascent made late in the season I found still of considerable extent. We have already seen that it is this peak which Albērūnī describes under the name of *Kulārjak*.[2] For an observer from the Panjāb plain about Gujrāt the appearance of the peak, with its glittering dome of snow, is very striking, notwithstanding the great distance (about 87 miles as the crow flies). I have sighted it on very clear days even from Lahore Minārs.

From Taṭakūṭi the chain continues at a great elevation for a considerable distance, the summit ridge keeping an average height between 14,000 and 15,000 feet. We find it crossed first by the Passes of *Sangsafēd*, *Nūrpūr* and *Cōrgalī*, all difficult routes leading down into the valley of Lohᵊrin, the ancient Lohara. It is only at the Tōṣᵊmaidān Pass that we meet again with an important and ancient line of communication.

Tōṣᵊ maidān Route.

49. This Pass being on the most direct route between the Kaśmīr capital and Lohara, was of special importance during the reigns of the later Kaśmīrian kings whose original home and safest stronghold was in Lohara. We

[1] See *Āīn-i Akb.*, ii. p. 348.

[2] Compare above, § 14.

find accordingly the route leading over the Tōṣ^a^maidān Pass often referred to in the last two Books of Kalhaṇa's Chronicle.

But apart from this historical connection the Tōṣ^a^maidān route must have always been prominent among the old lines of communication from Kaśmīr owing to its natural advantages. It was the shortest route into the Valley of Pūnch (Parṇotsa) and hence to that portion of the western Panjāb which lies between the Jehlam and Indus. It was besides under the old conditions of road and travel probably the easiest and safest route in that direction.[1]

This old route started from the present village of *Drang*, situated at the foot of the mountains in the Bīru Pargaṇa, circ. 33° 57′ lat. 74° 36′ long. The name of the village is, of course, nothing but the old term of *draṅga*, 'watch-station.' In old times the place was distinguished as KĀRKOṬADRAṄGA.[2] It may have received the distinctive first part of its name, *Kārkoṭa*, from the mountain-ridge now known as *Kākōdạr*, which is passed higher up on the route. Kś. *Kākōdạr* could well be derived form an earlier Skr. form like **Kārkoṭadhara*. The Tīrthasaṁgraha also mentions a *Kārkoṭanāga* somewhere in this direction.

From *Draṅg* where a customs-station exists to this day, the road ascends over an easy forest-clad slope to the edge of the *Tōṣ^a^maidān*. This is, as the name indicates, a large upland plateau of undulating grazing grounds, rising very gradually from a level of about 10,000 feet. At the point where the road strikes the northern edge of the plateau, there are several ruined towers. They seem to have been last repaired on occasion of the Sikh invasion of 1814 to be referred to below, but are probably far older. The spot is known to this day as *Barbal* which in Kś. means 'the place of the Gate' (Kś. *bar* < Skr. *dvāra*). In view of this designation and the commanding position of the place we can safely locate here the proper Dvāra or 'Gate' of this route.[3]

The route after crossing the Tōṣ^a^maidān plateau ascends over gently sloping grassy ridges to the Kākōdạr spur and passing along the south foot of the latter reaches the Pass. The ascent is so gradual and easy that though the elevation of the latter is over 13,000 feet, the construction of a cart-road would so far meet with little difficulty. The Pass itself is equally easy.

On its west side two routes are available. One descends in the

1 The historical references to this route will be found collected in Note *E* (*Rājat.* iv. 177) on Lohara, §§ 5–14.

2 Compare *Rājat.* vii. 140; viii. 1596 notes.

3 The term *dvāra* is actually used by Kalhaṇa, vii. 140, 1301, for a fortified post on this route. The village Drang is a suitable enough position for a customs and police station; the point for military defence, however, is higher up at 'Barbal.'

Gāgrī Valley past the village of *Chāmbar* mentioned in the Rājataraṅgiṇī by the name of Sārambara.[1] The other leads over a cross-spur in a south-westerly direction straight down into the valley now known as Lohᵃrin. The position of the ancient castle of Lohara which I was able to trace in the centre of this great and fertile valley, has been fully discussed by me in a separate note.[2] About 8 miles further down the valley and at the point where its waters meet the stream coming from Gāgrī, lies the large village of Maṇḍī. It marks the site of the old 'market of Aṭṭālikā,' repeatedly mentioned by Kalhaṇa.[3] From Maṇḍi onwards the route passes into the open valley of the Tohī (Tauṣi) of Prūnts which offers an easy line of communication down to the plains.

The historical importance of the Tōṣᵃmaidān route is best illustrated by the fact that it was chosen on two occasions for expeditions aiming at the invasion of Kaśmīr. We have already referred to Maḥmūd of Ghazna's expedition, probably of A.D. 1021, which Albērūnī accompanied, and to which we owe the valuable information recorded by him.[4] This attempt at invasion, perhaps the most serious of which we know during Hindu times, was frustrated by the valorous defence of the castle of Lohara and a timely fall of snow. Nor was Mahārāja Raṇjit Singh more successful when in 1814 he first attempted to invade Kaśmīr by this route.[5] The portion of the Sikh army led by him in person, safely reached the Tōṣᵃmaidān plateau where the Afghān defenders were posted near the towers above mentioned. Difficulties of supplies, however, and the news of a reverse sustained by the column marching by the Pir Pantsāl route forced on a retreat. This ended in a complete rout in the mountain defiles about Lohᵃrin.

It may yet be mentioned that the route over the Tōṣᵃmaidān was already in all probability followed by Hiuen Tsiang on his way to Parṇotsa or Prūnts.[6] It remained a favourite trade route until the recent Jehlam Valley cart-road was constructed. Owing to the elevation of the Pass, however, this route is always closed by snow longer than, *e.g.*, that of the Pīr Pantsāl. During the winter, therefore, the road from Lohara to Kaśmīr lay by the lower passes in the west leading into the Vitastā Valley below Bārāmūla.[7]

1 See *Rājat.* viii. 1875–77 note.

2 See Note *E*, iv. 177; also *Ind. Ant.* 1897, pp. 225 *sqq.*

3 See *Rājat.* viii. 581 note.

4 See above, § 14.

5 For a more detailed account of this expedition, see Note *E*, iv. 177, § 14.

6 Compare above, § 9.

7 See Note *E* (*Rājat.* iv. 177), §§ 7, 8, for Kalhaṇa's references to the occasions when this more circuitous route was used.

Not far to the north of the Tōsᵊmaidān Pass the range still attains a height of over 15,000 feet in a group of bold snowy peaks. Its summit ridge then gradually descends and is crossed by some lower passes from the neighbourhood of the well-known alpine plateau of Gulmarg. From a summit behind Gulmarg (marked 'Sallar' on the map) several spurs radiate. They form the northern end of the range, and descend very steeply and with faces of rugged cliffs into the narrow valley of the Vitastā.

Section III.—The Vitastā Valley.

Valley of Vitastā.

50. We have already spoken of the Vitastā Valley as the single outlet for the waters of Kaśmīr and as the great gate of the country. We may now cast a glance at the old route leading through it and at the defences by which nature has fortified it.

The Vitastā Valley below Bārāmūla is confined between two ranges of mountains. The one to the south is a branch of the Pīr Pantsāl Range separating from the main chain at a point behind Gulmarg. The range to the north belongs to a mountain-system which culminates in the Kājnāg Peak (14,400 feet) and is usually designated by the name of the latter. These two ranges accompany the course of the river for some eighty miles westwards down to the point near Muzaffarābād where the Vitastā makes its sudden bend to the south.

Along the whole length of the Valley, cross-ridges, more or less steep and rugged, run from both sides down to the river-bed. This consists from below Bārāmūla of an almost unbroken succession of rapids, the fall in level being nearly 3000 feet in the above distance. The Valley is throughout narrow and wanting in level ground. But for about 50 miles, down to the old Kaśmīr frontier line, it may more fitly be described as a narrow ravine. Only occasional alluvial terraces high above the river afford room here for settlement and cultivation.

Owing to this extremely confined nature of the Valley, communication on the route leading along it must have always been troublesome and risky in old times. The natural difficulties of this long defile were no doubt considerably increased by the restless disposition of the Khaśa tribe which has held it since ancient times. The Sikhs who were the last to fight their way through these passes, suffered more than one disaster at the hand of the hill-men. The line of forts erected by them along the valley attests to this day the trouble they experienced in holding the passage.[1] The military difficulties of a march through such a succession of dangerous defiles must have been even greater in old times which knew no fire-arms. The protection of the route against an active enemy who could easily seize and hold all commanding positions, was then, no doubt, a still more difficult task.

Vitastā Valley Route.

51. It is probably on account of the circumstances here briefly indicated that we hear in the Chronicles comparatively little of the route following the Vitastā. Being the shortest line of communication to the present Hazāra District and the Indus, it was certainly used from early times. We have seen that Hiuen Tsiang and Ou-k'ong coming from the ancient Gandhāra and Uraśā followed it on their way to Kaśmīr, and that it was well-known to Albērūnī.

But it seems probable that its importance, military and commercial, was then far smaller than that of the Pīr Pantsāl and Tōṣ*maidān routes. It is only in modern times that this western route has attained real prominence. This originated in the time of the Afghān rule over Kaśmīr when the route along the Vitastā to Muẓaffarābād and hence though Hazāra afforded the shortest and least exposed line of communication between Kaśmīr and Peshawar.[2] Subsequently after the annexation of the Panjāb, the establishment of the hill-station of Murree naturally drew traffic in this direction. The construction of the Tonga Road from Murree to Bārāmūla in our own time finally assured to this route its present supremacy.

There is at present a road on each side of the Valley leading down to Muẓaffarābād. But only the route along the right bank of the river can claim any antiquity. The one on the opposite bank has come into general use only within the last few decades since traffic towards Murree and Rawalpindi sprung up. The track chosen for the old road is easily accounted for by topographical facts. We have already noticed that the Vitastā Valley route was of importance chiefly as leading to Hazāra (Uraśā) and hence to the old Gandhāra. A glance at the map will show that the open central portion of Hazāra is most easily gained by crossing the Kiṣangaṅgā just above Muẓaffarābād and then passing the comparatively low ridge which separates this river from the Kunhār stream. The route here indicated finds its natural continuation towards

[1] Moorcroft's account of his attempt to use the Muẓaffarābād route in 1823 gives a graphic picture of the obstacles created by the rapacious hill-tribes; see *Travels*, ii. pp. 281 *sqq*. Compare also LAWRENCE, *Valley*, p. 200.

[2] Baron HÜGEL quite correctly notes a Kaśmīr tradition that the Bārāmūla route was properly opened up only about 80 years before his own visit (1835) on the arrival of the Paṭhāns; see *Kaschmir*, ii. p. 174.

Kaśmīr on the right bank of the Vitastā, the crossing of the latter being wholly avoided. It has already been shown above that this route, now marked by the stages of Abbottabad, Garhi Ḥabībullāh, Muẓaffarābād and Bārāmūla, is directly indicated in Albērūnī's itinerary.[1]

52. We may now proceed to examine the old notices regarding this route. It started in Kaśmīr from the twin towns of *Varāhamūla-Huṣkapura* which occupied the sites of the present Bārāmūla and Uṣkür, respectively. Huṣkapura on the left river bank, though the more important of the two places in ancient times, has dwindled down to a mere village. Varāhamūla-Bārāmūla, however, on the opposite bank is still a flourishing place and an emporium of trade. It occupies a narrow strip of open ground between the river and the foot of a steep mountain side.

Gate of Varāhamūla.

Close to the western end of the town a rocky ridge with a precipitous slope runs down into the river-bed. Only a few yards' space is left open for the road. At this point there stood till last year (1897) an old ruined gateway known to the people as the *Drang* or 'watch-station.' It had been occupied as a military police post; until the 'Rāhdārī' system was abolished, watch was kept here over those who entered or left the Valley. I had examined the gateway in 1892. When revisiting the spot in May, 1898, I could scarcely trace its foundations. The decayed walls had meanwhile been sold by auction, and its materials carried away by a contractor.

Though the structure I had seen, was scarcely older than the time of Sikh rule, there can be little doubt that it marked the site of the ancient 'Gate' of Varāhamūla. This is clearly indicated by the situation of the spot which is by far the most convenient in the neighbourhood for the purpose of a watch-station. Moorcroft does not mention the name *Drang*, but describes the gateway itself accurately enough. Here then, we may assume, stood in ancient times "the stone gate, the western entrance of the kingdom", through which Hiuen Tsiang had passed before he reached Huṣkapura (*Hu-se-kia-lo*), his first night's quarter in the Valley. Ou-k'ong too and Albērūnī, as we have seen, knew well this watch-station which is also mentioned by Kalhaṇa under the general designation of *Dvāra*.[2]

The road keeps close by the bank of the river as it winds in rapid fall through the rock-bound gorge. About two and a half miles below 'Drang' the hill sides recede slightly, leaving room for a small village

[1] See above, § 14. [The construction of a Tonga road between Abbottabad and Muẓaffarābād, recently sanctioned (1899), is sure to make the old route through Hazāra again popular.]

[2] See *Rājat.* viii. 413 note.

called *Nārān Thal*. Near it stands a little temple, with a spring close by which is visited by pilgrims and is probably identical with the *Nārāyaṇa-sthāna* of the Nīlamata.[1]

About a mile below this point and close to the village of Khādᵊ-niyār,[2] the river turns sharply round a steep and narrow spur projecting into the valley from the north-west. A ledge of rocks continues the spur below the river-bed and forms the first serious rapid of the Vitastā below which boats cannot pass (see map). The road crosses the spur by a narrow and deep cut, known as *Dyārᵊgul*. Kalhaṇa's Chronicle knows this curious cutting by the appropriate name of *Yakṣadara*, 'the demon's cleft.' According to the tradition there recorded the operations by which Suyya, Avantivarman's engineer, lowered the level of the Vitastā, extended to this point of the river bed.[3]

Old frontier in Vitastā Valley.

53. Two miles below Dyārᵊgul we pass near the village of Zehenpōr some ancient sites vaguely described by Vigne and Hügel. Still further down near the village of Gingal the map marks the ruins of a temple which I have not been able to visit. But no localities on this route are known to us from our old sources until after about three and a half marches we reach the side valley marked on the map as 'Peliasa.' This valley and the large village at its entrance are known indeed to the Pahāṛī population by the name of *Peliāsa*. But the Kaśmīrīs settled at several places along the Vitastā Valley call them *Buliāsa*. This form of the name which I ascertained by local enquiries, enables us to identify this locality with the Bolyāsaka of the Rājataraṅgiṇī.

Kalhaṇa in his account of S'aṁkaravarman's ill-fated expedition towards the Indus (A.D. 902) mentions *Bolyāsaka* as the place where the Kaśmīr army retreating from Uraśā reached the border of their own territory.[4] This reference is of special interest as it shows that Kaśmīr authority extended in Hindu times down to this point of the Valley. We can easily reconcile this fact with the existence of the 'Dvāra' at Varāhamūla.

The gorge at the latter place offered a convenient position for establishing a watch-station which was to secure control over the traffic and the collection of customs. But in regard to military defence a frontier-line in the immediate vicinity of the Kaśmīr Valley would have been very unsafe. I believe, therefore, that the Vitastā Valley

[1] See *Nīlamata*, 1179, 1315, 1349. The name occurs also repeatedly in the several Varāhakṣetramāhātmyas.

[2] Perhaps the *Khādanāvihāra* of *Rājat.* iii. 14.

[3] Compare *Rājat.* v. 87 note.

[4] See *Rājat.* v. 225 note.

below Varāhamūla was held as an outlying frontier-tract as far as the present Buliāsa. It is exactly a few miles below this place that ascending the Valley the first serious difficulties are encountered on the road. An advanced frontier-post could scarcely have occupied a strategically more advantageous position.

The conclusion here indicated is fully supported by what Kalhaṇa's narrative tells us of a locality almost exactly opposite to Buliāsa. Kalhaṇa mentions in two places a place called VĪRĀNAKA in connection with events which make it clear that it lay in the Vitastā Valley and just on the border of Kaśmīr territory.[1] I have been able to trace the position of Vīrānaka at the modern hill-village of *Vīran*, near the left bank of the Vitastā and only a short distance above Buliāsa. The valley below the old frontier thus marked is now known as *Dvārbidī*. Its ancient name is given by an old gloss of the Rājataraṅgiṇī which speaks of Bolyāsaka as situated in DVĀRAVATĪ. Local enquiries have shown me that even to the present day popular tradition indicates a ridge a short distance above Buliāsa as the eastern limit of Dvārbidī.[2]

In the account of Śaṁkaravarman's above-mentioned expedition six marches are reckoned from the capital of Uraśā to Bolyāsaka. This agrees exactly with the present reckoning which also counts six marches from the vicinity of Buliāsa to Abbottabad.[3] Near this place, the modern head-quarter of the Hazāra District, the old capital of Uraśā was in all probability situated.

Left bank of Vitastā.

54. It remains for us to notice briefly what is known of ancient localities on the left side of the Valley. As already explained there was no great line of communication on this side corresponding to the present Murree-Bārāmūla Road. Yet for two marches down the Valley, as far as Ūrī, the route of the left bank is likely to have been much frequented. From Ūrī a convenient route leads over the easy Hāji Pīr Pass to Prūnts or Parṇotsa. This pass owing to its small elevation, only 8500 feet, is never completely closed by snow. It is hence much used during the winter-months when the more direct routes to Kaśmīr *viâ* the Pīr Pantsāl, Tōṣᵃmaidān or other high Passes are rendered impracticable.

1 See *Rājat.* v. 214 and viii. 409. In the first passage we hear of an attack made on Vīrānaka by the chief commander of the frontier posts (*dvāreśa*). In the second *Vīrānaka* is referred to as a settlement of Khaśas which offered the first safe refuge to Sussala when defeated before Varāhamūla, A.D. 1111.

2 See *Rājat.* v. 225 and note v. 214.

3 Compare *Rājat.* v. 217 note; CUNNINGHAM, *Anc. Geogr.*, p. 104, and DREW, *Jummoo*, p. 528.

Marching down the valley from Uṣkür: Huṣkapura, we first cross the spur which bounds the gorge of Varāhamūla from the south. We then reach a fertile little plain, about two miles broad, charmingly situated in an amphitheatre of high pine-clad mountains and facing the Dyār^{a}gul ridge. It is known as *Nār^{a}vāv* and contains at the village of *Sīr* and *Fattegarh* considerable remains of ancient temples. On a small plateau which forms the western boundary of this plain by the river bank, lies the village of *Kiṭṣ^{a}hōm* It marks the site of the ancient Buddhist convent of *Kṛtyāśrama*, the foundation of which a curious legend related by Kalhaṇa attributes to the son of Aśoka.[1] Ou-k'ong refers to it as the 'monastère du mont *Kitché*.'

At Būniār, near the end of the first day's march we pass the well-preserved ruins of an ancient temple which are of considerable antiquarian interest. Its name and date cannot be traced in our extant records. Another similar ruin, but far more decayed, flanks the road about mid-way between Būniār and Ūrī.

From near the latter place the Vitastā Valley is held on the left bank chiefly by the Khakha tribe, on the right by the closely related Bombas. In the former we recognize the ancient *Khaśas* whose settlements lower down the Valley, at Vīrānaka, are distinctly mentioned by Kalhaṇa.[2] The predatory habits and restless ways of the Khaśas form a frequent theme in the Chronicle. The modern Khakhas and Bombas have up to the middle of the present century done their best to maintain this ancient reputation, just as their seats have remained the old ones.

[1] See *Rājat.* i. 147 note; also my *Notes on Ou-k'ong*, pp. 13 *sqq.* Kṛtyāśrama is mentioned already by Kṣemendra, *Samayam.* ii. 61.

[2] *Rājat.* viii. 409.

SECTION IV.—NORTHERN MOUNTAIN RANGE.

Range towards Karnau and Śardi.

55. The mountains which enclose the Kaśmīr Valley in the north-west and north, may be looked upon as one great range. Their chain nowhere shows any marked break though its direction changes considerably. The routes leading through these mountains have never been of such importance in the history of Kaśmīr as the routes towards India and the west. Hence our information regarding the old topography of this mountain range is also less detailed.

We are least informed about that portion of the range which joins on to the Kājnāg Peak north-west of Bārāmūla and then continues in the direction of south to north towards the upper Kiṣangaṅgā. The watershed of this portion forms the western boundary of Kaśmīr towards *Karnau*, the ancient KARṆĀHA.[1] This territory which may be roughly described as lying between the Kiṣangaṅgā and the Kājnāg Range, seems at times to have been tributary to Kaśmīr. Yet we hear of it only in the concluding portion of Kalhaṇa's Chronicle, and there too no details are given regarding the routes leading to it. These routes as the map shows, start from the ancient districts of *Samālā* (Hamal) and *Uttara* (Uttar).

At the point where the summit of the range comes nearest to the Kiṣangaṅgā, it takes a turn to the east and continues in this direction for more than 100 miles. The summit ridge keeps after this turn at a fairly uniform height of 12,000 to 13,000 feet for a long distance. From the northern parts of the Uttar and Lōlau Parganas several routes cross the range in the direction of the Kiṣangaṅgā.

Kalhaṇa has occasion to refer to these in connection with the expedition which took place in his own time against the *Śirahśilā* castle. This stood on the Kiṣangaṅgā close to the ancient Tīrtha of the goddess Śāradā still extant at the present Śardi.[2] One of these routes leads past the village of *Draṅg*, situated at 74° 18′ 45″ long. 34° 33′ 30″ lat. It is certain that the place took its name from an ancient watch-station here located and is identical with the DRAṄGA mentioned by Kalhaṇa in connection with the above expedition.[3] I have not been able to visit the place in person but was informed in the neighbourhood that remains of

[1] Compare *Rājat.* viii. 2485 note.

[2] Compare regarding the *Śāradātīrtha* and the castle of *Śirahśilā*, notes i. 36 (*B*) and viii. 2492 (*L*), respectively; also below, § 127.

[3] See *Rājat.* viii. 2507 note.

old watch-towers are still found on the path which leads up to the pass behind the village of Drang.

Besides the route marked by this old frontier-station there are others leading in the same direction. One is to the west over the Sītalvan Pass; the other lies in the west and passing through the valley of Krōras descends directly to S'ardi along the *Madhumatī* stream. The portion of the Kiṣangaṅgā Valley into which these routes lead, can never have been of much importance itself though there are indications of gold-washing having been carried on in it.[1] But from S'ardi starts a route leading very directly, by the Kankatōri (Sarasvatī) River and over a high pass, into Cilās on the Indus;[2] this line of communication may already in old times have brought some traffic to S'ardi.

Owing to the inroads made by Cilāsīs and the restless Bomba chiefs of the Kiṣangaṅgā Valley, the Paṭhān Governors found it necessary to settle Afrīdīs at Drang and the neighbouring villages to guard the passes. The presence of these Afghān colonies shows that the conditions which necessitated the maintenance of the old frontier watch-station at Draṅga, had altered little in the course of centuries.

Pass of Dugdhaghāta.

56. Above S'ardi the course of the Kiṣangaṅgā lies for a long distance through an almost inaccessible and uninhabited gorge. Hence for over 30 miles eastwards we find no proper route across the mountain range. Kalhaṇa gives us a vivid and interesting account of the difficulties offered by a winter-march along the latter when he describes the flight of the pretender Bhoja from S'irahśilā castle to the Darads on the Upper Kiṣangaṅgā.[3]

The line of communication we meet next is, however, an important one. It leads from the north shore of the Volur lake into that part of the Upper Kiṣangaṅgā Valley which is known as Gurēz, and connects with the routes leading to Astōr and the Baltī territory on the Indus. The road used in recent years, and now improved by British engineers into the 'Gilgit Transport Road,' crosses the range by the *Trāgᵃbal* or *Rāzdiangan* Pass, nearly 12,000 feet high. But the route frequented in ancient times lay some eight miles further to the east.

Kalhaṇa refers in several places to the hill fort of DUGDHAGHĀTA which guarded the mountain-route leading into Kaśmīr territory from inroads of the Darads. The latter can easily be shown to have held

[1] Compare Note *B* on S'āradā (*Rājat.* i. 36), §§ 2, 16. To this circumstance the of *Drang* owes probably the distinguishing designation of *Sunᵊ-Drang* 'the Gold Drang,' by which it is popularly known.

[2] See BATES, *Gazetteer*, p. 490.

[3] See *Rājat.* viii. 2710 *sqq.*

then as now the Kiṣangaṅgā Valley about Gurēz and the neighbouring territories to the north. From Kalhaṇa's description it is evident that this frontier fort stood on, or close to, the summit of a pass. Thanks to the indications of the Chronicle I was able to identify its site on the top of the *Dudᵊkhut* Pass.[1] The Pass (shown on the map by its ancient name *Dugdhaghāta*) is approached on the Kaśmīr side from the valley of the Baṇḍᵊpōr stream, still known to the Brahmans by its old name *Madhumatī*. At the small village of Ātavuṭh (map 'Atawat') a side valley is entered which is narrow and somewhat difficult below, but higher up widens. Its highest portion which forms the immediate approach to the pass, is an open alpine valley known to the mountain shepherds as *Vijje Marg*.

The term *Marg* which denotes any high alpine grazing ground frequented in the summer by herdsmen, is the modern Kaśmīrī equivalent, and direct derivative, of Skr. *maṭhikā*. It designated originally the small shelter-huts of stone or wood usually erected on such high plateaus or valleys by their summer occupants.[2] It is probably that Vijje Marg represents the *Prājimaṭhikā* which Kalhaṇa mentions as the position occupied by the Kaśmīr forces during their unsuccessful siege of the fort.

As a characteristic point it may be mentioned that the garrison depended for its water-supply on the storage of snow. This had become exhausted at the late summer season when the siege took place, but, luckily for the Darad defenders, was replaced by a fresh fall of snow. The latter is explained by the elevation of the pass which I estimated at about 11,500 feet. Snow-storms occur sometimes on the neighbouring *Trāgᵃbal* Pass so early as September.

From the Dudᵊkhut Pass an easy track over the ridge marked 'Kiser' on the map leads down to Gurēz, the chief place of the Valley. The latter corresponds probably to the DARATPURĪ of the Rājataraṅgiṇī. The route over the Dudᵊkhut, being very direct and comparatively easy during the summer, was much frequented by Dard traders until the recent construction of the 'Gilgit Transport Road.' It was used by the Sikhs for military convoys until a disaster caused by an avalanche above Ātavuṭh induced them to change it for the Trāgᵃbal route. It also seems to have been mentioned to Baron HÜGEL.[3] In Muhammadan

1 For detailed evidence regarding this location and a description of the site, see *Rājat.* vii. 1171 note.

2 Skr. *maṭhikā* is the diminutive of *maṭha* 'hut', 'Sarai.' The Kś. derivative of the latter term, *mar*, is still used regularly for the rude shelter-huts which are found on the higher passes particularly towards the north.

3 See *Kaschmir*, ii. p. 169.

times both routes were in charge of a 'Malik' who resided in the castle of *Banḍᵊkōṭh*, not far from the ancient *Mātṛgrāma* shown on the map.

In ancient times there probably existed in the same neighbourhood a watch-station or Draṅga. Ou-k'ong when speaking of the 'gate to the north' through which the road led to *Poliu* or Baltistān, may have meant either this Draṅga or the fort of Dugdhaghāta.

Mount Haramukuṭa.

57. To the east of the Dudᵊkhut Pass the summits of the range gradually get higher and higher until we reach the great mountain-mass of the Haramukh Peaks. Rising to close on 17,000 feet and surrounded by glaciers of considerable size, these Peaks dominate the view towards the north from a great part of the Kaśmīr Valley. Sacred legends have clustered around them from early times. The lakes below their glaciers belong still to the holiest of Kaśmīrian Tīrthas. The ancient name of the Peaks is HARAMUKUṬA, 'S'iva's diadem.' This is explained by a legend which is related at length in the Haracaritacintāmaṇi.[1] Their height is supposed to be S'iva's favourite residence.[2] Hence Kaśmīrian tradition stoutly maintains that human feet cannot reach the Peaks' summit.[3]

The lake which lies at the foot of the north-eastern glacier, at a level of over 13,000 feet, is looked upon as the true source of the Kaśmīr Gaṅgā or Sind River. It is hence known as UTTARAGAṄGĀ or popularly *Gangᵃbal*.[4] It is the final goal of the great 'Haramukuṭagaṅgā' pilgrimage which takes place annually in the month of Bhādrapada and is attended by thousands of pilgrims. The bones of those who have died during the year, are on that occasion deposited in the sacred waters. A short distance below this lake is another also fed by a glacier and now known as *Nundkōl*. Its old name *Kālodaka* or *Nandisaras* is derived from a legend which makes the lake the joint habitation of Kāla, *i.e.*, S'iva, and of his faithful attendant *Nandin*. From the

1 See *Haracar.* iv. 62 *sqq.*

2 The legends relating to S'iva's residence on Mount Haramukuṭa and his connection with the several sacred sites of Nandikṣetra, are given at great length in the *Nīlamata* 1049 *sqq.*

3 Owing to this superstition I had great difficulty in inducing any of my Kaśmīrī Coolies (Muhammadans!) to accompany me on the ascent I made to the Peaks in September, 1894. My Brahman friends could not give credence to my having reached the summit. According to their opinion the very fact of my having reached the Peak was a sufficient proof of this not having been Haramukuṭa. An argument as simple as incontrovertible to the orthodox mind.

4 See my note *Rājat.* i. 57. Another name often used in the Nīlamata and other texts is *Uttaramānasa*; see *Rājat.* iii. 448 note.

latter the whole collection of sacred sites takes the name of *Nandikṣetra* by which Kalhaṇa usually designates it.[1]

In the valley of the Kānkᵃnai stream (Skr. KANAKAVĀHINĪ) which issues from these lakes, lies the sacred site of S'iva BHŪTEŚVARA (now Buthⁱśēr). It is closely connected with the legends of Mount Haramukuṭa and often mentioned in the Rājataraṅgiṇī.[2] A series of interesting temple ruins marks the importance of this Tīrtha and that of the ancient *Jyeṣṭheśvara* shrine which immediately adjoins it.[3] Bhūteśvara is passed by the pilgrims on their way back from the sacred lakes, while on their way up they reach the latter by another route, passing the high ridge known as BHARATAGIRI and the smaller lake of BRAHMASARAS.

From the Gaṅgā lake a track passable for ponies leads over the *Satsaran* Pass to *Tilēl*, a Dard district on the Kiṣangaṅgā. It is probably the route by which King Harṣa's rebel brother Vijayamalla escaped from Lahara (Lār) to the Darad territory.[4]

North-eastern range.

58. Eastwards from the Haramukuṭa Peaks the range does not overlook on the south the main Valley of Kaśmīr, but that of the Sind River. The general level of the summits rises, and glaciers of fair size become frequent on their northern slopes. Close to the head of the Sind Valley, the range we have been so far following joins on to the great chain of snowy mountains which stretches from Mount Naṅgā Parvat in a south-easterly direction to the Nankun Peaks in S'ūru.[5] A few miles south of this junction we arrive at a gap in the mountains which forms the lowest watershed between the Indus and the Vitastā basins. It is the Pass known generally by its Ladākhī name of *Zōjī-Lā*. It leads at an elevation of 11,300 feet from Baltal, on the headwaters of the Sind, to a high-level valley draining into the Drās River and hence into the Indus.

Route over Zōjī-Lā.

The route leading over the Zōjī-Lā undoubtedly has been already in ancient times a most important thoroughfare. It connects Kaśmīr with Ladākh and thence with Tibet and China. Here too the natural watershed has in old as in modern times been also the ethnic boundary. Beyond the Pass begins the land of the *Bhauṭṭas* or *Bhuṭṭas*, as the Tibetan inhabi-

[1] See *Rājat.* i. 36 note.

[2] See regarding the history and remains of *Bhūteśvara*, Rājat. i. 107; v. 55 notes. The Tīrtha was rich enough to attract a special expedition of marauding hillmen in Kalhaṇa's time; see viii. 2756.

[3] See *Rājat.* i. 113 note.

[4] See *Rājat.* vii. 911.

[5] Compare regarding this great range which may fitly be called the main range of the mountain system around Kaśmīr, DREW, *Jummoo*, pp. 194 *sqq*.

tants of the Indus region are uniformly designated in our Kaśmirian texts (modern Kś. *Buṭ*).[1]

Ou-k'ong is the first who refers distinctly to this route when speaking of the road which leads through the gate in the east to Tou-fan or Tibet. Kalhaṇa has scarcely occasion to refer to it, as the regions beyond the Pass lay quite beyond the reach of the political power of the later Kaśmīrian kings. He probably means, however, the Zōji-Lā when mentioning the route of the *Bhuṭṭa*-land (*Bhuṭṭarāṣṭrādhvan*) by which the Darads offered to pass the pretender Bhoja into Kaśmīr, while the more direct routes from their own territory were closed by the winter.[2] An easy pass connects Tilēl at the head of the Kiṣangaṅgā Valley with the Drās territory to the east. From there Bhoja could then have entered Kaśmīr *viâ* the Zōji-Lā.

This Pass, the ancient name of which is not known to us, has more than once witnessed successful invasions of Kaśmīr. Through it came early in the 14th century the Turk (?) *Ḍulca* and the Bhauṭṭa *Riñcana* whose usurpation led to the downfall of Hindu rule in the Valley.[3] About two centuries later Mirzā Muḥammad Ḥaidar with his small Mughal force successfully fought here his entrance into Kaśmīr (A.D. 1532). The account he gives of this exploit in his *Tārīkh-i-Rāshidī*, is not without topographical interest.[4]

59. A high peak situated about 10 miles east-southeast of the Zōji-Lā, marks the point where the range forming the eastern boundary of Kaśmīr branches off from the main chain. This range runs in an almost southerly direction until it reaches the southernmost headwaters of the Vitastā. It then turns to the north-west and at the Bānahāl Pass joins on to the Pīr Pantsāl Range. Through this range there lead routes connecting Kaśmīr with the Maḍivāḍvan Valley (see § 84) which drains into the Cināb, and with Kaṣṭavār, the ancient Kāṣṭavāṭa, on the Cināb itself. Both these Valleys are confined, difficult of access, and scantily populated. They have hence never played an important part either in the foreign relations or trade of Kaśmīr. On this account our notices regarding the old topography of the dividing range are extremely meagre.

1 Compare *Rājat.* i. 312–316 note.

2 Compare *Rājat.* viii. 2887.

3 See *Jonar.* 142 *sqq.*, and for the stratagem by which Riñcana forced his way into Lahara (Lār), 165 *sqq.* The *Laharakoṭṭa* mentioned in the last passage probably represents the old watch-station of this route, but its position is uncertain.

4 See *Tārīkh-i-Rashīdī*, transl. by Messrs. Elias and Ross, pp. 423 *sqq.*, and below, § 131.

Tīrtha of Amaranātha.

At its northern end and close to the great snowy peak already mentioned, is the Tīrtha of AMAREŚVARA or AMARANĀTHA, known by its Kaśmīrī name as *Ạmburnāth.* Together with the sacred Gaṅgā-lake on Mount Haramukuṭa, it is now the most popular of Kaśmīrian pilgrimage places. Its Yātrā in the month of S'rāvaṇa attracts many thousands of pilgrims not only from Kaśmīr but from all parts of India.[1] Their goal is a cave situated at a considerable altitude and formed by a huge fissure on the south side of a snowy peak, 17,300 feet high (marked 'Ambarnath' on map). In this cave there is a large block of transparent ice formed by the freezing of the water which oozes from the rock. It is worshipped as a self-created (*svayaṁbhū*) Liṅga, and is considered the embodiment of S'iva-Amareśvara.

Judging from the scanty references made to this Tīrtha in the Rājataraṅgiṇī and the Nilamata, it appears doubtful whether it could have enjoyed in old times quite such great celebrity as now. But Jonarāja already relates a visit to this sacred site paid by Sultān Zainu-l-'ābidin,[2] and in the Māhātmya literature Amareśvara receives its due share of attention. The pilgrims' route described in great detail by the Amaranāthamāhātmya ascends the valley of the eastern branch of the Lid^{a}r or Ledarī.

There the lake of the Nāga SUŚRAVAS, now known as Suśramnāg or (with a popular etymology) S'eṣanāg, is visited at the north foot of a great glacier descending from the Kohenhār Peak. In this lake and a small rock-bound inlet of it called JĀMĀTṚNĀGA (Zām^{a}tur^{i} Nāg), the local legend, related by Kalhaṇa, i. 267 *sqq.*, and connected with the ancient site of Narapura, has placed the habitation of the Nāga Suśravas and of his son-in-law.[3] The route then crosses a high pass, known as Vāv^{a}jan (Skr. *Vāyuvarjana* in the Māhātmya), into a high-level valley drained by five streams which bear the joint designation of PAÑCATARAṄGIṆĪ. From there the pilgrims toil up a lofty spur to the north-east and descend into the narrow gloomy valley which lies at the foot of the Ạmburnāth Peak. It is watered by a stream (Amarāvatī) which comes from the glacier of a still higher peak to the east. Joining the Pañcataraṅgiṇī it flows through an inaccessible gorge down to the head of the Sind Valley near Baltal.

1 See for the old notices of the Tīrtha, *Rājat.* i. 267 note; for a description of the modern pilgrimage, VIGNE, *Travels*, ii. pp. 10 *sqq.*, and BATES, *Gazetteer*, pp. 121 *sq.*

2 Compare *Jonar.* (Bombay ed.) 1233 *sqq.*

3 Compare *Rājat.* i. 267 note.

Watershed range between Sindhu and Vitastā.

60. Connected with the eastern range is a mass of mountains which it will be convenient to mention here though it does not form part of the mountain-barriers of Kaśmīr. It fills the great triangular space which lies between the Sind Valley and the range in the east we have just noticed, the level ground along the right bank of the Vitastā forming as it were the base. This mass of mountains separates from the eastern ridge between the Kohenhār and Amburnāth Peaks. Trending westwards it soon culminates in the conspicuous pinnacle of Mount *Gāśᵊbrār* (map 'Kolahoi'), close on 18,000 feet in height. From this conspicuous mountain numerous spurs radiate with glaciers in their topmost hollows.

The highest of these ridges runs for about thirty miles along the Sind Valley, of which it forms the southern side. A high cross-spur, now known as Dūrün Nạ̄r, which descends to the north towards Sunᵃmarg, is probably identical with Mount DHUḌĀVANA, the scene of a siege related in the Rājataraṅgiṇī.[1] The extremity of this ridge in the west forms the amphitheatre of bold hills which encircle the Ḍal lake and S'rīnagar on the north. Here we have Mount MAHĀDEVA which is much frequented as a Tīrtha.[2]

Facing it from the south is the rocky spur which lines the eastern shores of the Ḍal. It bore in old days the name of S'RĪDVĀRA,[3] and is the site of a series of ancient pilgrimage places, such as Sureśvarī, Tripureśvara, Harṣeśvara, and Jyeṣṭheśvara, which will be discussed below. The extreme offshoot of this spur is the 'Hill of Gopa' (*Gopādri*), the present Ta<u>kh</u>t-i Sulaimān, which is so conspicuous a feature in the landscape of S'rīnagar. Other spurs descending into the vale further east form successively the semicircular side-valleys containing the Parganas of Vihī and Vular.

We now return once more to the eastern range. South of the Kohenhār Peak which is still over 17,000 feet high, its summit ridge gets gradually lower. It is crossed by the *Margan* Pass into Maḍivādvan. Of the latter valley I can find no old mention. Still further south we come to the *Marbal* Pass, at an elevation of 11,500 feet, which forms the usual route towards Kaṣṭᵃvār.

This territory which is now partially inhabited by Kaśmīrīs, is mentioned as an independent hill-state by Kalhaṇa.[4] The valley into

[1] See *Rājat.* viii. 595 note and below, § 131.

[2] It is mentioned in the *Nīlamata*, 1324, and frequently in the *S'arvāvatāra*.

[3] See *Rājat.* viii. 2422 note.

[4] Compare regarding the old *Kāṣṭhavāṭa* note vii. 588-590, where also the references in the later Chronicles are given.

which the route descends immediately after crossing the Marbal Pass, is known now as *Khaiśāl.* It is once mentioned as *Khaśālī* by Kalhaṇa and more frequently referred to in the last Chronicle by the name of KHAŚĀLAYA.[1] From the latter source we learn that it was inhabited by Khaśas to whose occupation it may have owed also its name. So we note here once more in the east the coincidence of the ethnic boundary with the natural watershed.

SECTION V.—UPPER COURSE OF THE VITASTĀ.

61. We have now completed the circuit of the great mountain-barriers which enclose the Kaśmir Valley, and can turn our attention to its interior. This is naturally divided into two great parts. One comprises the plain formed by the alluvium of the Vitastā and its main tributaries; the other consists of plateaus or Karēwas elevated above the river flats and largely caused by old lacustrine deposits. We shall first notice the alluvial plain and the river-system which has created it.

Name of Vitastā.

The great river which is the recipient of the whole drainage of the country, is now known to Kaśmīrīs by the name of *Vyath.* This modern designation is the direct phonetic derivative of the ancient Sanskrit VITASTĀ which we meet already among the river-names of the Rigveda.[2] The intermediary Prakrit form **Vidastā* underlies the *Hydaspes* of the Greeks in which we note, as so frequently in Greek renderings of foreign names, the modifying action of popular etymology.[3] In Ptolemy's *Bidaspes* we have another rendering which though later in date yet approaches closer to the sound of the Indian original.[4] The name *Jehlam* which is

[1] Compare *Rājat.* vii. 399 note.

[2] The line of phonetic development may be roughly represented as Skr. *Vitastā* > Pr. **Vidastā* > Ap. **Vi[h]ath* > Kś. *Vyath.*

The name Vitastā is still well-known to Kaśmīr Brahmans from the Māhātmyas and similar texts, and is currently used by them. The form 'Vedasta' which Drew and other writers indicate as the old name of the river "still used by those who follow Sanskrit literature," is due to some error of hearing. It is curious to meet a similar form **Vidastā* in the transcription of the Chinese Annals of the 8th century; see my *Notes on Ou-k'ong*, p. 31.

[3] The ending in the form *Hydaspes* is undoubtedly due to the influence of the numerous Persian names known to the Greeks which end in -ασπης (Old Persian *aspa*). For the rendering of initial *Vi-* by Ὑ compare Hystaspes: *Vishtāspa.*

[4] Ptolemy's *Bi* (for *Vi*) is the most exact phonetic reproduction possible in Greek characters. It is evident from Ptolemy's Panjāb river names that he did not take

now borne by the Vitastā in its course through the Panjāb, is wholly unknown to the genuine usage of Kaśmīr. It is apparently of Muhammadan origin and has been brought to Kaśmīr only by Europeans and other foreigners.[1]

The river to which the name Vitastā or Vyath is properly applied, is first formed by the meeting of the several streams which drain the south-eastern portion of the Valley. This meeting takes place in the plain close to the present town of Anatnāg or Islāmābād. But sacred tradition has not failed to trace the holiest of Kaśmīr rivers to a more specific source.

Legendary source of Vitastā.

An ancient legend, related at length in the Nīlamata and reproduced by the author of the Haracaritacintāmaṇi,[2] represents the Vitastā as a manifestation of S'iva's consort Pārvatī. After Kaśmīr had been created, S'iva at the request of Kaśyapa, prevailed upon the goddess to show herself in the land in the shape of a river, in order to purify its inhabitants from the sinful contact with the Piśācas. The goddess thereupon assumed the form of a river in the underworld, and asked her consort to make an opening by which she might come to the surface. This he did by striking the ground near the habitation of the Nīlanāga with the point of his trident (*śūla*). Through the fissure thus made which measured one *vitasti* or span, the river gushed forth, receiving on account of this origin the name *Vitastā*. The spring-basin where the goddess first appeared was known by the several designations of *Nīlakuṇḍa*, *S'ūlaghāta* ('spear-thrust') or simply *Vitastā*.[3] It is clear that the spring meant is the famous Nīlanāga, near the village of Vērnāg in the S͟hāhābād Pargaṇa. It is a magnificent fountain which amply deserves the honour of being thus represented as the traditional source of the great river.[4]

The legend makes Pārvatī-Vitastā subsequently disappear again from fear of defilement by the touch of sinful men. When brought to light a second time by Kaśyapa's prayer the goddess issued from the Nāga of *Pañcahasta*. In this locality we easily recognize the present

his nomenclature directly or indirectly from the historians of Alexander, but from independent sources. Bidaspes, Zaradros, Bibasis, Sandabal, these all represent unsophisticated attempts to reproduce in sound the genuine Indian forms. The same cannot be said of the names given by Arrian, Pliny, etc.

1 Alberūnī already knows the name *Jailam*; see above, § 14. S'rīvara when relating an expedition of Sultān Ḥaidar S͟hāh into the Panjāb, sanskritizes this name into *Jyalami*; see ii. 152.

2 See *Nīlamata*, 238 *sqq.*; *Haracar.* xii. 2–34.

3 See *Nīlamata*, 1290; *Haracar.* xii. 17.

4 Compare for the Nīlanāga and its round spring-basin (kuṇḍa), *Rājat.* i. 28 note

village of Pānzath, situated in the Div^{a}sar Pargaṇa and boasting of a fine spring which is still visited by the pious of the neighbourhood.[1] After another disappearance for a reason similar to the above, the goddess came forth a third time at *Narasiṁhāśrama*. This place I am unable to trace with certainty. Finally the goddess was induced to abide permanently in the land when Kaśyapa had secured for her the company of other goddesses, who also embodied themselves in Kaśmīr streams, like Lakṣmī in the Viśokā, Gaṅgā in the Sindhu, etc.

Another version of the legend which, however, seems of less ancient date, seeks the place of the Vitastā's second appearance in the spring of the modern *Vith^{a}vutur*, a small village situated about one mile to the N. W. of Vērnāg.[2] The place is known by the name of *Vitastātra* to Kalhaṇa who mentions Stūpas erected there by King Aśoka.[3] This notice certainly seems to indicate some sacred character attaching to the spot. Yet Kalhaṇa's direct mention of the Nīlakuṇḍa as the birthplace of the Vitastā leaves no doubt as to where the tradition prevalent in his own time placed the source of the sacred river.[4]

Headwaters of Vitastā.

62. The streams which unite close to Anatnāg and there form the true Vitastā river, are the *Sāndrạn*, the *Bring*, *Ār^{a}path* and *Lid^{a}r*. Of these the first and southernmost drains the Shāhābād (or Vēr) Pargaṇa and receives the water of the sacred springs mentioned in the preceding paragraph. Its old name I am unable to trace with any certainty. The next affluent, the *Bring*, comes from the side-valley which forms the Pargaṇa of the same name. The ancient name of the stream is unknown, the modern Vitastāmāhātmya which gives it as *Bhṛṅgī*, being but a doubtful authority. The Bring too is fed by the water of some well-known Nāgas, among which the famous Trisaṁdhyā fountain and the springs of Ardhanārīśvara (Nāṛ^{u}) may be specially mentioned.

The Ār^{a}path which comes from the north-east, is mentioned repeatedly in the Nīlamata by its ancient name of *Harṣapathā*.[5] The

[1] Compare *Rājat.* v. 24 note.

[2] This version is found in the Vitastāmāhātmya, ii. 37, *sqq.*, which calls the place *Vitastāvartikā*; see also VIGNE, i. p. 335.

[3] See *Rājat.* i. 102 note.

[4] *Rajāt.* i. 28. I am unable to account for the mention made in the *Mahābh.* iii. lxxxii. 90 of the Takṣaka Nāga in Kaśmīr as the Vitastā, *i.e.*, its source. No such distinction is claimed for the well-known Takṣaka spring near Zevan (Jayavana); see *Rājat.* i. 220. The author of the *Tīrthayātrā* in the Mahābh. shows no accurate knowledge of Kaśmīr and seems to have made a mistake here.

[5] See *Nīlamata*, 232, 1299, etc.

valley it drains is known as the Kōṭhēr Pargaṇa and takes its name from the sacred tank of *Kapaṭeśvara*. At the western end of the spur on the slope of which this Tīrtha is situated, issue the magnificient springs of Achᵃbal (Akṣavāla). They form a small stream by themselves, which flows into the Harṣapathā. A short distance below the village of Khanᵃbal (map 'Kanbal') where the three streams hitherto mentioned unite, their waters are joined from the north by those of the Lidᵃr.

This river, the ancient *Ledarī*,[1] receives a number of glacier-fed streams which drain the high range towards the Upper Sind Valley. It is hence in volume more considerable than any of the previously named affluents. The Ledarī spreads in several branches through the wide valley forming the Parganas of Dachünpōr and Khōvurpōr which take their names, 'Right Bank' and 'Left Bank,' respectively, from their position relative to this river. In old days a canal constructed on the hill-side to the east carried the water of the Ledarī, and with it fertility, to the barren plateau of Mārtāṇḍa or Maṭan.[2]

Vitastā's course in alluvial plain.

63. At Khanᵃbal the Vitastā becomes navigable and continues so on its whole course through the valley. There too the great flat plain begins which stretches on both sides of the river down to Bārāmūla in the north-west. In its course to the Volur lake, a direct distance of about 54 miles, the river falls only some 220 feet.[3] The slope in the general level of the plain is equally gentle. The bed of the river lies everywhere in the alluvial soil, the result of the deposition of sediment at flood times when the river overflows its banks. Down to Srinagar the river keeps in a single bed and its islands are but small, in fact mere temporary sandbanks. The course is in parts very winding. But as far we can judge from the position of the old sites along the river, no great changes are likely to have taken place in historical times in this portion of the river's course.

When the river is low as during the winter, the banks rise on an average about 15 feet above the water. But in the spring when the snow melts, the great volume of water brought down from the mountains rises to the top of the banks and often overflows it. Dangerous floods may also follow long and heavy summer-rains, and sometimes

1 See *Rājat.* i. 87.

2 The construction of this canal by Zainu-l-'ābidīn is described at length by *Jonar.* (Bo. ed.) 1232–60. It is probable that there existed earlier irrigation works on the same plateau. See below, § 111.

3 See DREW, *Jummoo*, p. 163.

cause immense damage to the crops over a great portion of the cultivated area of the Valley.[1]

Such floods and the famines which are likely to follow, were a danger well-known in old times already and are more than once mentioned by Kalhaṇa.[2] Against them the villages and riverside towns have always endeavoured to protect themselves by artificially raising the banks. The allusions found in the Chronicle suffice to show that the construction of embankments (*setu*, now *suth*), with the accompanying system of floodgates closing lateral drainage channels, has existed since ancient times.[3] One great regulation scheme which was directly designed to diminish these risks, and of which we possess a detailed historical account, will be discussed below. The equally elaborate system by which water was secured for the irrigation of the otherwise dry alluvial flats along the river, will also be specially noticed.

The navigable waters of the Vitastā have from ancient times to the present day formed the most important highway of Kaśmīr. The value of the river and of the numerous canals, lakes, and streams which are also accessible to boats, for the development of internal trade and traffic can hardly be overestimated. Until a couple of years ago there were nowhere in Kaśmīr, not even in the flattest parts of the Valley, roads fit for wheeled traffic. Carriages were practically things unknown to the population bred in the Valley. As long as the communication with the outer world was restricted to difficult bridle-paths or tracks passable only for load-carrying Coolies, the construction of such roads would have been, in fact, of very slight advantage. The importance of river-traffic in Kaśmīr may be estimated from the fact that the number of boatmen engaged in it (and their families) amounted according to the census of 1891 to nearly 34,000.[4] That boats were in old days, just as up to the present time, the ordinary means of travel in the Valley, is shown by the frequent references to river journeys in the Chronicles.[5]

Equally eloquent testimony to the historical importance of river navigation in Kaśmīr is borne by the position of the ancient sites. We

1 Compare for data as to modern floods, LAWRENCE, *Valley*, pp. 205 *sqq*.

2 See *Rājat*. vii. 1219; viii. 2449, 2786; also vii. 1624; viii. 1417, 1422; *Jonar*. 403 *sqq*.

3 See *Rājat*. i. 159; iii. 483; v. 91, 103, 120; viii. 2380, etc.; *Jonar*. 404, 887; *Śrīv*. iii. 191 *sq*., etc.

4 Compare regarding the *Hāṇz*ᶦ of Kaśmīr, LAWRENCE, *Valley*, p. 313; also *Rājat*. v. 101 note.

5 See *Rājat*. v. 84; vii. 347, 714, 1628, etc.

shall see that all the towns which from time to time were the capitals of the country, were built on the banks of the Vitastā, and that the great majority of other important places of ancient date were similarly situated. It is certain that then as now all produce of the country was brought to the great centres by water. Villages even when situated at a great distance, had, no doubt, just as at the present day, their landing places (Kś. *yārᵃbal*) on the river or the nearest navigable waterway. Kalhaṇa's description of the semi-legendary city of *Narapura* shows how closely the busy "coming and going of ships" was connected in the Kaśmīrian mind with the splendour of a large town.[1]

64. After these general remarks we may now proceed to follow the Vitastā's course through the Valley noticing its tributaries in due order as we reach the confluences. Below Khanᵃbal[2] the river receives in succession the several branches of the Ledarī and then passes the ancient town and Tīrtha of Vijayeśvara, the present Vijᵊbrör. About a mile lower down, its course lies between high alluvial plateaus or Karēwas. One on the left bank, the Tsakᵃdar Uḍar, will be noticed below as one of the most ancient sites of the Valley (Cakradhara).

The Gambhīrā.

About three miles further down and not far from the village of Marhōm (the old *Maḍavāśrama*), the Vitastā is joined by the Veśau and Rembyārᵊ Rivers which meet a short distance above their common confluence with the Vitastā. This river junction is known to the Māhātmyas by the name of GAMBHĪRASAṀGAMA ('the deep confluence') and is still visited as a Tīrtha.[3] The short united course of the Veśau and Rembyārᵊ bears the old name of GAMBHĪRĀ and is referred to under this designation repeatedly by Kalhaṇa. The Gambhīrā is too deep to be forded at any time of the year, and being on the route from Vijayeśvara to Śrīnagar, is of military importance. It was twice the scene of decisive actions. King Sussala's army on its retreat over the Gambhīrā (A.D. 1122) suffered a complete rout. Six years later Sujji, his son's general, gained an equally signal victory by forcing the passage in the face of a rebel army.[4]

1 See *Rājat.* i. 201 *sq.*

2 According to a gloss on *Nīlamata* 1307, Khanᵃbal, the port, so to say, of Anatnāg corresponds to the Khaṇḍapuccha Nāga of that text. This Nāga is elsewhere mentioned, but I have no distinct evidence for its identification.

3 See *Rājat.* iv. 80 note. Junctions of rivers and streams (*saṁgamas*) are everywhere in India favourite places for Tīrthas.

4 See *Rājat.* viii. 1063 *sqq.*, 1497 *sqq.*

The Viśokā.

The Veśau, frequently mentioned by its ancient name of VIŚOKĀ in the Chronicles, the Nīlamata and other texts,[1] is a considerable river. It receives all the streams coming from the northern slope of the Pīr Pantsāl Range between the Sidau and Bānᵃhāl Passes. Its traditional source is placed in the Kramasaras or Kōnsᵃr Nāg Lake below the Peak of Naubandhana. The Nīlamata, 271 *sqq.* relates a legend which identifies the Viśokā with Lakṣmī and accounts for its name ('free from pain'). The fine waterfall which is formed by the stream of the Kōnsᵃr Nāg not far from the village of Sidau, is now known as *Ahrᵃbal.* The Nīlamata calls it *Ākhor bila* 'the mousehole,' which may possibly be the origin of the modern name.[2] As soon as the Viśokā emerges from the mountains, numerous irrigation canals are drawn from it which overspread the whole of the old Parganas of *Karāla* (Āḍᵊvin) and *Devasarasa* (Divᵊsar).

One of these canals is the *Sunᵊmaṇⁱ Kul* which is mentioned in the Rājataraṅgiṇī by its ancient name of SUVARṆAMAṆIKULYĀ.[3] If the story of its construction by King Suvarṇa, reproduced from Padmamihira, could be trusted, we should have to ascribe to this canal a high antiquity. It leaves the Viśokā near the village shown as 'Largoo' on the map and rejoins it near the village of Āḍᵊvin (map 'Arwin'). Another old canal, called *Nāndī* (not shown on the map), leaves the Viśokā near Kaimuh, the ancient Katimuṣa, and irrigates the land between the lower course of this river and the Vitastā. Its name is connected perhaps with that of the village *Nandaka* which is referred to in connection with Avantivarman's drainage operations.[4] The Viśokā is navigable up to Kaimuh.

The Ramanyāṭavī.

The *Rembyārᵊ* which joins the Viśokā a little above Gambhīrasaṁgama, we have met already before as the river uniting the streams from the Pīr Pantsāl and Rūprī Passes. Kalhaṇa mentions it by its ancient name RAMAṆYĀṬAVĪ when relating the legend of the burned city of Narapura.[5] The Rembyārᵊ after leaving the mountains below Hürᵊpōr flows divided in many channels within a wide and mostly dry bed of rubble and boulders. This strip of stony waste along the river attains a width of over two miles near the village of Tsüran (map 'Charran').

The local legend referred to attributes the creation of this waste to

[1] See *Rājat.* iv. 5 note.

[2] Compare *Nīlamata,* 271 *sqq.*, and for *Ākhor bila,* 283.

[3] See *Rājat.* i. 97.

[4] See *Rājat.* v. 85 note.

[5] See *Rājat.* i. 263–265, note.

the Nāgī Ramaṇyā. She had come down from the mountains carrying masses of stone to assist her brother, the Suśravas Nāga, in the destruction of Narapura. When she learnt that he had already completed his task, she dropped the stones 'more than a Yojana' from the site of the doomed city. The distance indicated corresponds exactly to that of the village of Lit^a^r where the Rembyār^a^ leaves behind its stony bed and passes into alluvial soil. The village land for five Yojanas above that place was buried by the mighty boulders which Ramaṇyā left along her trail. Similar tales regarding the origin of stone-wastes ("Murren") are well-known to European alpine folk-lore.

The Vitastā near Śrīnagar.

65. Below Gambhīrasaṁgama the Vitastā receives from the right the stream which drains the ancient district of Holaḍā, the present Vular. It then passes close to the foot of the Vastarvan spur, near the old town of Avantipura. No important stream joins the river from the right until we reach S'rīnagar. The affluents on the left like the Rāmuṣa are also of small volume. Some do not reach the river direct but end in low marshes, communicating with the latter only by gates made in the river embankments. Of the ancient sites situated along the river, the town of PADMAPURA, the present Pāmpar, is the most considerable. As we approach S'rīnagar we pass the site of the ancient capital, PURĀṆĀDHIṢṬHĀNA, marked by the present village of Pāndrĕṭhan. It lies between the right river bank and the southern foot of the ridge which encircles the Ḍal. For the streams we have next to notice, a reference to the special map of Ancient S'rīnagara is necessary.

Just before we reach the area of the city proper, the Vitastā is joined by a stream which drains the lake to the east of the city. This lake, known as *Ḍal* (Skr. Ḍala), is fed by plentiful springs and by streams which reach it from the north. Its surplus waters flow out towards the Vitastā by a canal which is now called Tsūṇṭh Kul, but in ancient times bore the name of MAHĀSARIT.[1] This canal passes through an ancient embankment (*setu*) which protects the city as well as the low shores of the Ḍal from floods of the river, and already figures in the traditional account of the foundation of S'rīnagar. The position of the gate which closes the outflow of the Mahāsarit is marked on the map by the entry 'Durgāgalikā.'

A small channel from the river—whether artificial or natural cannot

[1] For the identification of the Tsūṇṭh Kul and the Mār canal in the city with the *Mahāsarit*, my note on Rājat. iii. 339–349 should be consulted. In addition to the evidence there recorded, it should be noted that the Mahāsarit is twice mentioned by its old name also in the *S'arvāvatāra* iii. 74; iv. 120 *sq*.

be ascertained now—joins the Mahāsarit at this very point and turns the ground between it and the river into an island. This is now known by the name of Māy*sum, derived from the ancient MĀKṢIKASVĀMIN. We shall have to refer to it again in our account of the topography of S'rinagar. From Durgāgalikā downwards the Mahāsarit or Tsūṇṭh Kul was in old times the south-eastern boundary for that part of S'rīnagar which lies on the right bank of the Vitastā. Being a natural line of defence it is frequently referred to in the narrative of the various sieges of the capital.[1]

The confluence of the Mahāsarit and Vitastā which is just opposite to the modern palace, the Shērgaṛhi, has been a Tīrtha from early times and is mentioned by its correct name in Maṅkha's description of Kaśmīr.[2] S'rīvara refers to it by a more modern name, *Mārīsaṁgama*, where *Mārī* is an evident adaptation from the Kś. form *Mār*.[3] The latter name, itself a derivative of Mahāsarit, is applied at the present day to another branch of the Ḍal outflow. This turning to the west passes through the marsh known as Bṛāṛ[i]nambal (*Bhattāranadvalā*) and then enters the city.

This canal is of considerable importance for the internal traffic of the city as it opens a convenient waterway to the Ḍal and greatly facilitates the transport of its manifold produce.[4] After passing behind the whole of the city quarters on the right river-bank the Mār issues near the quarter of Narvor (Skr. *Naḍavana*) into the marshes of the Anch[i]ār. Through the latter a connection is thus secured with the Sind river delta. This extension of the Mār to the west seems, however, of later date, as S'rīvara attributes the construction of a navigable channel towards the Sind to Zainu-l-'ābidīn.[5]

66. The lake which supplies the water of the Mahāsarit, is in some respects one of the most favoured spots of the whole Valley. Its limpid water, the imposing aspect of the mountain amphitheatre which encloses it on three sides, and the charming gardens and orchards around it have made the Ḍal justly famous.

The Ḍal lake.

[1] See *Rājat.* viii. 733, 753, 3131.

[2] See *S'rīkaṇṭhac.* iii. 24, *Mahāsaridvitastayoḥ ... saṁgamaḥ.* Here too as in former translations of the Rājataraṅgiṇī, Mahāsarit has been wrongly taken as an common noun and explained as 'great river.'

[3] The term *Mārī* is also elsewhere used in the later Chronicles and the Māhātmyas; comp., *e.g.*, *S'rīv.* i. 442; iv. 298; Fourth Chron. 145, etc.

[4] It is this narrow canal, more picturesque than sweet-smelling, which has led to the frequent comparisons of S'rīnagar with Venice. It has not received much attention in recent years and for want of dredging seems in danger of silting up.

[5] See *S'rīv.* i. 440 *sq.*

The Ḍal measures about four miles in length and two and a half in width where it is broadest. Its depth nowhere exceeds 30 feet, and in most parts it is far more shallow. At its southern end it is fringed by lagoons, and a great portion of it is covered by the famous floating gardens. Notwithstanding the superabundance of water-plants and vegetable matter, the water everywhere retains an admirable clearness and freshness. This is, no doubt, due to the ampleness of the springs which rise within the lake. Though we find no direct mention of the lake in the Rājataraṅgiṇī, and though it does not claim any particular sanctity, there is no want around its shores of ancient and holy sites.

The earliest reference to the lake itself occurs in the Chronicle of S'rīvara who describes at length how King Zainu-l-'ābidīn diverted himself on the lake and adorned its vicinity.[1] S'rīvara calls the lake Ḍala, while the few Māhātmyas which condescend to mention it, use the form *Dala*.[2] He also mentions the two small artificial islands called *Laṅkā*, and now distinguished as *Rupᵊlānk* and *Sunᵊlānk* ('the Silver Laṅkā,' 'Golden Laṅkā'). Different names are given to several distinct portions of the lake. But of these only Hastavālika, the present Astᵊvōl, can be traced in the Chronicles.

The sacred sites of Gopādri, Jyeṣṭheśvara, Thedā, S'ureśvarī, etc., with their numerous Nāgas line the eastern shores of the Ḍal. They will be mentioned below in the description of the vicinity of the capital. The well-known gardens of S͟hālimār, Nis͟hāt and Nasīm are creations of the Mug͟hal Emperors who did much to enhance the natural beauties of the lake.

Besides the springs of the lake itself the latter is fed also by a stream which comes from the Mār Sar lake, high up in the mountains to the east. The old name of this stream, marked 'Arrah' on the map, is uncertain. The S'arvāvatāra seems to extend to it the name *Mahāsarit*.[3] In its lower course where it approaches the north shore of the Ḍal, it now bears the name of Tᵊlbal Nāl (stream). An earlier form is furnished by S'rīvara who calls the stream at this point, by the name of Tilaprasthā; the latter is also found in several Māhātmyas.[4]

67. From the junction with the Mahāsarit downwards the Vitastā flows for over three miles between almost unbroken lines of houses raised high above the water on stone embankments. The latter consist now-a-days chiefly of large blocks of stone which belonged to ancient

1 *S'rīv*. i. 418 *sqq*.
2 See, *e.g.*, *Vitastāmāh*, xxi. 39.
3 See *S'arvāv*. iii. 75; iv. 129.
4 See *S'rīv*. i. 421; *S'arvāv*. iv, *sqq*., etc.

temples and other structures of pre-Muhammadan date. Judging from their size and careful carving we can well picture to our mind the splendid appearance which the river-banks must have here presented in bygone days.

The Kṣiptikā.

The river within the city flows first in one long reach due north. Near the fourth bridge in the heart of the city, it makes a great bend and turns to the south-west. A canal which leaves the left bank of the river between the Shērgaṛhi palace and the quarter of Kāṭhül (Kāṣṭhīla), and rejoins the river near the last bridge, allows boats to cut this great bend. It now bears the name Kuṭᵊkul, derived from the ancient designation of KṢIPTIKĀKULYĀ.[1] The Kṣiptikā is often mentioned in the later portions of Kalhaṇa's Chronicle which relate the sieges of S'rīnagar witnessed in his own time. It forms to this day the natural line of defence for that part of the city which occupies the left river-bank, and which could be successfully attacked only by crossing the Kṣiptikā.[2] No information is available to us as to the origin of this canal. Judging from its position it is likely to have been a natural side-channel of the river which was subsequently maintained or improved for the convenience of navigation.

The Dugdhagaṅgā.

A few hundred yards lower down the Vitastā is joined on its left bank by a considerable river now known as the *Dūdgaṅgā*, 'the milk Gaṅgā,' or *Chaṭsᵊkul*, 'the white stream.' Its ancient name is given as *Dugdhasindhu* in Bilhaṇa's description of S'rīnagar.[3] The Māhātmyas know it by the name of *Svetagaṅgā*, 'the white Gaṅgā,' to which the alternative modern designation, Chaṭsᵊkul, exactly corresponds.[4] Its waters come from the central part of the Pīr Pantsāl Range round Mount Taṭakūṭi, its chief sources being the mountain-streams marked as 'Sangsofed' (Saṅgsafēd) and 'Yechara' on the map. The confluence of the Vitastā and Dūdgaṅgā, opposite to the old quarter of Diddāmaṭha, is still a Tīrtha of some repute and is probably alluded to already by Bilhaṇa.[5]

[1] Kś. *kul* < Skr. *kulyā* is the ordinary term for small streams or canals.

[2] For detailed evidence of this identification, see *Rājat.* viii. 732 note.

[3] *Vikramāṅkac.* xviii. 7.

[4] See *Vitastāmāh.* xxii; *S'vetagaṅgāmāh.*, etc. Skr. *śveta* becomes in Kś. by regular phonetic conversion *chuth*, fem. *chaṭsᵊ*.

The Nīlamata curiously enough does not mention the Dūdgaṅgā unless it is meant by *Kṣīranadī*, 1281. The latter name, meaning 'the river of milk,' is given to the Dūdgaṅgā by a passage of the modern Vitastāmāhātmya, xxii.

[5] See *Vikram.* xviii. 22.

SECTION VI.—LOWER COURSE OF THE VITASTĀ.

68. Immediately below S'rīnagar we come to marshes which stretch along both sides of the river for a considerable distance. Those on the left bank, of which the Hukh^{a}sar and Panz^{i}nōr Nambal are the nearest, are fed by mountain-streams of smaller volume. The marshes to the north of the river are more extensive and belong to the Delta of the Sind River, the greatest tributary of the Vitastā within the Valley.

The Sindhu.

Our survey of the northern range of mountains has already taken us to the true headwaters of the Sind near the Zōji-Lā and the Amburnāth Peak. Its traditional source in the sacred Gaṅgā-lake on Mount Haramukh has also been noticed. This great river has a course of over sixty miles and drains the largest and highest portion of the mountain-chain in the north. Its ancient name, SINDHU, means simply 'the river' and is thus identical with the original designation of the Indus.[1] The Rājataraṅgiṇī mentions the river repeatedly, and it figures largely in the Nīlamata, Haracaritacintāmaṇi and the Māhātmyas.[2] Everywhere it is identified with the Gaṅgā, as already by Alberūnī's informants. The valley of the Sind forms the district of Lār, the ancient Lahara, one of the main subdivisions of Kaśmīr territory.

Where this valley debouches into the great Kaśmīr plain, near the village of Dud^{a}rhōm, the old *Dugdhāśrama*, the river spreads out in numerous branches. These form an extensive Delta, covered in its greatest portion by shallow marshes and known as *Anch^{i}ār*. Its eastern side extends along the strip of high ground which connects S'rīnagar with the foot of the spur at the mouth of the Sind Valley. The western

1 It is customary in Kaśmīr to distinguish the two rivers by giving the designation of 'the Great Sind (Buḍ Sind),' to the Indus. This is found as '*Bṛhatsindhu*,' already in the Haracaritacintāmaṇi, xii. 45.

The identity of the two river names has led to a great deal of confusion in geographical works down to the beginning of the present century. The Sind River of Kaśmīr was elevated to the rank of one of the chief sources of the Indus, or else represented as a branch of the great river taking its way through Kaśmīr (!). This curious error is traceable, *e.g.*, in the map of 'L'Empire du Grand Mogol' reproduced in Bernier's *Travels*, ed. Constable, p. 238, from the Paris Edition of 1670, and in the map of Ancient India attached to TIEFFENTHALER, *Description de l' Inde*, 1786, p. 60. Compare HÜGEL, *Kaschmir*, i. p. 330. Even WILSON, writing in 1825, says of the Kaśmīr Sind that "it is not improbably a branch of the Indus."

2 See *Rājat.* i. 57 note; also iv. 391; v. 97 *sqq.*; viii. 1129; *Jonar.* 982; *S'rīv.* iv. 110, 227, etc.

side of the delta is marked by an alluvial plateau which continues the right or western side of the lower Sind Valley down to the river's confluence with the Vitastā. The base of the triangle is the Vitastā itself which between Śrīnagar and this junction flows in a bed separated by artificial banks from the marshes on either side. The waters of the Sind after spreading over this wide Delta leave it in a single channel at its western extremity, opposite to the village of Shād[i]pūr.

Confluence of Vitastā and Sindhu.

The confluence of the Vitastā and Sindhu has from early times enjoyed exceptional sanctity as a Tīrtha. Kaśmīr tradition, as recorded already in the Nīlamata, identifies the Vitastā and Sindhu, the largest and holiest rivers of the country, with the *Yamunā* and *Gaṅgā*, respectively. Their junction represents, therefore, the Kaśmīrian equivalent of the famous *Prayāga* at the confluence of the great Indian rivers. The VITASTĀSINDHUSAṂGAMA is often referred to as an important Tīrtha in the Rājataraṅgiṇī, the Nīlamata and numerous other texts. It is actually known by the name of PRAYĀGA to the modern tradition and the Māhātmyas.[1] A small island built of solid masonry rises in the river-bed at the point where the waters of the two rivers mingle. It is the object of regular pilgrimages on particular Parvans throughout the year. On it stands an old Cinār tree which to the pious Kaśmīrian represents the far-famed Ficus Indica tree of the real Prayāga.

Notwithstanding the accumulated holiness of this Tīrtha there is most explicit evidence to show that its present position dates back only to about a thousand years. We owe the knowledge of this interesting fact to the detailed account which Kalhaṇa has given us of the great regulation of the Vitastā carried out under King Avantivarman (A.D. 855-883). As the change in the confluence of the Vitastā and Sindhu forms one of the most striking results of this regulation, Kalhaṇa's account of the latter may conveniently be noticed in the present place. I shall restrict myself to an indication of the main facts connected with these operations, referring for all detailed evidence to Note *I* (v. 97-100) of my translation.

Suyya's regulation of the Vitastā.

69. Kalhaṇa tells us in his opening notice[2] that the produce of Kaśmīr had in earlier times been greatly restricted owing to disastrous floods, particularly from the Mahāpadma or Volur lake, and the general water-locked condition of the country. Drainage operations

[1] For a detailed account of the references to the Vitastā-Sindhusaṃgama and the ancient remains near it, see Note *I* (*Rājat.* v. 97-100), §§ 14, 16; also note iv. 391.

[2] See *Rājat.* v. 68 *sqq.*

under King Lalitāditya had led to an increase of agricultural produce. But these works were apparently neglected under his feeble successors, and disastrous floods, followed by famines, became again frequent. In Avantivarman's time *Suyya*, a man of conspicuous talents but low origin, offered to remedy these troubles. Receiving the king's assent for his scheme and the necessary means, he set about regulating the course of the Vitastā with a view to a better drainage of the whole Valley. Omitting legendary details with which evidently popular tradition has embellished Suyya's story, the course adopted was briefly the following.

The operations commenced in Kramarājya at the locality called Yakṣadara where large "rocks which had rolled down from the mountains lining both river banks," obstructed the Vitastā.[1] We have already when describing the Vitastā Valley route, referred to Yakṣadara, the present Dyārᵊgul, as a spur projecting into the river-bed some three miles below the commencement of the Bārāmūla gorge. Its rocky foot forms the first rapid of the river. By removing the obstructing rocks the level of the river was lowered. Then a stone-dam was constructed across the bed of the river, and the latter thus blocked up completely for seven days. During this time "the river-bed was cleared at the bottom, and stone walls constructed to protect it against rocks which might roll down."[2] The dam was then removed, and the river flowed forth with increased rapidity through the cleared passage.

I must leave it to competent engineering opinion to decide to what extent and at which point of the Bārāmūla gorge the operations so far described were practicable with the technical means of that age. What follows in Kalhaṇa's account is so matter-of-fact and so accurate in topographical points, that a presumption is raised as to the previous statements also resting, partially at least, on historical facts.

Wherever inundation breaches were known to occur in times of flood, new beds were constructed for the river. One of these changes in the river-bed affected the confluence of the Vitastā and Sindhu, and this is specially explained to us in v. 97-100. The topographical indications here given by Kalhaṇa are so detailed and exact that they enabled me to trace with great probability what I believe to have been the main course of the Vitastā before Suyya's regulation.

Change of confluence of Vitastā and Sindhu.

70. Kalhaṇa describes to us successively the position of the old and the new confluence relative to certain temples situated at the village of Trigrāmī and other points on the river-banks. Most of these structures I have been able to identify, and a close examination of the

[1] See v. 87 *sqq.*

[2] Compare v. 92 *sq.*

general topographical features in their neighbourhood has fully borne out the correctness of Kalhaṇa's account. Without the help of a larger-scale map it would, however, be impossible to explain here accurately the topographical evidence collected.[1] I must, therefore, once more refer to the above-quoted detailed note in my forthcoming work, where a special map, on the scale of one inch to the mile, has been inserted for the illustration of this tract. In the present place I must restrict myself to indicating the main results of my enquiries.

These have shown that while the new confluence which Kalhaṇa knew in his own time, is identical with the present junction opposite S̱ẖạdⁱpūr,[2] the old one lay about two miles to the south-east of it, between the village of Trigām and the Parᵊspōr plateau. The latter is the site of the great ruins of *Parihāsapura*, first identified by me and shown on the map (see below, § 121.) Trigām marks the position of the ancient *Trigrāmī*, and a short distance south of it stands the temple ruin which I identify with the shrine of Viṣṇu *Vainyasvāmin*.

Kalhaṇa mentions this temple as the point near which "the two rivers, the Sindhu and Vitastā, formerly met flowing to the left and right of Trigrāmī, respectively." Standing on the raised ground before the ruin and turning towards S̱ẖạdⁱpūr, we have on our left a narrow swamp about a quarter of a mile broad which runs north-east in the direction of Trigām. In this swamp and a shallow Nāla continuing it towards S̱ẖạdⁱpūr, we can yet recognize the old bed of the Sindhu. On the right we have the Badrihōl Nāla which divides the alluvial plateau of Trigām and Parᵊspōr. This Nāla is clearly marked as an old river-bed by the formation of its banks and is still known as such to the villagers of the neighbourhood.

The Badrihōl Nāla connects the great swamp to the east known as *Pạnzⁱnōr Nambal* with the extensive marshes stretching west and north-west of Parᵊspōr towards the Volur. This channel still serves regularly as an outflow for the Pạnzⁱnōr Nambal whenever the latter is flooded from the Vitastā at times of high-water. Were it not for the great embankments which guard the bed of the Vitastā towards the low Pạnzⁱnōr Nambal, the latter would still form a regular course of the

[1] In the copies of the map accompanying this memoir the faint outlines by which the engraved Atlas of India sheet marks the low alluvial plateaus, the marshes, and similar features of this tract, have become much effaced. A reference to the original groundmap or the larger Survey map (2 miles to the inch) is hence recommended.

[2] S̱ẖạdⁱpūr is a modern contraction for *S̱ẖahābuddinpūr*, the name given to the place by Sultān S̱ẖahābu-d-dīn (A.D. 1354–73) who founded it, as Jonarāja, 409, tells us, at the confluence of the Vitastā and Sindhu.

river. Even so it is still liable to be invaded by the Vitastā at times of flood. For the swamp as well as the fertile village lands reclaimed around it, lie below the level of the river-bed.[1]

The old course of the rivers here briefly indicated explains the curious position of the Nōr (map 'Noroo'). This canal which is of importance for navigation leaves the Vitastā on the left bank just opposite to the present junction with the Sindhu and practically continues the southwesterly course of the latter for some distance. Only about ⅓ mile of low ground divides the Nōr from the end of the swamp which marks the bed of the Sindhu at the point of its old junction opposite the Vainyasvāmin ruin.

Similarly the position of *Parihāsapura* which King Lalitāditya chose for his splendid capital, becomes now intelligible. The plateau or Karēwa of Par[ə]spōr which still preserves its name is now flanked on the east by the Paṇz[i]nōr Nambal and on the west by the marshes of Hār[a]traṭh. Neither of them affords in their present condition the convenient waterway we find invariably near all other Kaśmīr capitals. Before Suyya's regulation, however, the Vitastā flowed as we have seen, immediatly to the north of the plateau and at the very foot of the great temples erected here by King Lalitāditya.

Results of Suyya's regulation.

71. The object and result of the change of the confluence can, I think, also be traced yet. By forcing the Vitastā to pass north of Trigām instead of south of it, the reclamation of the marshes south of the Volur lake must have been greatly facilitated. The course thus given to the river carries its waters by the nearest way into that part of the Volur which by its depth and well-defined boundaries is naturally designed as a great reservoir to receive the surplus water of dangerous floods. The southern shores of the lake are still to this day the scene of a constant struggle between the cultivator and floods. The reclamation of land which has gone on for centuries in these low marshy tracts,[2] could never have been undertaken if the Vitastā had been allowed to spread itself over them from the south, the direction marked by its old course.

The change in the confluence of the Vitastā and Sindhu was a necessary condition for the subsequent course given to the united rivers. It

[1] See LAWRENCE, *Valley*, pp, 210 *sq*. Kalhaṇa's account shows that the huge embankments guarding the Paṇz[i]nōr tract must be far older than the times of the Mug͟hals to which they are popularly attributed.

[2] Compare DREW, *Jummoo*, p. 116, for a description of these tracts and the amphibious ways of the inhabitants who get their living as much from the water as the land around.

was thus closely connected with the general scheme of regulation and drainage. Kalhaṇa indicates this by referring immediately after the above passage to stone-embankments constructed along the Vitastā for seven Yojanas (circ. 42 miles) and the damming-in of the Volur lake.[1]

On the land reclaimed new populous villages were founded. From the circular dykes which were built around these villages, they are said to have received the popular designation of *kuṇḍala*, 'ring.' We actually still find two villages on the low ground near the Volur showing in their modern names the ending *kuṇḍᵊl*, derived from Skr. *kuṇḍala*. Uts̱ᵊkuṇḍᵊl (map wrongly 'Watr koondl') and Marᵊkuṇḍᵊl are situated both close to the left bank of the Vitastā before it enters the marshes at the south-eastern end of the Volur. Their names and position seem to support the assumption that the present northerly course of the river above Trigrāmī and S̱hādⁱpūr is directly due to Suyya's operations.

Kalhaṇa adds that even in his own time, *i.e.*, two and a half centuries later, there were "seen, growing on the banks of the former river-beds, old trees which bore the marks of the boat ropes fastened to them."[2] Similarly the observant Chronicler noted the old pales securing the embankments "which the rivers displayed when low in the autumn."[3] We must be grateful to him for the evident interest with which he ascertained and recorded the details of Avantivarman's operations. For he has thus enabled us even at the present day to trace some of the important changes then effected in the hydrography of the whole Valley.

Course of Vitastā towards the Volur lake.

72. Following the course of the Vitastā below its present confluence with the Sindhu we soon pass the village of Sambal where the route from Śrīnagar to the north of the Volur lake and thence to the Trāgᵃbal Pass, crosses the river. Here at some distance from the left bank is the site of the ancient *Jayapura*, the capital founded by King Jayāpīḍa in the second half of the eighth century.[4] It is marked by the village of Andᵊrkōṭh situated on an island between the Sambal marsh and a branch of the canal known as Nōr. An ancient causeway connects the island with the strip of land separating the marsh from the present course of the Vitastā.

[1] See v. 103 *sqq.*

[2] v. 101.

[3] It is still the common belief in Kaśmīr that "no embankment on the riverside is sound unless it has a foundation of piles"; LAWRENCE, *Valley*, p. 211. Considering the peaty nature of the soil along the lower course of the river, this belief may be justified by old experience.

[4] See for the identification of this site, *Rājat.* v. 506 note, and below, § 122.

We should have some difficulty in understanding the position chosen for a town which was intended to be a place of importance if we did not know the great change effected in the course of the river by the subsequent regulation of Avantivarman. In King Jayāpīḍa's time one of the main branches of the Vitastā probably followed the line of the Nōr in this neighbourhood. The island of And^{a}rkōṭh which forms a small alluvial plateau, raised perhaps artificially in parts, was then a convenient site. This is no longer the case since the river flows to the east of And^{a}rkōṭh and at a considerable distance. We can safely attribute to this change the fact that Jayapura like the similarly situated Parihāsapura had fallen into insignificance already before Kalhaṇa's time.

Close to Sambal the river passes the foot of an isolated hill known as *Āh^{a}tyung*, rising about a thousand feet above the plain. Under its shelter on the north is the small lake of *Mānasbal* which is mentioned by the name of *Mānasa[saras]* in the Nīlamata and by Jonarāja.[1] It is about two miles long, and occupying a rock-basin is deeper than the other lakes of the Kaśmīr plains. It is connected with the river by a short channel and partially fed by an irrigation canal carried into it from the Sind River.[2] Its ancient name is derived from the sacred lake on Kailāsa, famous in the Purāṇas and Epics and usually located in the Mansarōvar of the Tibetan highlands.

A short distance lower down the villages of Utṣ^{a}kuṇḍ^{a}l and Mar^{a}-kuṇḍ^{a}l already referred to above, are passed on the left bank. There are various indications which make it probable that in old times the Volur lake reached much closer to these villages than it does at present. Kalhaṇa's reference seems to indicate that these villages enclosed by circular dykes were actually reclaimed from the lake, and Jonarāja still places them on the very shore of the lake.[3] In the same way Śrīvara speaking of the villages stretching from Samudrakoṭa,[4] the present Sud^{a}rkōṭh, to the vicinity of Dvārikā, near And^{a}rkōṭh, seems to place them along the shore of the Volur.

A glance at the map shows that the land on the left bank of the river below the 'Kuṇḍala' villages projects like a peninsula into the lake.

[1] As *Jonarāja*, 864 *sq.*, makes the ancient name quite certain, the latter could have safely been shown on the map. In some passages of the Nīlamata and Māhātmyas it might be doubted whether this lake or the Uttaramānasa on Mount Haramukh is intended; see however *Nīlamata*, 1338, where the Mānasa lake is mentioned after the Vitastāsindhusaṁgama.

[2] The construction of this canal is ascribed by Jonarāja, 864 *sq.*, to Zainu-l-'ābidīn.

[3] See *Rājat.* v. 120, and *Jonar.* 1230, (Bo. ed.).

[4] See *Śrīv.* i. 400 *sq.*

It can be safely assumed that the creation of this strip of land which now accompanies the river-channel for some seven miles farther, is due to the continual deposits of silt. This silting-up process is still going on in this as in other portions of the Volur where streams enter it, and is likely to reduce the expanse of the lake still further in the future.[1]

A striking proof for the gradual change thus effected is afforded by the position of the artificial island known now as Zain^{a}lānk. It was constructed by King Zainu-l-ʿābidin from whom it took its proper designation of *Jainalaṅkā*. It was then, according to Jonarāja's description, in the middle of the Volur where the water was deep.[2] It is now situated in a shallow marsh close to the present embouchure of the river.

Volur lake.

73. The great lake, with the southern shores of which we have already become acquainted, is a very important feature in the hydrographic system of Kaśmīr. It acts as a huge flood-reservoir for the greatest part of the drainage of Kaśmīr and gives to the western portion of the Valley its peculiar character. Its dimensions vary at different periods, owing to the low shores to the south being liable to inundation. In normal years the length of the lake may be reckoned at about 12 and its width at 6 miles, with an area of about 78 square miles. In years of flood the lake extends to about 13 miles in length and 8 miles in width.[3] Its depth is nowhere more than about 15 feet and is continually lessening in those parts where the streams debouch into it. Notwithstanding this slight depth navigation on the lake often becomes dangerous when violent storms sweep over it from the mountains in the north. The boundaries of the lake are ill-defined in the south and partly in the east; the marshes and peaty meadows merge almost imperceptibly into the area of the lake. On the north the shores slope up towards an amphitheatre of mountains from which some rocky spurs run down to the water's edge. The fertile tract at the foot of these mountains forms the ancient *Khūyāśrama*, the modern Pargaṇa of *Khuy^{a}hōm*.

Mahāpadma Nāga.

The ancient name of the lake is MAHĀPADMASARAS, derived from the Nāga *Mahāpadma*, who is located in the lake as its tutelary deity. This designation is by far the most common in the Chronicles, the Nīlamata, and other old

1 Compare DREW, p. 166, and LAWRENCE, *Valley*, p. 20. The latter author is probably reproducing a popular tradition when mentioning that in King Zainu-l-ʿābidin's time the waters of the Volur stretched south to Aśam and Saṃbal.

2 See *Jonar.* (Bo. ed.) 1227 *sqq.* The name Jainalaṅkā was mutilated in the Calcutta edition; else it would have been shown on the map.

3 See LAWRENCE, p. 20.

texts.[1] It is also used, as we have seen, in the description of Kaśmīr given by the T'ang annals.

The name *Ullola* from which the present Volur (*vulgo* 'Woolar') seems to be derived, is found only in one passage of Jonarāja's Chronicle and in a single modern Māhātmya.[2] Skr. *ullola* can be interpreted to mean 'turbulent' or '[the lake] with high-going waves.'[3] Those who have experienced the sensation of crossing the lake with a strong wind, will readily allow the appropriateness of this designation. Yet it is impossible to dismiss altogether the suspicion that the name which seems wholly unknown to the older texts, may be only a clever adaptation of the Kaśmīrī name Volur or its earlier representative. It is certainly curious that in modern Māhātmyas we meet with Ullola as a nam for the Vul/ar Pargaṇa, the genuine ancient designation of which is Holaḍā.[4] Jonarāja in his commentary on Śrīkaṇṭhacarita, iii. 9, uses Ullola as a paraphrase for Mahāpadma.

Legends of Mahāpadma Nāga.

74. From an early date various legends seem to have clustered around this, the greatest of Kaśmīr lakes. The Nīlamata relates at length how the lake became the habitation of the Mahāpadma Nāga.[5]

Originally it was occupied by the wicked Nāga Ṣaḍaṅgula who used to carry off the women of the country. Nīla, the lord of Kaśmīr Nāgas, banished Ṣaḍaṅgula to the land of the Dārvas. The site left dry on his departure was occupied by a town called *Candrapura* under King Viśvagaśva. The Muni Durvāsas not receiving hospitable reception in this town, cursed it and foretold its destruction by water. When subsequently the Nāga Mahāpadma sought a refuge in Kaśmīr and asked Nīla for the allotment of a suitable habitation, he was granted permission to occupy Candrapura. The Mahāpadma Nāga thereupon approached King Viśvagaśva in the disguise of an old Brahman and asked to be allowed to settle in the town with his family. When his prayer was agreed to he shewed himself in his true form and announced to the King the approaching submersion of his city. At the Nāga's direction the King with his people emigrated and founded two Yojanas further west the new town of *Viśvagaśvapura*. The Nāga then converted the city into a lake, henceforth his and his family's dwelling place. A recollection of this legend still lives in popular tradition, and the ruins of the doomed city are supposed to be sighted occasionally in the water.

[1] For detailed references see *Rājat.* iv. 593 note.

[2] See *Jonar.* (Bo. ed.) 1227–30; *Dhyāneśvaramāh.* 30, 33.

[3] See Bühler, *Report*, p. 9.

[4] See *Vitastāmāh.* v. 48; *Haridrāgaṇeśamāh.*

[5] See *Nīlamata*, 976–1008, and Bühler, *Report*, p. 10.

Another legend has found a lengthy record in Kalhaṇa's narrative of King Jayāpīḍa's reign,* iv. 592 *sqq*. The Nāga Mahāpadma being threatened with desiccation by a Dravidian sorcerer, appeared to the King in his dream and asked for protection. As a reward he promised to show a gold mine to the King. Jayāpīḍa agreed to the Nāga's prayer. Curiosity, however, induced him to let the Draviḍian first try his magic on the lake. When the waters had been dried up so far that the Nāga and his dependents were seen as human-faced snakes wriggling in the mud, the king interfered and caused the lake to be restored. The Nāga, however, resented the insult and showed to the king only a rich copper ore instead of the gold mine.

With reference to a Purāṇic legend the Mahāpadma is sometimes identified with the Nāga *Kāliya* who was vanquished by Kṛṣṇa. As the foot of the god when touching the Nāga's head made lotuses (*padma*) appear on it, Mahāpadma is treated by Kaśmirian poets as another form of Kāliya.[1]

Lower affluents of Vitastā.

75. Of the streams which fall into the Volur lake besides the Vitastā, the stream of the *Banḍᵃpōr* Nāla is the most considerable. It drains the range between Mount Haramukh and the Trāgᵃbal Pass and forms a small Delta of its own to the north of the lake. Its ancient name is *Madhumatī*.[2] It is repeatedly mentioned in the Rājataraṅgiṇī in connection with the route leading to the Dard territory, but must be distinguished from another, smaller Madhumatī which flows into the Kiṣangaṅgā near the Śāradātīrtha.

The outflow of the lake's waters is at its southwest corner about two miles above the town of Sōpūr. The latter is the ancient *Suyyapura*, founded by Suyya and commemorating his name.[3] If we may judge from the position of the town and the words used by Kalhaṇa in another passage,[4] it appears probable that the operations of Avantivarman's great engineer extended also to the river's bed on this side of the lake.

About four miles below Sōpūr the Vitastā which now flows in a winding but well-defined bed, receives its last considerable tributary within Kaśmīr. It is the Pohur which before its junction has collected the various streams draining the extreme northwest of the Valley.

[1] Compare *Śrīkaṇṭhac*. iii. 9; *Jonar*. 933, and my note *Rājat*. v. 114.

[2] See *Rājat*. vii. 1179 and note 1171; also viii. 2883; *Nīlamata* 1259 *sqq*., 1398, etc.

[3] See *Rājat*. v. 118 note.

[4] V. 104: "Trained by him, the Vitastā *starts* rapidly on her way from the basin of the Mahāpadma lake, like an arrow from the bow."

This portion of the country figures but little in Kalhaṇa's narrative ; hence we find in the Rājataraṅgiṇī no reference to the Pohur or any of its affluents. The old name of the river is uncertain. Jonarāja in a passage which is found only in the Bombay edition, calls this river *Pahara* ; the Māhātmyas vary between *Prahara* and *Prahāra*.[1] Of the side-streams the Māvᵘr (map 'Maur') flowing through the Machⁱpōr Pargaṇa is named in the Nīlamata as *Māhurī*.[2] The name of the Hamal stream is identical with that of the Pargaṇa through which its course lies, the ancient *Samālā*.[3]

About 18 miles from the point where the Vitastā leaves the Volur, it reaches the entrance of the gorge of Bārāmūla. Through this defile we have already before followed the course of the river. At Bārāmūla navigation ceases. After passing with a violent current the ravine immediately below the town, the river, so placid within the Valley, turns into a large torrent rushing down in falls and rapids.

SECTION VII.—SOIL AND CLIMATE OF THE VALLEY.

Alluvial Plateaus (Uḍar).

76. Our survey of Kaśmīr rivers has taken us along that great flat of river alluvium which forms the lowest and most fertile part of the Valley. We must now turn to the higher ground of the Vale which consists of the peculiar plateaus already alluded to.

The genuine Kaśmīrī term for these plateaus is *uḍar*, found in its Sanskrit form as *uḍḍāra* in the Chronicles. Another modern designation of Persian origin now often used, is *karēwa*. The word *uḍḍāra* is twice found as an ending of local names in the Rājataraṅgiṇī [4], while the latter Chronicles use it frequently in designations of well-known plateaus.[5] An earlier Sanskrit term no longer surviving in use, is *sūda*, originally meaning 'barren waste ground.' Kalhaṇa employs it when speaking of the well-known Dāmᵃdar Uḍar.[6]

The Uḍars of the Kaśmīr Valleys are usually considered by geologists to be due to lacustrine deposits. They appear either isolated by

[1] See *Jonar.* (Bo. ed.) 1150, 1152 ; *Vitastāmāh.* xxvii. 2 ; *Svayambhūmāh.*

[2] *Nīlamata*, 1322 *sqq.*

[3] See *Rājat.* vii. 159 note.

[4] *Locanoḍḍāra* and *Dhyānoḍḍāra*, *Rājat.* viii. 1427 note.

[5] See *Gusikōḍḍāra, the* Uḍar of Gūs near Rāmuh, *Śriv.* iv. 465, 592, 596 ; *Dāmodaroḍḍāra*, the Dāmᵃdar Uḍar, *Śriv.* iv. 618 ; *Laulapuroḍḍāra*, Fourth Chron. 175, etc.

[6] See *Rājat.* i. 156 note.

lower ground around them or connected by very gentle slopes with spurs descending from the mountains. Often the tops of these plateaus seem almost perfectly flat, forming table lands of varying dimensions. They rise generally from 100 to 300 feet above the level of the ravines and valleys which intersect them, and through which the streams from the mountains and their own drainage find their way to the Vitastā. Most of the Uḍars are found on the south-western side of the Valley, stretching from S'upiyạu to Bārāmūla. But they also occur across the river on the north-eastern side of the Valley, and at both extremities of the river-flat in the south-east and north-west.

Owing to the inferiority of the soil and the difficulty of irrigation, the Uḍars show a marked difference in point of fertility from other parts of the Valley. Those which slope down from the foot of the mountains have been brought under cultivation with the help of water-courses conducted over them from the higher ground behind. Most of these irrigation-channels are, no doubt, of ancient date, and some are specially mentioned in the Chronicles. To other Uḍars, particularly those which are entirely isolated, water could not be brought. These are either barren wastes covered with low jungle or if cultivated, yield only precarious crops owing to the uncertainty of the rainfall.

Some of the Uḍars, owing to their position near the Vitastā or for other reasons, are sites of importance in the ancient topography of Kaśmīr. Such are the plateaus of Mārtāṇḍa, Cakradhara, Padmapura, Parihāsapura. Another, the 'Uḍar of Dāmodara,' plays an interesting part in the legendary lore of the country. All these will be duly noticed in the next chapter.

Kaśmīr climate.

77. Climatic conditions are so closely connected with a country's topography that the few old notices and references which we have regarding those of Kaśmīr, may fitly find mention here.

The only distinct account of the Kaśmīr climate is given by Albērūnī.[1] He clearly indicates the reason why Kaśmīr is exempt from the heavy Monsoon rains of India proper. When the heavy clouds, he explains, reach the mountains which enclose Kaśmīr on the south, "the mountain-sides strike against them, and the clouds are pressed like olives or grapes." In consequence "the rain pours down and the rains never pass beyond the mountains. Therefore Kaśmīr has no *varṣakāla*, but continual snowfall during two and a half months, beginning with Māgha, and shortly after the middle of Caitra continual rain sets in for a few days, melting the snow and cleansing the earth. This rule has seldom an exception; however, a certain amount of extraordinary meteorological occurrences is peculiar to every province in India."

[1] See *India*, i, p. 211.

That this description is on the whole as accurate as Albērūnī's other data regarding Kaśmīr, will be easily seen by a reference to the detailed statements of Mr. LAWRENCE and Mr. ELIOT.[1] What chiefly characterizes the climate of Kaśmīr as against that of the Indian plains, is the absence of a rainy season and the equally marked absence of excessive heat. The moderate temperature of the Kaśmīr summer is ensured by the high elevation of the Valley, and has at all times been duly appreciated by its inhabitants as well as its visitors.

Kalhaṇa already proudly claims this exemption from the torments of a fierce sun as one of the favours accorded to his country by the gods.[2] His enthusiastic description of a Kaśmīr summer passed "in the regions above the forests" shows that he was no stranger to the charms of that season in the alpine parts of the country.[3] More than once he refers to the sufferings which the heat of an Indian summer outside the Valley inflicts on Kaśmīrian exiles. Even in the hill regions immediately to the south of Pīr Pantsāl the hot season with its accompanying fevers has often proved disastrous to the Kaśmīrian troops employed there.[4]

On the other hand we find also the rigours of a Kaśmīr winter duly illustrated by the Chronicle's narrative. We may refer to the description of the heavy and continued snowfall which followed Sussala's murder in Phālguna of 1128 A.D., the freezing of the Vitastā in the winter of 1087-8 A.D., etc.[5] The graphic account of Bhoja's flight to the Upper Kiṣangaṅgā Valley shows us in full detail the difficulties which attend a winter-march over the snow-covered mountains to the north of the Valley.[6] Nor do we fail to be reminded otherwise of the great differences in climate which are implied by the varying altitudes of Kaśmīr localities.[7]

Exceptionally early snowfall in the autumn such as saved the garrison of the frontier fort on the Dugdhaghāta Pass, has always been known and dreaded even low down in the Valley. The danger it represents for the rice crops is illustrated by Kalhaṇa's account of the famines resulting from such premature snowfalls.[8]

1 See LAWRENCE, p. 24 *sqq.*

2 See i. 41.

3 ii. 138.

4 Compare vii. 970; viii. 1634, 1830, 1836, 1865; regarding the fever-season of Rājapurī and neighbouring districts, my note viii. 1873.

5 *Rājat.* viii. 1376 *sqq.*; 1434 *sqq.*; vii. 592.

6 See viii. 2710 *sqq.* It must be remembered that as much as forty to sixty feet of snow falls in a severe winter on the higher ranges around Kaśmīr; see also viii. 411.

7 Compare vii. 916; viii. 2511; ii. 138.

8 See ii. 18 *sqq.*; viii. 2449.

In this as in other respects there is nothing to suggest any material change of the climatic conditions during historical times. Kalhaṇa, it is true, in describing the reign of Abhimanyu I., speaks of deep snow as "falling each year to cause distress to the Bauddhas" and obliging the king to pass six months of the cold season in Dārvābhisāra. But the whole story there related is nothing but a mere rechauffé of the ancient legend told in the Nīlamata of the annual migrations caused by the presence of the Piśācas. It therefore can claim no historical value whatever.[1]

78. Cultivation such as appears to have been carried on in Kaśmīr since the earliest historical period, must necessarily leave its traces in the topography of a country and may hence claim a passing notice.

Cultivation.

Rice has as far as we can go back, always been the largest and most important produce of the Valley. Its character as the main cereal is sufficiently emphasized by the fact that it is usually referred to in the Chronicles by the simple term of *dhānya* 'grain.'[2] The conditions of its cultivation presuppose an extensive system of irrigation, and for this the Kaśmīr Valley with its abundance of streams and springs is admirably adapted by nature. The elaborate arrangements which exist at present for taking water from the streams large and small and distributing it over all the ground capable of irrigation, will be found fully detailed in Mr. LAWRENCE's valuable and exhaustive account of Kaśmīr agriculture.[3] There is every reason to believe that they have come down with little, if any, change from a very early period.

Irrigation.

Many of the larger irrigation channels which intersect the fertile alluvial flats, or skirt the terraced slopes of the Uḍars and mountain-sides, are shown on the map; see, *e.g.*, the tracts on the lower course of the Lidar, Veśau, Sind, and other rivers. In old times when the population was larger than now, much land which is at present allowed to lie waste on the hill-sides, on the Uḍars and in the low-lying tracts by the marshes, must have been under cultivation.[4] I have often come across traces of old irrigation-cuts long ago abandoned, which brought down the water of the melting snows from alpine plateaus high above the forest zone. Their distance from any lands capable of rice-cultivation is so great

[1] See i. 180, and note i. 184.

[2] "The Kashmiris, so far, have considered no crop worthy of attention save rice;" LAWRENCE, *Valley*, p. 319.

[3] See *Valley*, pp. 323 *sq*.

[4] Compare *Valley*, pp. 239 and 356, as to the extensive areas which were once cultivated and are likely to be so again in future.

and the trouble of their construction must have been so considerable that only a far greater demand for irrigation than the present one can account for their existence.

In the earliest traditions recorded by Kalhaṇa the construction of irrigation canals plays already a significant part. The *Suvarṇamaṇikulyā* which is ascribed to King Suvarṇa and which still brings water to a great part of the Āḍ[a]vin district, has already been noticed.[1] The reference to the aqueduct by which King Dāmodara is supposed to have attempted to bring water to the great Uḍar named after him, though legendary in the main, is also characteristic.[2] Lalitāditya is credited with having supplied villages near Cakradhara (T̲sak[a]dar) with the means of irrigation by the construction of a series of water-wheels (*araghaṭṭa*) which raised the water of the Vitastā.[3]

To Suyya, however, Avantivarman's engineer, is ascribed the merit of having on an extensive scale secured river-water for village-lands. From Kalhaṇa's detailed description it is evident that Suyya's regulation of the Vitastā was accompanied by systematic arrangements for the construction of irrigation channels. For these the water of various hill-streams was utilized as well as that of the main-river. The size and distribution of the water-course for each village was fixed on a permanent basis. He is thus said "to have embellished all regions with an abundance of irrigated fields which were distinguished for excellent produce." The increase in produce consequent on these measures and the reclamation of new lands from the river and marshes is said to have lowered the average price of a Khāri of rice from two hundred to thirty-six Dinnāras.[4]

The importance of irrigation from a revenue point of view must have always been recognized by the rulers of the country. Hence even in later times we find every respite from internal troubles marked by repairs of ancient canals or the construction of new ones. The long and peaceful reign of Zainu-l-ʿābidīn which in many respects revived the traditions of the earlier Hindu rule, seems in particular to have been productive of important irrigation works. Jonarāja's and S'rīvara's Chronicles give a considerable list of canals constructed under this king.[5] Among these the canal which distributed the water of the Pohur River over the Zain[a]gir Pargaṇa, and the one by which the

1 See above, § 64.

2 See *Rājat.* i. 156 *sq.* note.

3 See *Rājat.* iv. 191 note.

4 See *Rājat.* v. 109–112 and note.

5 See *Jonar.* (Bo. ed.) 1141–55, 1257 *sqq.*; *S'rīv.* i. 414 *sqq.* For repairs of old canals, see *Rājat.* viii. 2380.

water of the Lidᵃr was conducted to the arid plateau of Mārtāṇḍa, deserve special mention. In the latter locality some work of this kind must have existed already at a far earlier period. Or else we could scarcely understand how it could have been chosen as the site for Lalitāditya's magnificent temple and the flourishing township which once surrounded it.[1]

Saffron-cultivation.

Of the other products of the Valley only two may be mentioned here, since they have from old times received special attention in all descriptions of the country. Already Kalhaṇa in his introduction designates saffron and grapes among "the things that even in heaven are difficult to find but are common there."[2] Saffron (*kuṅkuma*) has to the present day remained a famous product of Kaśmīr. Its cultivation has apparently from an early time specially flourished about Padmapura, the present Pāmpᵊr, where the Uḍar lands are still chiefly utilized for it. The Fourth Chronicle describes at length the plant and its treatment. Abū-l-Faẓl mentions it also in the same locality and devotes to it a long notice.[3]

Grapes.

The grapes of Kaśmīr which Kalhaṇa mentions repeatedly,[4] have not retained their area of cultivation with equal persistence. They must have enjoyed reputation outside Kaśmīr, because the name *Kaśmīrā* is given by Sanskrit Kośas as the designation of a special variety of grapes.[5] They were once plentiful at Mārtāṇḍa where both Kalhaṇa and the Fourth Chronicle mention them, and at many other localities.[6]

In Akbar's time grapes were abundant in Kaśmīr and very cheap; but Abū-l-Faẓl notes that the finer qualities were rare.[7] Since then, viticulture among the people generally has greatly declined. Though vines of remarkable size and age can still be found in many places, they are mostly wild. The produce of grapes is now restricted to a few old gardens at the mouth of the Sind Valley and to the new vineyards established on the Ḍal shores by the late Mahārāja for the cultivation of French vines.[8]

1 See *Rājat.* iv. 192.

2 i. 42.

3 See Fourth Chron. 926 *sqq.*; *Āin-i-Akb.*, i. pp 357 *sq.*

4 *Rājat.* i. 42; iv. 192; vii. 498.

5 See *Böhtlingk-Roth*, s. v.

6 Fourth Chron. 851, 928.

7 *Āin-i-Akb.*, i. p. 349.

8 For a detailed account of Kaśmīr vineyards, see LAWRENCE, *Valley*, pp. 351 *sq.*

Old ethnography of Kaśmīr.

79. It will be useful to refer here briefly to the data we possess regarding the old ethnography of Kaśmīr and the adjacent hill regions.

As far as Kaśmīr itself is concerned our information does not allow us to connect any particular localities with ethnic divisions. Judging from Kalhaṇa's Chronicle and what other sources of information are available to us, the population of Kaśmīr has shown already in old times the same homogeneity that it does at present. The physical and ethnic characteristics which so sharply mark off the Kaśmīrī from all surrounding races, have always struck observant visitors to the Valley and have hence often been described.[1] Hiuen Tsiang's brief sketch reproduced above is the earliest in date and yet applies closely to the modern inhabitants.

That the Kaśmīris form a branch of the race which brought the languages of the Indo-Aryan type into India, is a fact established by the evidence of their language and physical appearance. But when their settlement in the country took place, and from which direction they immigrated, are questions beyond the present range of historical research. The purity of race which has often been noted as distinguishing the great mass of the Kaśmīr population, may be admitted with a qualification. It is probably due not only to the country's natural isolation but also to a curious faculty for absorbing foreign elements. Colonies of Mughals, Paṭhāns, Panjābīs, and Pahāris, settled within comparatively recent times in the Valley, are being amalgamated with remarkable rapidity through intermarriage and other means.

Absorption of foreign ethnic elements.

The complete absorption of these settlements which is going on under our own eyes as it were, furnishes a likely analogy for the ethnic history of earlier times. We have reason to assume that Kaśmīr has also in Hindu times been often under foreign rule. It is difficult to believe that the reign of foreign dynasties has not been accompanied also by settlements of immigrants of the same nationality. But it is not likely that these foreign colonies were ever extensive. In any case we find no trace of their having retained a distinct and independent existence.

Various tribal sections of the population are mentioned in Kalhaṇa's narrative, but we have no means of deciding to what extent they were based on race or caste distinctions. The names of the *Lavanyas* and *Tantrins* survive in 'Krāms,' or tribal names, still borne by sections of

[1] For a general account of the Kaśmīrī population DREW's remarks, *Jummoo*, pp. 174 *sqq.*, may still be recommended. Fuller details regarding the various classes, castes, etc., will be found in Mr. LAWRENCE's work, pp. 302 *sqq.*

the Muhammadan rural population (*Lūnⁱ* and *Tāntrⁱ*).[1] But whatever distinctions of race or caste may have originally been indicated by these 'Krāms,' they have long ago disappeared.

It is equally certain from an examination of the Chronicle that these sections were never confined to particular territorial divisions, but spread all over the Valley. The humblest of these sections is probably the one which has least changed its character during the course of centuries. The modern Ḍūmbs, the descendants of the old *Ḍombas*,[2] are still the low-caste watchmen and village-menials as which they figure in Kalhaṇa's narrative. They, like the still more despised Vātals or scavengers, cannot intermarry with other Kaśmīrīs. They have thus retained in their appearance a distinctive type of their own which points to relationship with the gipsy-tribes of India and Europe.

It is difficult to come to any definite conclusion as regards the *Ki-li-to* whom Hiuen Tsiang mentions as a low-born race settled in Kaśmīr from early times and opposed to the Bauddhas.[3] Their name, usually transcribed *Kritiya*, cannot be traced in indigenous records. There is nothing to support their identification with the *Kīras*, as suggested by General Cunningham.[4] The latter seems to have been a tribe settled somewhere in the vicinity of Kaśmīr.[5]

80. The ethnography of the territories immediately adjoining Kaśmīr can be traced quite clearly from the notices of the Rājataraṅgiṇī.

Races on Kaśmīr borders.

In the south and west the adjacent hill-regions were occupied by *Khaśas*. Their settlements extended, as shown by numerous passages of the Chronicle, in a wide semi-circle from *Kaṣṭᵃvār* in the south-east to the Vitastā Valley in the west.[6] The hill-states of Rājapurī and Lohara were held by Khaśa families; the dynasty of the latter territory succeeded to the rule of Kaśmīr in the 11th century. I have shown elsewhere that the *Khaśas* are identical with the present *Khakha* tribe to which most of the petty chiefs in the Vitastā Valley below Kaśmīr and in the neighbouring hills belong. We have already seen that the

[1] Compare notes v. 248; vii. 1171.

[2] See *Rājat.* note iv. 475; also v. 353 *sqq.*, vi. 84, 182; vii. 964, 1133, viii. 94. These passages show that the Ḍombas also earned their bread as hunters, fishermen, buffoons, quacks, etc., and their daughters as singers and dancers. Their occupations thus closely resembled those of the gipsies whose name, *Rom*, is undoubtedly derived from Skr. *ḍomba*; see *P. W.* s. v.

[3] See *Si-yu-ki*, transl. Beal, i. pp. 150, 156 *sqq.*

[4] See *Anc. Geogr.*, p. 93.

[5] Compare my note viii. 2767.

[6] See *Rājat.* i. 317 note.

Khakhas have until very recent times worthily maintained the reputation which their forefathers enjoyed as marauders and turbulent hillmen.

North of the Vitastā Valley and as far as the Kiṣangaṅgā we now find the Bombas as the neighbours of the Khakhas to whom they are closely related. It is probable that the Karnāv district was held by them already in old times. Kalhaṇa seems to comprise them, viii. 3088, under the designation of Khaśa.

The upper Kiṣangaṅgā Valley above S'ardi was in old days already as at present inhabited by Dards (Skr. *Darad*, *Dārada*) who are often referred to by Kalhaṇa as the neighbours of Kaśmir on the north.[1] Their seats extended then too probably much further to the north-west, where they are now found in Citrāl, Yāsin, Gilgit and the intervening regions towards Kaśmīr. Megasthenes already knew them in the Upper Indus regions. Kalhaṇa relating events of his own time speaks of *Mlecchas* further to the north. These might have been Muhammadanized Dards on the Indus, and beyond.[2]

The regions immediately to the north-east and east of Kaśmīr were held by the *Bhauṭṭas*. We have already seen that these represent the people of Tibetan descent, the modern *Buṭ*ᵃ, of Drās, Ladākh and the neighbouring mountain districts.[3]

[1] See *Rājat.* i. 317 note.

[2] See note viii. 2762-64.

[3] See above, § 58.

CHAPTER IV.

POLITICAL TOPOGRAPHY.

SECTION I.—FRONTIERS OF ANCIENT KAŚMĪR.

81. Our account of the political topography of ancient Kaśmīr may conveniently open with a survey of its frontiers. These agree so closely with the natural boundaries of the Valley that we have already had occasion to trace them when dealing with the mountain ranges enclosing the latter. It will however be useful to supplement our information regarding these frontiers by a brief notice of the territories which lay beyond them and formed the neighbours of the Kaśmīr kingdom in Hindu times.

Territories S. E. of Kaśmīr.

Beginning in the south-east we have first the Valley of KĀṢṬHAVĀṬA, the present Kaṣṭᵃvār (' Kishtwar ' of the maps) on the upper Cināb. It is mentioned by Kalhaṇa as a separate hill state in the time of Kalaśa.[1] Its Rājās who were Hindus till Aurangzeb's time, practically retained their independence until the conquest of their territory by Mahārāja Gulāb Singh.

The hill-district of Bhadravāh lower down on the Cināb is once named in the Rājataraṅgiṇī as *Bhadrāvakāśa.*[2] Its Rājās were tributary to Cambā in recent centuries. This was probably the case also in earlier times as we do not find a ruler of Bhadrāvakāśa referred to in Kalhaṇa's lists of hill Rājās.

[1] See *Rājat.* vii. 590 note.

[2] See *Rājat.* viii. 501 note.

The Rājās of Cambā, the ancient CAMPĀ, on the other hand figure often in the Kaśmīr Chronicle.[1] Their territory has since early times comprised the valleys of the sources of the Rāvī between Kāngra, the ancient Trigarta, and Kāṣṭhavāṭa. The ancient Rājpūt family which rules this hill state to the present day, often intermarried with the Lohara dynasty which reigned in Kaśmīr.

To the west of Campā and south of Bhadrāvakāśā lay the chiefship of VALLĀPURA, the modern Ballāvar.[2] Its rulers are repeatedly referred to in Kalhaṇa's narrative and retained their independence as petty hill-chiefs till the rise of the Jammu family early in this century. 'Ballāwar' was known also to Albērūnī.

Of the political organization of the hill-territories between Vallāpura in the south-east and Rājapurī in the north-west we have no distinct information. The Hindu inhabitants of this tract including Ballāvar call themselves now *Dogrās* and their country *Dugar*. This name is traditionally derived from Skr. **Drigarta*,[3] but this term is nowhere found in our historical texts and has probably been created for the sake of an etymology in analogy of the ancient Trigarta. The original of the name seems to be *Durgara*.[4]

It is very probable that the region of the lower and middle hills between the limits indicated was already in old times divided into a number of small chiefships. Of these some eleven seem to have existed up to the time of the extension of the Sikh power into the Panjāb Kōhistān.[5] They were all absorbed in the growing state of Jammu which was originally one of them.

Among these small hill-chiefs of limited territory but ancient descent, we have probably to class the Ṭhakkura Deṅgapāla on the Cināb who gave his daughter to the pretender *Bhikṣācara* in marriage.[6] Also the Rājā of KĀNDA must probably be located in this hill tract.[7] Other Ṭhakkuras in this region are mentioned as levying blackmail on Prince Mallārjuna when on his march to Kaśmīr from the plains.[8] Immediately at the foot of the Bānahāl Pass in the territory of VIṢALĀṬĀ we find the castle of a 'Khaśa lord,' who gave shelter to Bhikṣācara and at the time

[1] Compare *Rājat.* vii. 218 note, and CUNNINGHAM, *Anc. Geogr.*, p. 141.

[2] See *Rājat.* vii. 220 note, and CUNNINGHAM, *Anc. Geogr.* p. 135.

[3] See DREW, *Jummoo*, pp. 43 *sq.*

[4] Compare the Cambā copperplate, edited by Prof. KIELHORN, *Ind. Ant.*, 1888, p. 9.

[5] See CUNNINGHAM, *Anc. Geogr.* pp. 133 *sqq.*, where a useful synopsis of the hill-states in the central portion of the Panjāb Kōhistān is given.

[6] See *Rājat.* viii. 554 *sqq.*

[7] See note vii. 590.

[8] viii. 1989 *sqq.*

was evidently independent.[1] Temporarily the Khaśas of the hills immediately south of the Pīr Pantsāl Range may have acknowledged the suzerainty of strong Kaśmīr rulers. But during the greatest part of the period which is known to us from historical sources, they appear to have held their own and rather to have levied subsidies, *i.e.*, blackmail from the Kaśmīr rulers.[2]

Frontier territories to the south-west and west.

82. Some of the petty hill states here referred to must have been included in the region which by its ancient name was known as DĀRVĀBHISĀRA. I have elsewhere shown that this name, as a geographical term, was applied to the whole tract of the lower and middle hills between the Candrabhāgā and Vitastā.[3] The combined names of the Dārvas and Abhisāras are found already in the ethnographical lists of the Mahābhārata and Bṛhatsaṁhitā. A chief of this region figures by the ethnic appellation of *Abisares* in the accounts of Alexander's Indian campaign.

The most important of the hill-states in this territory was certainly the ancient RĀJAPURĪ represented by the modern district of Rajaurī.[4] It comprised the valleys drained by the Tohī of Rajaurī and its tributaries. Owing to its position on the most direct route to the Panjāb, Rājapurī was necessarily often brought into political relations with Kaśmīr. When Hiuen Tsiang passed through it, the 'kingdom of Rājapurī' was subject to Kaśmīr. From the 10th century onwards we find the chiefs of Rājapurī as practically independent rulers, though the Chronicle tells us of numerous expeditions undertaken into their territory by the later Kaśmīr kings. The upper valley of the Tohī of Prūnts leading to the Pīr Pantsāl Pass, was included in Rājapurī territory.[5] Here lay probably the famous strong-hold of *Rājagiri* known also to Albērūnī.[6]

Rājapurī took its name from its capital which is repeatedly mentioned by Kalhaṇa and undoubtedly occupied the position of the present town of Rajaurī.[7] The ruling family belonged to the Khaśa tribe. Its descendants were the Muhammadanized Rājpūt chiefs who retained this territory down to the present century.

On the north-west Rājapurī was adjoined by the territory of

[1] viii. 1665 *sqq.*

[2] See *Rājat.* viii. 2283 note.

[3] See note i. 180.

[4] For a detailed account, see *Rājat.* vi. 286 note.

[5] See *Rājat.* viii. 959 note.

[6] See vii. 1270 note.

[7] See vii. 973 *sqq.*

LOHARA.[1] The chief valley belonging to this hill-state was the present Lohᵃrin which we have already visited when examining the Tōṣᵃmaidān route. Lohara became important for Kaśmīr from the end of the 11th century when a branch of its ruling family acquired the Kaśmīr throne. Subsequently this branch succeeded also to Lohara which thus became united to Kaśmīr under the same ruler. As the ancestral home and stronghold of the dynasty, the castle of Lohara has played a great part during the last reigns related by Kalhaṇa. The chiefs of Lohara are distinctly named as belonging to the Khaśa tribe.

Lohara seems to have included in those times also the town and district of PARṆOTSA corresponding to the present Pūnch or Prūnṭs (the Kaśmīrī form), in the lower valley of the Tohī (Tauṣī).[2] In Hiuen Tsiang's time Parṇotsa gave its name to the whole hill-state which was then tributary to Kaśmīr. The Muhammadan Rājās of Prūnṭs, closely related to the Khakhas of the Vitastā Valley, remained more or less independent till the conquest of Mahārāja Gulāb Singh. Their territory forms now a separate small principality under a branch of the Jammu family. Parṇotsa being on the great route to the western Panjāb is often mentioned in the Kaśmīr Chronicles. The large percentage of the Kaśmīrī element in the population of Prūnṭs attests the closeness and ancient date of its relations to Kaśmīr.

The hills to the south-west of Prūnṭs were held till early in this century by petty chiefs, known as the Rājās of *Kōṭlī*. It is possible that the small hill-state of KĀLIÑJARA repeatedly referred to by Kalhaṇa and known also to Ferishta, lay in this direction.[3]

Proceeding to the north-west of Parṇotsa we come to the valley of the Vitastā. This, as has already been shown above, was held in old times as an outlying frontier-district of Kaśmīr as far down as BOLYĀSAKA, the present Buliāsa. Beyond this point it was occupied by Khaśas. In Muhammadan times the valley was divided between several petty chiefs of the Khakha and Bomba clans who seem to have acknowledged as their nominal head the Khakha Rājā of Muzaffarābād. The portion of the valley between Muzaffarābād and Buliāsa bore the old name of DVĀRAVATĪ from which the modern designation of this tract, *Dvārbidī*, is derived (see above, § 53).

1 Compare for the history of *Lohara* and its various localities, Note *E*, *Rājat.* iv. 177, reproduced in *Ind. Ant.*, 1897, pp. 225 *sqq.*

2 See for details note iv. 18. Hiuen Tsiang's reference shows that the town of *Parṇotsa* must be older than the time of Lalitāditya to whom Kalhaṇa ascribes its foundation.

3 See note *Rājat.* vii. 1256.

Uraśā-Hazāra.

83. Further to the west and beyond the course of the Vitastā after its great bend, lay the ancient kingdom of Uraśā.[1] Its greatest part is comprised in the British district of Hazāra, between the Vitastā and Induṣ. It is the Οὔαρσα or Ἄρσα of Ptolemy; its ruler figures as *Arsakes* in the accounts of Alexander's campaigns. Hiuen Tsiang mentions the territory by the name of *Wu-la-shi* and found it tributary to Kaśmīr. Though this dependence seems soon to have ceased we find Uraśā often referred to in the Rājataraṅgiṇī. The account of S'aṁkaravarman's ill-fated expedition in this direction furnishes us with a clue as to the position of the old capital of Uraśā. It probably lay between the present Mansahra and Abbottabad.[2] Kalhaṇa's notice of an expedition undertaken in his own time mentions in Uraśā the town of Atyugrapura.[3] I have shown in my note on the passage that this locality is probably represented by the modern *Agrōr*, situated on the border of Hazāra towards the 'Black Mountains.' We have an intermediary form of the name in Ptolemy's Ἰθάγουρος, given as the designation of a town in Uarsa or Arsa north of Taxila.

In Muhammadan times Uraśā was included in the region known as Pakhlī. This is defined by Abū-l-Faẓl as comprising the whole of the hill territory between Kaśmīr in the east and the Indus on the west.[4] To Pakhlī belonged also the lower valley of the Kiṣangaṅgā and the valleys of the streams which flow into the latter from the Kājnāg Range and the mountains to the north-west of Kaśmīr.

Kiṣangaṅgā Valley.

This tract which is now known as *Karnau*, bore the old name of Karṇāha. It seems to have been held by small chiefs nominally tributary to Kaśmīr even in later Hindu times.[5] It is but rarely mentioned in the Chronicle. The inhabitants were Khaśas,[6] who are represented by the modern Bomba clans still holding Karnau. Their Rājās were practically independent till the Sikh conquest and often harried the north-western parts of Kaśmīr.[7] The last irruption of the Karnau Bombas and their allies, the Khakha chiefs of the Vitastā Valley, occurred as late as 1846.

1 For a detailed synopsis of the old notices, see *Rājat.* v. 217 note.

2 See *Rājat.* v. 217 note and Cunningham, *Anc. Geogr.*, p. 104.

3 Compare note viii. 3402.

4 See *Āin-i-Akb.*, ii. pp. 390 *sq.*

5 Compare *Rājat.* viii. 2485 note.

6 See viii. 2756, 3006, 3088.

7 Compare for the modern Karnau, Bates, *Gazetteer*, p. 228.

The valley of the Kiṣangaṅgā above its junction with the Karnau river and as far as S'ardi, forms a separate tract known as *Drāva.* This is possibly the DURĀṆḌA mentioned in a passage of Kalhaṇa's Chronicle.[1] The northernmost portion of the tract seems to have been a dependency of Kaśmīr even during the later Hindu reigns. At S'ardi we find the shrine of S'āradā, one of the most sacred Tīrthas of old Kaśmīr. To this as well as an old feudal stronghold in its neighbourhood we shall have occasion to refer thereafter (§ 127).

Through S'ardi leads a route to Cilās on the Indus. But this territory as well as the other portions of the Upper Indus Valley lay apparently quite beyond the sphere of Kaśmīr political influence. Hence we meet nowhere in the Chronicles with their ancient names.

Darad territory.

84. Immediately above S'ardi the valley of the Kiṣangaṅgā turns, as we have seen, into a narrow uninhabited gorge. At the other end of this gorge we reach the territory of the Darads. Their settlements on the Upper Kiṣangaṅgā and its tributaries seem to have formed a separate little kingdom, called by a general name DARADDEŚA in the Chronicle.[2] Its inhabitants who bore Hindu names, more than once attempted invasions of Kaśmīr. DARATPURĪ, 'the town of the Darads,' which was the capital of their chiefs, may have occupied the position of the modern Gurēz (map 'Goorais').[3] The latter is the chief place of the valley where the Nawābs governing it till the Sikh conquest resided. The 'Mleccha' chiefs who on two occasions figure as the Darad Rājās' allies from the north, were perhaps rulers of other Darad tribes further towards the Indus who had early been converted to Islām.[4]

Bhauṭṭas.

Crossing from the head-waters of the Kiṣangaṅgā to those of the Drās River we arrive in high-level valleys inhabited by people of Tibetan race and language, the *Bhauṭṭas* of the Chronicles. The Rājataraṅgiṇī tells us nothing of the political organization or topography of the Bhauṭṭa territories. It is, however, possible that we have a reference to *Leh,* the capital of Ladākh, in the "foreign country called LOḤ," which Kalhaṇa names in iii. 10.

Nor do the later Chronicles supply us with any details in this direction, though the several invasions which Kaśmīr suffered from this side give Jonarāja and S'rīvara occasion to refer more frequently to the Bhauṭṭas and their rulers. It may, however be noted that S'rīvara

[1] See viii. 2709 note.

[2] Compare *Rājat.* vii. 911; for other references to the Darads, i. 312 note.

[3] See vii. 911 note.

[4] See viii. 2762 note.

already knows the terms 'Little and Great Bhuṭṭa-land.'[1] They refer to Baltistān (Skardo) and Ladākh which have continued to be known to the present day as 'Little and Great Tibet,' or among Kaśmīrīs as *Lukh Buṭun* and *Buḍ Buṭun*.[2] These terms are in fact of a far older date, as they are found already in the Chinese Annals as *Little and Great Poliu*.[3]

The eastern frontier of Kaśmīr is, as we have seen, formed by a mountain range which runs from the Zōji-Lā almost due south towards Kaṣṭᵃvār. Along this range on the east lies a long narrow valley marked as Maru-Wardwan on the map (in Kaśmīrī *Maḍivāḍvan*). It is drained by a large river which joins the Cināb near the town of Kaṣṭᵃvār. Owing to its high elevation and the rigours of its climate it is inhabited only by a scanty population. According to Mr. Drew's race map and other authorities, this consists now chiefly of Kaśmīrīs. Whether this was already the case in old times, is uncertain. The Valley is nowhere mentioned in our old Kaśmīrian texts.[4] It is hence doubtful whether it belonged to Kaśmīr territory in Hindu times. Yet Abū-l-Faẓl counts it among the Parganas of Kaśmīr.[5] Beyond it to the east stretches an uninhabited belt of high mountains and glaciers, dividing Maḍivāḍvan from the Tibetan tracts of Sūru and Zanskar. To the south we reach once more the territory of Kāṣṭhavāṭa from which our present survey has started.

[1] See *Śrīv*. iii 445 (*Sūkṣmabṛhadbhuṭṭadeśau*).

[2] *Buṭun* (connected with the ethnic term *Buṭ*ᵊ < Bhauṭṭa; see above, § 58), is the Kaśmīrī term for Tibet in general.

[3] Compare A. Rémusat, *Nouveaux mélanges asiatiques*, i. p. 194; and Sir H. Yule, *Cathay*, p. lxx.

[4] The Trisaṁdhyāmāhātmya which refers to the Valley as *Maḍavāṭira*, cannot claim any particular antiquity.

[5] See *Āin-i-Akb*., ii. p. 369.

Section II.—Ancient Political Divisions.

Kramarājya, Maḍavarājya.

85. The Valley of Kaśmīr to which we may now return has from early times been divided into two great parts, known by their modern names as *Kamrāz* and *Marāz*. These terms are derived from Skr. Kramarājya and Maḍavarājya, which are found very frequently in the Rājataraṅgiṇī as well as the later Chronicles.[1] The original form of the modern Kamrāz was known to the tradition of the S'rinagar Paṇḍits generally. With the old name Maḍavarājya, however, I found only those few acquainted who, like the late Paṇḍit Dāmodara and Paṇḍit Govind Kaul, had specially studied Kalhaṇa's Chronicle.

According to the generally prevailing notion Marāz comprises the districts on both sides of the Vitastā above S'rīnagar, and Kamrāz those below. The present tradition places the boundary of the two great divisions more accurately at the Shērgaṛhi palace. That the boundary was already in old times indicated by a line drawn through the capital is easily proved by an examination of all passages in the Rājataraṅgiṇī and other Chronicles naming Maḍavarājya and Kramarājya. They invariably show localities situated above S'rīnagar in the former and those below in the latter division.

We arrive at the same result on a reference to the Āīn-i Akbarī. Abū-l-Faẓl distinctly informs us that "the whole kingdom was divided under its ancient rulers into two divisions, *Marāj* on the east and *Kamrāj* on the west."[2] He then proceeds to tabulate the thirty-eight Parganas into which Kaśmīr was divided under Akbar's administration, separately under the two main-heads of Marāj and Kamrāj. The city of S'rinagar is counted with the former, and so are also all Parganas above the capital, while those below are shown in Kamrāj.

The term of Kamrāz has in modern times occasionally been used also in a more restricted sense, for the designation of the Parganas to the west and north-west of the Volur lake. This usage probably arose from the fact that at various periods several of the small Parganas in this portion of the Valley were for administrative purposes grouped together in one Pargaṇa, to which the name Kamrāz was given.[3] This

1 See my note on *Rājat.* ii. 15.

2 Compare *Āīn-i-Akb.*, ii. p. 368.

3 Thus Abū-l-Faẓl's table seems to show that in Akbar's time the old Parganas of Uttar, Lolau, Hamal and Machipūr were embodied in the large Pargaṇa of 'Kamrāj;' see *Āīn-i Akb.*, ii. p. 371. In Moorcroft's and Baron Hügel's list the Pargaṇa Kamrāj includes Uttar, Hamal and Machipūr. Owing to the frequent changes

circumstance explains the different accounts referred to by Prof. Bühler in his note on the term Kramarājya.[1]

Though the terms Maḍavarājya and Kramarājya are so often employed in the Chronicles, we have no distinct evidence of the two divisions having in Hindu times formed separate administrative units or provinces. It is possible that this was the case at one or the other period. But Abū-l-Faẓl's account as well as the usage traceable from his time to the present day show that the terms in their popular geographical significance could maintain themselves quite independently of actual administrative divisions.[2]

Administrative Districts.

86. The whole of the Valley has from an early date been subdivided for administrative purposes into a considerable number of small districts known in recent times as 'Parganas.' Their ancient designation was *viṣaya*.[3] The number, names and limits of these subdivisions have been subject to considerable variations during the period over which our documents extend.

The great majority of the Parganas known in recent times can be safely assumed to have existed already during the Hindu rule. This is proved by the fact that the names of numerous Parganas are found in their ancient forms already in the Rājataraṅgiṇī and the other Chronicles. But these texts do not furnish us anywhere with a complete list of the Parganas. It is hence impossible for us to restore in full detail the map of the administrative sub-divisions for any particular epoch

of the Pargaṇa divisions (see below) the extent of the 'Pargaṇa Kamrāj' has also varied from time to time.

[1] See *Report*, p. 11.

[2] The only trace I can find of a general division of Kaśmīr other than that into Maḍavarājya and Kramarājya, is contained in an unfortunately corrupt and fragmentary passage of the Lokaprakāśa, iv. It seems to divide the twenty-seven Viṣayas or Pargaṇas of Kaśmir (see below) into three tracts, *viz.* (i) *Kramarājya* from Khōyāśrāmika onwards (Khuyāhōm, the old Khūyāśrama is meant); (ii) *Madhyamarājya* from the Cānūlā [river ?] to Lahara or Lār; (iii) *Maḍavarājya* from *Śrīvantaka* (?).

The text is in a deplorable condition and the explanation of Cānūlā and Śrīvantaka quite uncertain. The former may be the river of doubtful name and i[illegible]ntity referred to in Rājat. note v. 109. It appears as if at the time to which the [L]okaprakāśa's notice goes back, an intermediate slice of territory had been [f]ormed between Kramarājya and Maḍavarājya and dubbed *Madhyamarājya* 'the [m]iddle province.' Five thousand villages out of the 66,063 with which the text [c]redits Kaśmir, are attributed to this intermediate division.

[3] Compare for the term *viṣaya Rājat.* v. 51; viii. 1260, 1413, 2697.

The expression Pargaṇa may have been introduced by the Mughal administration. Its Skr. origi[n]al **puragaṇa* is not found in the Chronicles.

during Hindu times. The Lokaprakāśa, it is true, tells us of the division of Kaśmir into twenty-seven Viṣayas and enumerates some nineteen of the latter. But several of the names are so corrupt as to be beyond recognition, while others bear a distinctly modern look. In any case it is impossible to fix the date to which this notice may belong or to judge of its authenticity.[1]

Abū-l-Faẓl's account is the first which presents us with a systematic statement of Kasmir Parganas. It is of special interest because it shows us how their list could be increased or re-adjusted within certain limits according to fiscal requirements or administrative fancies. The return of Āsaf Khān reproduced by Abū-l-Faẓl shows thirty-eight Parganas, while the earlier one of Qāẓī 'Alī contained forty-one. The difference is accounted for by the amalgamation of some and the splitting-up of other Parganas. The Parganas varied greatly in size, as shown by the striking contrasts in the revenue-assessments. Thus, *e.g*, Paṭan was assessed at circ. 5300 Kharwārs, while the revenue from 'Kamrāj' amounted to 446,500 Kharwārs.

The number of Parganas had changed but little during Mughal and Paṭhān times. For the Sikhs on their conquest of the Valley seem to have found thirty-six as the accepted traditional number. But there had been various changes in the names and extent of these Parganas. These changes became still more frequent under the Sikh administration, as is seen by a comparison of the lists given by Moorcroft (1823), Baron Hügel (1835) and Vigne (circ. 1840). They all show a total of thirty-six Parganas but vary among themselves in the names of individual Parganas.

These frequent changes and redistributions of the Parganas continued during Dogrā Rule. The most accurate list I am able to refer to for this most recent period, is that given by Major Bates. It shows a total of forty-three Parganas for the year 1865.[2] Subsequent reforms introduced Taḥsīls after the fashion of British provinces with a view to reducing the number of sub-divisions. The latest list shows eleven Taḥsīls.[3] In their constitution little regard was paid to the historical divisions of the country. Fortunately, however, Kaśmiris are as con-

1 Of the Lokaprakāśa's Viṣayas *Khoyāśramī, Samālā, Laharī, Auladiya, Nīlāśa, Khaḍūviya* correspond clearly to the Khūyāśrama, Samālā, Lahara, Holaḍā, Nīlāśva, Khaḍūvī of the Rājataraṅgiṇī. *Ekena, Devasūvi* may possibly be corruptions for Evenaka and Devasarasa. *Krodhana, Dvāviṁśati, Bhṛṅga, Phāgvā* probably represent the modern Parganas of Kruhin, Dūntṣ, Bring, Phākh. *Cālana, Vitasthā, Satrava, Svanavārī, Nīlā, Hārī, Jalahaḍiya*, are quite uncertain.

2 See *Gazetteer*, p. 2 *sqq*.

3 Compare the sketch-map attached to MR. LAWRENCE'S *Valley*.

servative in their topographical nomenclature as in many other matters. The old Pargaṇa names are hence still in ordinary use and likely to remain so for some time to come.[1]

The absence of a complete list of Pargaṇas for an earlier period and the changes in their constitution during more recent times make a systematic exposition of the ancient territorial divisions impracticable. In a separate note I have given a comparative table of the Pargaṇa lists we possess since Akbar's time. There too I have indicated the ancient equivalents of the Pargaṇa names, as far as they can be traced in the Sanskrit Chronicles.[2] We shall have occasion to refer to these names and their history in the course of our detailed survey of ancient localities in the Valley.

Density of population in old Kaśmīr.

87. The large number of administrative sub-divisions which as we have seen goes back to an early date, may be taken as an indication of the dense population then occupying the Valley. We have no means of forming any accurate estimate as to the number of the population which the country contained in Hindu times. But there is every reason to believe that even at a later period it was far larger than at the present day. The existence of a very great number of deserted village-sites, in all parts of the country, the remains already alluded to of a far more extended system of irrigation, the number of great temple ruins, and the uniform tradition of the people,—all point to the same conclusion.

The present century has witnessed in Kaśmir a series of appalling famines and epidemics, which wrought terrible havoc in the mass of the rural population particularly. The last famine, 1878–79, alone is supposed to have removed three-fifth of the population from the Valley.[3] The political vicissitudes of the first half of the century had a baneful influence on the economical condition of Kaśmir and brought about an extensive emigration both among the industrial and agriculturist classes. Notwithstanding all these trials the population which in 1835 was estimated at about 200,000 souls, had risen to 814,000 according to the census of 1891.

These figures indicate great powers of recuperation. Yet it is held by competent judges that the present agricultural population is by no means sufficient even for the land actually under cultivation. I would hence manifestly be hazardous to make any guess as to the umbers

[1] The Survey of India maps indicates the approximate extent of the Pargaṇas recognized in the fifties.

[2] See Supplementary Note BB.

[3] Compare for this and other statistical details Mr. LAWRENCE's *Valley*, p. 223 *sqq*.

which the country might have supported in the most prosperous times of Hindu rule.

The fact of Kaśmīr having possessed a far greater population in ancient times helps to explain the curious traditional verse which puts the number of villages of Kaśmīr at 66,063. The verse is found twice in the Lokaprakāśa and still lives in the oral tradition of the Brahmans throughout the Valley. It has been reproduced from the latter in Paṇḍit Sāhibrām's Tīrthasaṁgraha.[1] That it can claim some antiquity is evident from the allusion made to the number in Jonarāja's Chronicle.[2]

Though that figure must have at all times implied a considerable exaggeration, it is nevertheless characteristic of the popular notion on the subject. Even Sharīfu-d-dīn whose information, collected about A.D. 1400, is generally accurate and matter-of-fact, records: "It is popularly believed that in the whole of the province—plains and mountains together—are comprised 100,000 villages. The land is thickly inhabited."[3] It is curious that Mirzā Ḥaidar who had ruled Kaśmīr himself copies this statement without modification or dissent.

Section III.—The old and new Capitals.

88. The ancient divisions of Kramarājya and Maḍavarājya are separated by a line drawn through S'rīnagar. This fact as well as the great historical interest attaching to S'rīnagar as the capital of the country make it the convenient starting-point for our survey. The history of Kaśmīr has always been reflected as it were in that of its capital. The site of the latter has not changed for more than thirteen centuries. It is thus easy to account for the ample historical data which enable us to restore in great part the ancient topography of S'rīnagar and to trace back the city's history to the time of its foundation.

Śrīnagara in the Hiuen Tsiang's time.

Hiuen Tsiang who visited the Kaśmīr capital about A.D. 631, and whose record is the earliest we possess, found it already in the position of the present S'rīnagar. He describes it as situated along the

[1] *Ṣaṣṭir grāmasahasrāṇi ṣaṣṭir grāmaśatāni ca | ṣaṣṭir grāmās trayo grāmā hyetat Kaśmīramaṇḍalam* ||; comp. Lokaprakāśa, *Ind. Studien*, xviii. p. 375.

[2] See *Jonar.* (Bo. ed.), 153.

[3] See *Tārīkh-i-Rashīdī*, p. 430. Ritter who reproduces the passage of the Zafarnāma from De la Croix's translation, shows the number of villages as 10,000; see *Asien*, ii. p. 1123. It may be noted in passing that according to the Census of 1891 the number of villages in Kaśmīr was then reckoned at 2870.

east bank of a great river, *i.e.* the Vitastā, 12 or 13 *li* long from north to south and 4 or 5 *li* broad from east to west About 10 *li* to the south-east of this, "the new city," the pilgrim notices a Buddhist convent which lay between a high mountain on the north and the site of 'the old city' on the south.

It is the merit of General Cunningham to have first recognized that the situation here indicated for the new capital of Hiuen Tsiang's time corresponds exactly to that of the modern S'rīnagar.[1] A glance at the map shows that the position and dimensions ascribed by Hiuen Tsiang to the new city apply closely to that part of S'rīnagar which occupies the right or eastern riverbank, and which, as we shall see, forms the older portion of the city. The two and a half miles represented by the 12 or 13 *li* of the Chinse measurement, agree accurately with the length of the city within its ancient limits along the eastern bank of the Vitastā. The estimate of its breadth at somewhat less than one mile (4 or 5 *li*) is equally correct.

Purāṇādhiṣṭhāna.

89. The position of 'the old city' is marked by the present village of *Pāndrēṭhan* which derives its name from the appellation PURĀṆĀDHIṢṬHĀNA, meaning 'the Old Capital.' It lies to the south-east of S'rīnagar just as Hinen Tsiang says, at the south foot of a mountain spur which rises with bold slopes to a height of about 3000 feet above the village. Measured from the nearest point of old S'rīnagar, the distance to the presumptive site of the monastery between Pāndrēṭhan and the steep hill-side is exactly two miles or 10 *li*.

The history of 'the Old Capital' is so closely connected with that of S'rīnagara that it will be useful to acquaint ourselves first with the data bearing upon it. The name of PURĀṆĀDHIṢṬHĀNA meets us first in Kalhaṇa's account of the reign of King Pravarasena I. (or S'reṣṭhasena) who is said to have erected there a shrine known as that of S'iva *Pravareśvara*.[2] At the beginning of the tenth century the minister Meruvardhana built at Purāṇādhiṣṭhāna a Viṣṇu temple called after his own name. This has been rightly identified by General Cunningham with the well-preserved little temple which still stands in the village of Pāndrēṭhan and has often been described by European travellers.[3]

[1] Gen. CUNNINGHAM's identification was first indicated in his paper on the architecture of Kaśmir temples, *J. A. S. B.*, 1848, p. 283. For a fuller account, see *Anc. Geogr.*, pp. 93 *sqq.*

[2] See *Rājat.* iii. 99 note, where detailed references have been given regarding the site

[3] See v. 267 note, also for descriptions of the temple.

Even in Kalhaṇa's own time pious foundations are recorded at this ancient site.

The identity of Pāndrēṭhan with the site named in the Chronicle as 'the Old Capital' is proved by ample evidence. It is indicated in the old gloss on Rājat. v. 267 and is still known to Paṇḍit tradition. Śrīvara in describing the flight of some troops which had been defeated in Śrinagar and were retiring along the Vitastā to the east, speaks of the road from the Samudrāmaṭha (Sudᵃrmar on the right bank of the river near the second bridge) to *Purvādhiṣṭhāna* as covered with the corpses of the slain.[1] It is clear that by the latter designation which also means 'the Old Capital,' he refers to our present Pāndrēṭhan. This name itself is the direct phonetic derivative of *Purāṇādhiṣṭhāna*.[2]

Aśoka's Śrīnagarī.

90. General Cunningham has assumed that 'the Old Capital' marked by the site of Pāndrēṭhan was in reality the ancient Śrīnagarī which Kalhaṇa mentions as the capital founded by the great Aśoka.[3] His assumption was based on another passage of the Chronicle which mentions the foundation of the shrine of Jyeṣṭharudra at Śrinagarī by Jalauka, the son of Aśoka. General Cunningham thought he could recognize this shrine in the extant temple on the top of the Takht-i Sulaimān hill, below which at a distance of about one and a half miles Pāndrēṭhan is situated.

I have shown in my note on the passage that no reliance can be placed on the alleged tradition which General Cunningham had adduced as the sole proof of his location of the shrine. Yet at the same time the evidence recorded by me proves that Jyeṣṭharudra must have been worshipped either on the hill itself or in its close vicinity. Accordingly Aśoka's Śrīnagarī may safely be looked for in the same neighbourhood. Our present data do not allow us to decide with absolute certainty whether its site was at Pāndrēṭhan or elsewhere. But there are at least sufficient indications to make General Cunningham's view appear very tempting and probable.

1 See Śrīv. iv. 290.

2 The Kś. derivative of Skr. *Purāṇa* is *prᵃnⁱ* 'old'; this forms, with assimilation of the initial double consonant, the first part, *Pān-*, of the modern name. The elision of the second *ā* in the assumed intermediary form * P[u]*rān*[*ā*]*dēṭhan* is accounted for by the influence of the stress accent which lies on the second syllable of the modern name. The development of the combination *nd* into *ndr* is paralleled by similar cases in other Indo-Aryan Vernaculars; comp. Dr. Grierson, Phonology of Indo-Aryan Vernaculars, *Z.D.M.G.*, l. p. 37, § 115. The nazalisation of *ē* may be of recent date, as the old gloss of A_2 on Rājat. v. 267 shows the name as *Pāmydrṭhan*, i. e. *Pᵃnⁱdreṭhan*.

3 See Note *C*, i. 124.

There is in the first place the significant name *Purāṇādhiṣṭhāna*, 'the Old Capital,' which shows that the site of Pāndrēṭhan must have once been occupied by an important city. Next it is to be noted that Kalhaṇa's narrative knows nothing of any other capital which might have been founded in this vicinity previous to the new capital built by Pravarasena II. on the site of the present S'rīnagar. Lastly we have an indication in the very name *S'rīnagara* which Pravaraśena's city has come to bear in general usage instead of its proper and official designation *Pravarapura.*

If Aśoka's S'rīnagarī actually lay at or near the present Pāndrēṭhan the transfer of its name to the new capital is most readily accounted for. General Cunningham already has rightly pointed out the numerous analogies for such a transfer furnished by the history of other Indian capitals.[1] Pravarasena's city was practically contiguous to the older S'rīnagarī and existed for centuries side by side with it. We can hence easily understand that popular usage retained for the new capital the old familiar designation.[2] Exactly in the same way the several new cities founded by successive kings in the vicinity of Delhi all continued to be known simply by the name "Delhi," though each of them was originally intended to bear the distinctive name of its founder.

Though Purāṇādhiṣṭhāna had sunk to small importance already in Hindu times, extensive remains of ancient buildings can still be traced on the terraced slopes rising immediately to the north and north-east of Pāndrēṭhan. Foundations of old walls, carved slabs, and architectural fragments cover the foot of the hill-side for about one and a half miles. Broken Liṅgas of colossal dimensions are scattered among them. All the remains above ground, however, are far too much decayed to permit of a distinction of individual structures.[3]

The advantages of Pāndrēṭhan as the site for a great city cannot be compared with those offered by the position of S'rīnagar. Yet the close vicinity of the Vitastā, coupled with the security from floods which the near hill-slopes afford, must have been appreciated in an earlier

1 See *Anc. Geogr.*, pp. 97 *sq.*

2 The feminine form *S'rīnagarī* is used also for the new capital; [c]omp. *Rājat.* i. 104 note. There is thus no difference in the name as applied to bot[h] Aśoka's and Pravarasena's cities. *S'rīnagara* or *S'rīnagarī* means the "City of [S']rī", *i.e.* of Lakṣmī, the Goddess of Fortune. For a whimsical etymology of Eu[ro]pean growth, which has turned S'rīnagar into the "City of the Sun", see above § [illegible] note.

3 Compare for an account of these ruins, CUNNINGHAM, *J. A. S. B.*, 1848, pp. 283 *sq.*, *Anc. Geogr.* 95 *sq.* [The remarks made in the latter place as to the supposed cause of the desertion of Purāṇādhiṣṭhāna rest on a misinterpretation of certain Rājataraṅgiṇī p[ass]ages. The reconstruction of an alleged 'Pravareśva[ra] symbol' at Pāndrēṭhan, *J. A. S. B.*, 1848, pp. 324 *sq.*, is also unsupported by evidence.]

period when probably the riveraine flats of the valley were less drained. The small semi-circular glens which are formed between projecting spurs both north and east of the present village, with their gentle slopes offer convenient building sites. The fertile shores of the Ḍal are also within easy reach of Pāndrēṭhan through the gap in the hill-range which separates the Takht-i Sulaimān hill from the greater heights to the east. It is probably in this direction that we have to look for the Saṅghārāma mentioned by Hiuen Tsiang in connection with 'the old city.'

Pravarasena's capital.

91. Kalhaṇa's Chronicle furnishes us with a full account of the origin of the new city which was the capital of the Kaśmīr in his time and destined to remain so to the present day.[1] Kalhaṇa attributes the foundation of this capital to King Pravarasena II. The topographical details of his description make it clear beyond all doubt that its site was that of the present S'rīnagar.

The identity of the latter with Pravarasena's town was duly recognized by General Cunningham who referred to the close agreement between the general features of Kalhaṇa's description and the situation of the present capital. He also pointed out that Kalhaṇa distinctly mentions as one of the pious buildings founded in Pravarasena's city that very *Jayendravihāra* in which Hiuen Tsiang resided during his long stay in the Kaśmīr capital.[2] Subsequently Professor Bühler noticed the survival of several old local names for parts of the modern city which also prove its identity with Pravarasena's capital.[3] The most convincing evidence, however, is contained in the long list of ancient buildings and localities which Kalhaṇa mentions in Pravarasena's town. In the course of our survey we shall be able to identify many of them within the modern S'rīnagar and its environs.

The attribution of this new capital to King Pravarasena rests on equally strong proof. Through a chain of references extending over nearly twelve centuries we can trace the use of the name PRAVARAPURA, shortened (*bhīmavat*) for *Pravarasenapura*, as the official and correct designation of the city occupying the site of the present S'rīnagar. We have found this appellation already in the record of the T'ang Annals going back to the commencement of the eighth century. It is also found in the works of Kṣemendra, Bilhaṇa, and numerous other Kaśmīrian authors. It has continued to be used to the present day in colophons of Sanskrit Manuscripts, in horoscopes and similar documents.[4]

1 See *Rājat.* iii. 336-363.

2 See *Anc. Geogr.*, p. 97; also *Rājat.* iii. 355 note.

3 Compare *Report*, p. 16.

4 For detailed references see my note *Rājat.* iii. 339-349. *S'rī-Pravarapure* for

The date of King Pravarasena II. whose name the above designation of the new capital was intended to preserve, cannot be fixed with accuracy. Various historical and numismatic indications, however, make it probable that he ruled at some period of the 6th century. Thus we can easily understand that at the time of Hiuen Tsiang's visit (A.D. 631) Śrīnagara or Pravarapura was still the 'new city.'

Legend of foundation of Pravarapura.

92. The traditional account of the foundation of Pravarapura as recorded by Kalhaṇa is of considerable interest. Though largely interwoven with legendary matter it preserves for us a series of exact topographical data. Kalhaṇa's story is contained in verses 336–349 of the Third Book, and runs briefly as follows.[1]

When King Pravarasena II. had returned from his victorious expeditions abroad, he desired to found a new capital which was to bear his name. He was then residing in the city of his grandfather Pravarasena I., *i.e.*, in Purāṇādhiṣṭhāna.[2] From there the king went forth at night in order, as the text says, "to ascertain in a supernatural way the proper site and the auspicious time for the foundation of the new city." On his way he reached a stream which skirted a burning ground, and was illuminated by the glow of funeral pyres. Then on the other bank of the stream there appeared to him a demon of terrible form. Promising him fulfilment of his desire, the demon invited the king to cross over to his own side by the embankment he was preparing for him. Thereupon "the Rākṣasa stretched out his own knee from the other bank, and thus caused the water of the Mahāsarit to be parted by an embankment (Setu)." The courageous Pravarasena drew out his dagger (*kṣurikā*), cut with it steps into the flesh of the Rākṣasa, and thus crossed over to the place which has since been known as *Kṣurikābala*. The demon then indicated to him the auspicious time and disappeared, after telling him to build his town where he would see the measuring line laid down in the morning. This line (*sūtra*) of the Vetāla the king eventually discovered "at the village of *Sāritaka* at which the goddess *Sārikā* and the demon *Aṭṭa* resided." There he built his city in which the first shrine erected was the famous one of Śiva *Pravareśvara*.

Śripravarasenapura is often written in the abbreviated form *Śrīp* n the formulas of the Lokaprakāśa, almanacs, etc. Kalhaṇa often uses the simple *Pura* for Pravarapura and *Nagara* for Śrīnagara.

[1] For all detailed references in connection with this story, note iii. 339–349 should be consulted.

[2] That *Purāṇādhiṣṭhāna* is meant is proved by iii. 99. There Kalhaṇa, speaking of a foundation Pravarasena I. in his capital, by a kind of anachronism uses the designation of Purāṇādhiṣṭhāna.

Keeping in view the details of the ancient topography of S'rīnagar, we can still follow up step by step the localities by which the legend here related leads King Pravarasena to the site of his new city. We have already seen that the *Mahāsarit* is the stream now known as Tsūṇṭh Kul which flows from the Ḍal into the Vitastā. Near its confluence with the Vitastā which we have also found already mentioned as a Tirtha, there existed, until the times of Mahārāja Raṇbīr Singh, a much frequented Hindu burning Ghāṭ. It was undoubtedly of ancient date. Kalhaṇa relates how the body of King Uccala, murdered in his palace at S'rīnagar, was hurriedly cremated at the burning place situated on the island at the confluence of the *Mahāsarit* and *Vitastā*.[1] It is certain that the island of Māyᵊsum (Skr. Mākṣikasvāmin) is meant here, at the western end of which the Mahāsarit or Tsūṇṭh Kul falls into the Vitastā.

The stream flowing from the Ḍal is bounded on its northern bank by an old embankment which stretches from the west foot of the Takht-i Sulaimān close to the high bank of the Vitastā near the Second Bridge. This embankment which is the most substantial at or around S'rīnagar and known only by the general designation of *Suth* (from Skr. *setu*), 'dyke,' is undoubtedly of very early date. It protects the whole of the low-lying portions of the city on the right river-bank as well as the floating gardens and shores of the Ḍal which would otherwise be exposed to annual inundations from the Vitastā. A tradition still heard by Mr. Vigne ascribed the construction of this embankment to King Pravarasena.[2] It is indeed evident that its construction was a necessary condition for the safety of the newly founded city.

Several topographical indications warrant the conclusion that it was this old dyke in which the popular legend recorded by Kalhaṇa recognized the leg and knee of the demon. A glance at the map shows that the eastern portion of the 'Suth' turns sharply at a right angle and thus curiously resembles a bent knee. *Kṣurikābala* was the name of the place where Pravarasena according to the legend was supposed to have reached firm ground after crossing the stream. I have shown that this name in the form of its Kaśmīrī derivative *Khudᵃbal* still attaches to the city quarter which lies at the western end of the Suth.[3]

Finally it will be seen from the map that Kalhaṇa's words regarding the 'Setu' dividing the waters of the Mahāsarit, describe exactly the present embankment which has on one side the Tsūṇṭh Kul and on the other side the various marshes and canals fed by the Mār. It

[1] See viii. 339.

[2] See VIGNE, *Travels*, ii. p. 69.

[3] See note iii. 339-349.

has been shown above that this second outflow of the Ḍal also shared the old name of Mahāsarit.[1]

Old limits of Pravarapura.

93. The name of the village *Sārīṭaka* where the demon showed to the king the proper site for his city, has long ago disappeared. Its position, however, is sufficiently marked by the mention of the goddess *Sārikā*. The latter, a form of Durgā, has since ancient times been worshipped on the hill which rises to the north of the central part of Srīnagar and is still called after her. The modern name of the hill, *Hārᵃparvat,* is the regular phonetic derivative of Skr. *Sārikāparvata.* By this name it is designated in the latter Chronicles and Māhātmyas.[2]

Another passage of the Rājataraṅgiṇī shows that the term *Vetālasūtrapāta,* 'the demon's measuring line,' clearly connected with the above legend, was also in later times applied to the limits of the oldest part of Pravarapura[3]. But our materials do not enable us to ascertain these limits in detail. Kalhaṇa it is true, has not failed to specify them, as he mentions the temples of *Vardhanasvāmin* and *Viśvakarman* as marking the extreme ends of Pravarasena's city[4]. Unfortunately the position of neither of these structures can now be traced.

So much, however, is clear that the new city was at first confined to the right bank of the river. Kalhaṇa tells this distinctly,[5] and those sites and structures which he particularly mentions in his description of Pravarasena's capital, are all found as far as they can be identified, on the right bank. The account of Hiuen Tsiang and the T'ang Annals show that even in the 7th century Pravarapura extended mainly along the eastern bank of the river.[6]

Kalhaṇa's description of Pravarapura.

Kalhaṇa follows up his account of the foundation of the city with a brief description of its splendours[7]. He notes the extravagant story of its having once counted thirty-six lakhs of houses, and

[1] Compare § 65.

[2] See note iii. 339-349. *Hārᵃ* is the Kaśmīrī name of the goddess *Sārikā* as well as of the *Sārikā* bird (Maina); comp. BÜHLER, *Report*, pp. 16 *sq.*

Panjābis and other foreign visitors from India have by a popular etymology turned the 'Hill of Sārikā' into the 'Hill of Hari (Viṣṇu)' or the 'Verdant Hill.' The latter interpretation could be justified only on the principle of *lucus a non lucendo;* for verdure is scarce indeed on the rocky faces of the Sārikāparvata. DR. BERNIER already, *Travels*, p. 398, was told this popular etymology, probably by his friends from Delhi.

[3] See vi. 191 note.

[4] iii. 357.

[5] iii. 358.

[6] See ante, §§ 8, 10.

[7] iii. 357-363.

refers to the regularly arranged markets with which its founder had provided it. The city of his own time still boasted of "mansions which reached to the clouds" built, no doubt, mostly of wood just as the mass of private houses in modern S'rīnagar.[1]

When he mentions "the streams meeting, pure and lovely, at pleasure-residences and near market streets," he means evidently the numerous canals from the Ḍal and Anchhār lakes which intersect the suburbs and also pass through the heart of the city. They and the river still serve as the main thoroughfares for the market traffic, and all principal Bazars are built along their banks.[2] The S'ārikāparvata receives due mention as "the pleasure-hill from which the splendour of all the houses is visible as if from the sky." Nor does he forget to praise the cool water of the Vitastā which the citizens find before their very houses on hot summer-days.

Finally he refers to the abundance of magnificent temples with which successive kings had adorned Pravarapura, and of which so many are particularly mentioned in his narrative. Of the number and imposing appearance of these structures we can even at the present day form some idea if we examine their massive remains which meet us in every part of modern S'rīnagar. The high embankments which now line the river's course within the city, are mainly composed of carved slabs, columns and other ancient stone materials. Their profusion and imposing dimensions must even to a superficial observer suggest an idea of the architectural splendour of ancient S'rīnagar.

Advantages of the site of Śrīnagar.

94. It can scarcely be the result of chance that Pravarasena's city has escaped the fate of so many Indian capitals, of being superseded by later foundations.

There had indeed not been wanting attempts on the part of later rulers to transfer the capital to other sites which they had chosen for their own cities. The great Lalitāditya, then Jayāpīḍa, Avantivarman,

1 Both Mirzā Ḥaidar and Abū-l-Faẓl speak with admiration of the many lofty houses of S'rīnagar, built of pine wood. This material was used, then as now, as being cheap and more secure against earthquakes. According to Mirzā Ḥaidar "most of these houses are at least five stories high and each story contains apartments, halls, galleries and towers" (*Tārīkh-i-Rashīdi*, p. 425). That the mass of private dwellings in S'rīnagar were already in Hindu times constructed of wood, is shown by *Rājat.* viii. 2390. The many disastrous fires recorded point to the same conclusion.

2 Useful and convenient as these canals undoubtedly are, it is rather difficult to concede to them now the epithets of 'pure and lovely.' They add, however, greatly to the picturesqueness of the city and certainly make the want of carriage roads less felt.

and Śaṁkaravarman, had successively endeavoured to effect this object. The great ruins of Parihāsapura, Jayapura and Avantipura show sufficiently that the failure of the first three kings was not due in any way to deficient means or want of purpose.

Of Lalitāditya the Chronicle distinctly records that he proposed, Nero-like, to burn down the ancient capital to assure the predominance of his own creation, Parihāsapura. And the long list of splendid edifices erected at the latter place during his own reign shows plainly that for a time at least that monarch's pleasure had succeeded. Yet each one of these temporary capitals speedily sank into insignificance, while Pravarapura continued to be the political and cultural centre of Kaśmīr down to the present day.

We can safely attribute this exceptional position of Śrīnagar to the great natural advantages of its site. Occupying a place close to the true centre of the Valley, Śrīnagar enjoys facilities of communication which no other site could offer. The river along which the city is built provides at all seasons the most convenient route for trade and traffic, both up and down the Valley. The two lakes which flank Śrīnagar, offer the same facilities for the fertile tracts which lie immediately to the north. The lakes themselves furnish an abundant supply of products which materially facilitate the maintenance of a large city population. The great trade route from Central Asia debouches through the Sind Valley only one short march from the capital.

Natural defences of Śrīnagar.

Nor can we underrate the security which the position of Śrīnagar assures both against floods and armed attack. The neck of high ground which from the north stretches towards the Vitastā and separates the two lakes, is safe from all possible risk of flood. It is on this ground, round the foot of the Śārikā hill, that the greatest part of the old Pravarapura was originally built. The ancient embankment which connects this high level ground with the foot of the Takht-i-Sulaimān hill sufficed to secure also the low-lying wards fringing the marshes of the Ḍal. A considerable area, including the present quarters of Khānayār and Rāṇivōr (Skr. *Rājānavāṭikā*), was thus added to the available building ground on the right bank and protected against all ordinary floods.

The frequent sieges which Śrīnagar underwent during the last reigns related by Kalhaṇa, give us ample opportunity to appreciate also the military advantages which the city's position assured to its defenders. With the exception of a comparatively narrow neck of dry ground in the north, the Śrīnagar of the right river-bank is guarded on all sides by water. a the south the river forms an impass defence.

The east is secured by the Ḍal and the stream which flows from it. On the west there stretch the broad marches of the Anch[i]ār divided from the Vitastā by a narrow strip of firm ground.

From the north, it is true, the city can be approached without passing such natural obstacles. But the map shows that just to the north of the S'arikā hill inlets from the two lakes approach each other within a few thousand feet. The narrow passage left between them could at all times easily be guarded. It is curious to note that the successful attacks on the city of which the Chronicle tells us, were delivered from the north, treachery or the defenders' weakness having opened this passage.[1]

The later and smaller portion of S'rīnagar occupying the left river-bank, does not share the same natural advantages as the old one. The present level of the ground on which it stands appears to have been raised gradually by the accumulated débris of centuries. We do not know exactly when the extension of the city in this direction began. The number of ancient sites on this side is comparatively small. The royal residence was transferred to it only in the reign of Ananta (A.D. 1028-63). There too we find a natural line of defence. It is the Kṣiptikā or Kuṭ[a]kul which flows round the western edge of this part of the city and is also often mentioned in the accounts of the later sieges.

Section IV.—Ancient sites of S'rīnagara.

95. Having thus reviewed the origin and the general position of the Kaśmīr capital, we may proceed to a brief survey of the more important ancient sites which our available materials permit us to trace in it. We can conveniently start on our circuit from the Hill of S'ārikā to which the legendary account of the city's foundation had taken us.

Hill of Śārikā.

The goddess S'ārikā which has given to the hill its name, has been worshipped since ancient times on the north-west side of the hill. Certain natural markings on a large perpendicular rock are taken by the pious to represent that kind of mystical diagram which in the Tantraśāstra is known as *Srīcakra*.[2] This 'Svayambhū' Tīrtha is still a much frequented pilgrimage place for the Brahmans of the city and has been so probably since early times.[3] The S'ārikāmāhātmya now in use relates

1 Compare for Uccala's entry into S'rīnagar, vii. 1530 *sqq.*; that of Sussala, viii. 944 *sqq.*; compare also note viii. 1104–1110.

2 Compare *Rājat.* note i. 122, regarding the worship of such diagrams.

3 Compare *Jonar.* (Bo. ed.) 472, 767.

that the hill was carried to its present position by Durgā who had taken the shape of a Sārikā bird. The goddess is supposed to have thus closed a gate of the Daityas dwelling in hell. This legend is alluded to already in the Kathāsaritsāgara.[1]

Another ancient designation of the Hārᵃparvat is 'Hill of Pradyumna' (*Pradyumnapīṭha,-giri,-śikhara*, etc.), often found in the Chronicles and elsewhere.[2] The Kathāsaritsāgara accounts for the origin of this name by a story which connects the hill with the love of Uṣā and Aniruddha, the son of Pradyumna. Kalhaṇa mentions a Maṭha for Pāśupata mendicants which King Raṇāditya built on the hill. The eastern slopes of the latter are now occupied by extensive buildings connected with the famous Ziārats of Muqaddam Ṣāhib and Ākhūn Mullā Shāh. It is probable that these Muhammadan shrines have taken the place of Hindu religious buildings, as at so many old sites of Kaśmīr.

Close to the foot of the southern extremity of the hill lies a rock which has from ancient times received worship as an embodiment of Gaṇeśa, under the name of BHĪMASVĀMIN. A legend related by Kalhaṇa connects this 'Svayambhū' image with Pravarasena's foundation of Srīnagar.[3] From regard for the pious king the god is there said to have turned his face from west to east so as to behold the new city. The rock is covered by the worshippers with so thick a layer of red lead that it is not possible to trace now any resemblance to the head of the elephant-faced god, still less to see whether it is turned to the west or east. In fact, if we are to believe Jonarāja, the rock image has subsequently changed its position yet a second time. This Chronicler relates that Bhīmasvāmin from disgust at the iconoclasm of Sikandar Būtshikast has finally turned his back on the city.[4] This last turn would, no doubt, most satisfactorily account for the present amorphous look of the sacred rock.

There is nothing in the Chronicles that would lead us to assume that the hill of Sārikā was ever fortified in Hindu times. The great bastioned stone-wall which now encloses the hill and the ground around its foot (Nāgar-nagar), was built by Akbar as an inscription still extant over the main-gate proclaims.[5] The fort which now crowns the summit of the hill, is of even more modern origin.

[1] See lxxiii. 107 *sqq.*

[2] See *Rājat.* iii. 460 note.

[3] See iii. 352 note.

[4] See *Jonar.* (Bo. ed.), 766.

[5] Compare Fourth Chron. 939 *sqq.*

Temple of Pravaresa-vara.

96. A short distance to the south-east of the Bhimasvāmin rock, and outside Akbar's fortress, lies the Ziārat of Bahāu-d-dīn Ṣāhib, built undoubtedly with the materials of an ancient temple. The cemetery which surrounds it contains also many ancient remains in its tombs and walls. At the south-west corner of this cemetery rises a ruined gateway built of stone-blocks of remarkable size, and still of considerable height. This structure is traditionally believed by the S'rinagar Paṇḍits to have belonged to the temple of S'iva PRAVAREŚVARA which Kalhaṇa mentions as the first shrine erected by Pravarasena in his new capital.[1]

An old legend related by Kalhaṇa and before him already by Bilhaṇa, makes the king ascend bodily to heaven from the temple of Pravareśvara. Bilhaṇa speaks of the temple as "showing to this day a gap above, resembling the gate of heaven through which King Pravara bodily ascended to heaven."[2] Kalhaṇa, writing a century later, also saw at the temple of Pravareśvara "a gate resembling the gate of heaven." Its broken stone roof was supposed to mark the king's passage on his way to S'iva's abode.

This tradition still attaches to the roofless stone-gate above described, which may indeed be the very structure seen by Bilhaṇa and the Chronicler. As far as its architecture is concerned, it might well belong to the earliest monuments of S'rinagar. It owes its preservation perhaps to the exceptional solidity of its construction and the massiveness of its stones. Stone-blocks measuring up to sixteen feet in length with a width and thickness equally imposing were no convenient materials for the builders of Muhammadan Ziārats, Ḥammāms, etc., who have otherwise done so much to efface the remains of ancient structures in S'rinagar. The position of the ruin is very central and might well have been chosen by the founder of Pravarapura for a prominent shrine in his new city.

Position of Raṇa-svāmin temple.

Not far from Bahāu-d-dīn Ṣāhib's Ziārat to the south-west stands the Jāmi' Masjid, the greatest Mosque of S'rinagar. Around it numerous ancient remains attest the former existence of Hindu temples. Proceeding still further to the south-west in the midst of a thickly built city quarter, we reach an ancient shrine which has remained in a comparatively fair state of preservation probably owing to its early conversion into a Ziārat. It is now supposed to mark the resting place of the saint styled Pir Ḥāji Muḥammad. It consists of an octa-

1 See *Rājat.* iii. 350 note.

2 See *Vikram.* xviii. 28.

gonal cella of which the high basement and the side walls are still well-preserved. The quadrangular court in which it stands is enclosed by ancient walls and approached by ornamented gateways.

The position of this shrine has suggested to me its possible identity with the ancient temple of Viṣṇu RAṆASVĀMIN which Kalhaṇa mentions as founded by King Raṇāditya.[1] This temple must have enjoyed considerable celebrity till a comparatively late period. Maṅkha refers to it as an object of his father's devotion and Jonarāja in his comments on the passage speaks of Viṣṇu Raṇasvāmin as one of the chief shrines of Pravarapura.[2]

In his own Chronicle Jonarāja indicates this temple as the furthest point up to which Zainu-l-'ābidin carried the canal flowing through *Jainanagarī*.[3] The latter locality corresponds to the S'rīnagar quarters of Sangin Darwāza and Naushahr, and the canal itself is the one now known as *Lachᵃm Kul*.[4] It brings the waters of the Sind River *viâ* Amburhēr to the northern suburbs of S'rīnagar, and after flowing past the Jāmi' Masjid empties itself into the Mār canal near the bridge called Kāḍⁱ Kadᵃl. In the corner formed by the two canals stands the ruined temple above described. If it could be shown that the present termination of the Lachᵃm Kul is the same which Jonarāja knew in the middle of the fifteenth century, the identity of those remains with the Raṇasvāmin temple might be considered as certain.

Bhaṭṭārakamaṭha; Diddāmaṭha.

97. Crossing the Mār to the south we reach the city quarter known as *Braḍⁱmar*, occupying the right bank of the river between the Fourth and Fifth Bridge. It derives its name from the ancient BHAṬṬĀRAKAMAṬHA which is repeatedly referred to in the Rājataraṅgiṇī as a building of considerable size and strength.[5] Bilhaṇa too notices it specially in his descripton of S'rīnagar. Like other Maṭhas built originally to serve the purposes of a Sarai, it was used on occasion as a place of defence. Queen Diddā sent her infant son there at the time of a dangerous rising.

[1] *Rājat.* iii. 453 *sq.* note.

[2] See *S'rīkaṇṭhacar.* iii. 68.

[3] See *Jonar.* 872.

[4] Compare *Rājat.* iii. 453–454 note. The Lachᵃm Kul is mentioned by Abū-l-Faẓl, ii. p. 355. It probably took its name (equivalent to *Lakṣmikulyā) from Lakṣmī, the queen of Shahābu-d-din, in whose honour the quarter of Lakṣmīnagarī was found in the vicinity of the present Sangin Darwāza; see *Jonar.* 407 *sq.*

[5] See *Rājat.* vi. 240 note; viii. 2426; *Vikram.* xviii. 11. For the derivation of *Braḍⁱ* from *Bhaṭṭāraka* comp. *Brārⁱnambal* < *Bhaṭṭāranaḍvalā*, below. That Bhaṭṭārakamaṭha was the old name of this locality, is known to the tradition of the Paṇḍits; see BÜHLER, *Report*, p. 16.

The Chronicle shows us often the Maṭhas of Śrinagar utilized as places of refuge in the times of internal troubles, occasionally also turned into prisons.[1] We may hence conclude that they were substantially built, probably like modern Sarais in the form of detached quadrangles, and thus better adapted for defence than other city-buildings.

That Maṭhas more than once left their names to the city-quarters in which they stood, is shown by the designation of other wards. Thus the large quarter of *Did^{a}mar* which forms the western end of the city on the right river-bank, retains the name of the DIDDĀMAṬHA.[2] It was built by Queen Diddā for the accommodation of travellers from various parts of India. As a local name Diddāmaṭha meets us often in the later Chronicles. Above Did^{a}mar we find near the Sixth Bridge the quarter of *Balanḍimar*.[3] It represents in all probability the *Balāḍhyamaṭha* of the later Chronicles which Jonarāja mentions as having been built by Balāḍhyacandra under King Rājadeva in the 13th century.[4]

Skandabhavana; Naḍavana.

A little to the north of the Sixth Bridge lies the Mahalla known by the name of *Khand^{a}bavan*. It has received its appellation from the ancient Vihāra of SKANDABHAVANA, a foundation of Skandagupta whom Kalhaṇa mentions among the ministers of Pravarasena II.'s successor Yudhiṣṭhira.[5] The site of the Vihāra has been traced by me in the close vicinity of the Ziārat of Pīr Muḥammad Bāsur. Certain ancient remains there were locally known and worshipped till the middle of the present century as a Tīrtha sacred to Skanda.[6]

The ground immediately to the north-east of Khand^{a}bavan is now an open waste space used partly for Muhammadan graveyards. It seems to have been unoccupied already in old times. For it was chosen as the burning place for the widows of the murdered king Sussala when a rebel force hovering around the capital rendered the usual burning ground on the island of Mākṣikasvāmin inaccessible.[7]

The quarter of *Narvor* still further to the north is probably identical with the old NAḌAVANA, mentioned by Kalhaṇa as the site of a Vihāra built by one of King Meghavāhana's queens. I have shown in my note on the passage that the modern name goes back to a form

[1] Compare *Rājat.* vi. 223; viii. 374, 1052, 2309.

[2] See *Rājat.* vi. 300 note.

[3] Its old name could not be shown on the map owing to want of room.

[4] See *Jonar.* 82.

[5] See iii. 380.

[6] Compare Note *K*, vi. 137, also for the temple of *Parvaguptेśvara* which stood close by.

[7] *Rājat.* viii. 1441 *sq.*

***Naḍavāṭa.**[1] The termination *vāṭa* 'garden,' frequent in Kaśmīr local names, may safely be taken as the equivalent of *vana* in Kalhaṇa's form of the name.

98. Before we continue our survey further up the river, it will be useful to make a brief reference to the bridges which connect the two river-banks within the city.

Bridges of old Śrīnagara.

Śrīnagar has now seven bridges across the Vitastā. Their number has remained unchanged for at least five hundred years.

Already Sharifu-d-dīn had heard that of the thirty boat-bridges constructed across the great river of Kaśmīr, there were seven in the town of Śrīnagar. The boats were bound together by chains, and through the bridges a way could be opened for the river traffic.[2] Sharīfu-d-dīn's notice is of interest because it shows clearly that down to the end of the Hindu period permanent bridges across the Vitastā where unknown in Kaśmīr.

I had been led to the same conclusion by an examination of the Rājataraṅgiṇī passages bearing on the subject.[3] Kalhaṇa distinctly says of the two bridges the construction of which he specially records, that they were built with boats. Elsewhere this inference may be drawn from the rapidity with which the bridges are broken at the approach of the enemy or in danger of fire.[4]

The first bridge of this kind is ascribed by Kalhaṇa to Pravarasena II. who built the 'Great Bridge' (*Bṛhatsetu*) in his new capital.

Bṛhatsetu.

"Only since then is such construction of boat-bridges known."[5] This 'Great Bridge' is subsequently mentioned in connection with a great conflagration which destroyed the city in the time of Sussala (A.D. 1123). This fire arose at the southern end of Śrīnagar, and Kalhaṇa mentions that the smoke first rising from Mākṣikasvāmin: Māyasum had scarcely been noticed from the 'Bṛhatsetu' when the fire was already spreading over the whole city.[6] Kalhaṇa evidently refers to the 'Great Bridge' as a comparatively distant point from Mākṣikasvāmin. Considering that the river forms an almost straight reach from this locality to the present Fourth Bridge, it appears to me likely that Pravarasena's bridge was somewhere in the vicinity of the latter. The position is in the

1 Compare *Rājat.* iii. 11 note.
2 See *Tārikh-i-Rashidi*, p. 431.
3 See note iii. 354.
4 See *Rājat.* vii. 909, 1539; viii. 1182; *Śrīv.* i. 308, 720; ii. 70, 122.
5 *Rājat.* iii. 354.
6 Compare *Rājat.* viii. 1171-72 note.

very heart of the city. It is just here that Zainu-l-'ābidīn subsequently constructed the first permanent bridge over the Vitastā named after him Zaina Kad^{a}l (*Jainakadali*).[1]

Another old boat-bridge had been established by Harṣa just opposite to his palace.[2] The latter as we shall see was situated on the left bank somewhere near the present Second Bridge (Haba Kad^{a}l). The bridge proved fatal to Harṣa's fortunes, because it enabled the rebels to make their final and successful assault on the palace.

There can be little doubt that the first permanent bridge across the Vitastā was of wood and showed the same peculiar cantilever construction which the Kaśmīr bridges have preserved to this day. The latter have attracted the attention of all modern travellers and have often been described.[3] But it is curious that none of them can be traced back beyond the time of Zainu-l-'ābidīn. The explanation may lie in the fact that that stone-architecture in which the engineers of the Hindu period were so proficient, did not permit of the construction of bridges with a sufficient span. For their Muhammadan successors working chiefly in wood it was easier to overcome this difficulty.

Among the most characteristic features of the river-scene as it now presents itself within Śrīnagar, are the numerous wooden bathing cells moored before all city Ghāṭs. They have been there already in Hindu times. For Kalhaṇa mentions more than once the *snānakoṣṭhas* of the river.[4] From a humorous sketch of city-life which Kalhaṇa draws for us, we can see that they formed, then as now, the favourite meeting-place of the idle and curious.[5]

Eastern quarters of Śrīnagara.

99. Resuming our walk up the river-bank we pass the remains of more than one old temple near the present Ziārats of Bad Shāh (Zainu-l-'ābidīn), Shāh Hamadān and elsewhere. But we have no data for their identification. An old site is marked by the present Ghāṭ Sōm^{a}yār, below the Second Bridge, which represents the SOMATĪRTHA of the Rājataraṅgiṇī.[6] The place is still visited as a Tīrtha, and some old Lingas are found by the river-side. The quarter in which the Somatīrtha lies, is known as *Sud^{a}rmar*. It owes its name to the SAMUDRĀMAṬHA built by Samudrā, the queen of Rāmadeva, in

[1] See *Śrīv.* i. 231 *sq.*, 296.

[2] *Rājat.* vii. 15[illegible].

[3] See, *e.g.*, V[illegible], *Travels*, ii. 23; LAWRENCE, *Valley*, p. 37.

[4] Compare *R[illegible]at.* viii. 706, 1182, 2423. Also Kṣemendra, *Samay.* ii. 38, know the term *snānak[illegible]ṭhaka* which lives in the present *K[illegible]rāngkuṭh*.

[5] See *Rājat.* viii. 706–710.

[6] See *Rājat.* viii. 3360 note.

the 13th century. The numerous passages in which the Samudrāmaṭha is mentioned by the later Chronicles, makes this identification quite certain.[1]

A little higher up, if we can trust local tradition, stood the ancient temple of VARDHAMĀNEŚA mentioned already in King Saṁdhimat's reign. The site so designated by the Purohitas of the adjoining Mahalla is close to the Mal^{a}yār Ghāt. I have referred already in a previous note to the curious manner in which an ancient Linga supposed to be that of Vardhamāneśa was recovered a few years ago from a neighbouring Mosque and a Māhātmya composed for the newly established shrine.[2]

The confluence of the Tsūṇṭh Kul or Mahāsarit with the Vitastā we have also had occasion to notice.[3] It is the Tīrtha now known as MĀRĪSAṀGAMA. Beyond it lies the great island of *Māy^{e}sum*, the ancient MĀKṢIKASVĀMIN, now chiefly occupied by the houses and camps of European residents and visitors. From the way it is referred to by Kalhaṇa, it appears that it was already partly inhabited in old times.[4] Following up the right bank of the Mahāsarit above the junction we reach the quarter of *Khuḍ^{a}bal* already identified with the *Kṣurikābala* of King Pravarasena's story.

Here begins the old embankment or *Setu*, noticed in connection with the latter.[5] To the north of this embankment stretches an extensive marsh fed by canals coming from the Ḍal and known as *Brāṛ^{i}nambal*. It is the *Bhaṭṭāranaḍvalā* of the Chronicle into which the body of one of Harṣa's ministers was thrown after his execution.[6]

At the eastern end of the Setu where it joins the rocky foot of the Takht-i Sulaimān hill, there has been for at least a century a gate through which the Tsūṇṭh Kul flows out from the lake. It is closed at times of flood when the Vitastā rises higher than the level of the Ḍal. It is highly probable that this gate is very old and contemporary with the construction of the embankment itself. Beyond it lies the suburb of *Drug^{a}jan*. This is identified in an old gloss of the Rājataraṅgiṇī with DURGĀGALIKĀ, where according to tradition the blind King Yudhiṣṭhira I. was imprisoned after his abdication.[7]

[1] See *Jonar*. 111; *Śrīv*. iv. 121, 169, 290; Fourth Chron. 504, 618.

[2] See above, § 31 note 2.

[3] See above, § 65.

[4] See *Rājat*. iv. 88 note.

[5] Compare § 92.

[6] See *Rājat*. vii. 1038. *Nambal*, from Skr. *naḍvalā*, is the regular Kś. word for 'marsh.' *Brāṛ^i* is a direct phonetic derivative of Skr. *bhaṭṭāra* 'god.'

[7] See *Rājat*. ii. 4.

Leaving the Setu where it makes its great bend and going north across low ground flanked by marshes, we reach the quarter of *Nāv*ᵃ*pūr*. The bridge which leads here over the Mār or Mahāsarit, is repeatedly mentioned as NAUPURASETU by Srīvara, in connection with later sieges of Srinagar.[1] By breaking it, the south-eastern parts of the city were rendered more secure. Continuing our route to the north we come to the great suburb of *Rāṇ*ⁱ*vōr*. It is traversed by numerous canals coming from the Ḍal. Kalhaṇa mentions it repeatedly by its ancient name of RĀJĀNAVĀṬIKĀ as a place largely inhabited by Brahmans. Their solemn fasts (*prāyopaveśa*) gave no small trouble to King Sussala in his worst straights.[2] Rāṇⁱvōr has continued to the present day a favourite place of residence for city Brahmans.

Left river bank.

100. We have now completed our circuit of the ancient city as far as it lay on the right bank of the river and may proceed to the smaller and later portion which occupies the left bank. Just opposite to the 'Mārīsaṁgama' stands the Shērgaṛhi, the modern palace of the Dogrā rulers. Its site was apparently first chosen by the Paṭhān governors for their fortified residence.

Immediately below the palace the Kuṭᵃkul or *Kṣiptikā* branches off from the river. We have already noticed its value as a line of defence for this part of the city.[3] The quarter of *Kāṭhül* which lies next between the Kuṭᵃkul and the river is of ancient date. It is mentioned as *Kāṣṭhīla* by Kalhaṇa and other writers, Bilhaṇa speaking of it particularly as a locality inhabited by Brahmans.[4]

Site of Royal Palace.

At the northern end of the Kāṭhül quarter and close to the present Second Bridge, we must assume the palace of the later Hindu kings to have stood. Its position is indicated by an interesting passage of the Rājataraṅgiṇī which informs us that King Ananta (A. D. 1028–63) abandoned the palace of the former dynasties and transferred the royal residence to the vicinity of the shrine of SADĀŚIVA.[5] The new site was adhered to by subsequent kings probably till long after Kalhaṇa's time. The mention of the Sadāśiva shrine and the fre-

[1] See *Srīv.* iv. 122, 243.

[2] See *Rājat.* viii. 756, 768, 899. For the phonetic relation of *Rāṇi* < Skr. *Rājāna*, see viii. 756 note; *vōr* is common in Kś. local names and derived from Skr. *vāṭikā* 'garden.'

[3] See above, § 67.

[4] See *Rājat.* viii. 1169 note, and *Vikram.* xviii. 25.

[5] Compare *Rājat.* viii. 186-187, and for detailed proof of the identification, the note thereon.

quent references to the Kṣiptikā as flowing near to the royal palace (*rājadhānī*) enable us to fix the position of the latter with fair accuracy. In the note on the above passage I have shown that the Sadāśiva temple stood opposite to the Samudrāmaṭha which occupies the right river bank just below the Second Bridge. Exactly in the position thus indicated we find now an ancient Liṅga, on the river Ghāṭ of Puruṣᵃyār, which the tradition of the local Purohitās knows by the name of *Sadāśiva*.

It is in this neighbourhood, then, that the palace stood which had witnessed so many tragic scenes related in the last two Books of Kalhaṇa's Chronicle. Its great height is specially referred to by Bilhaṇa. This suggests that it was in part at least built of wood, just like a later palace described by Mirzā Ḥaidar.[1] "Sultān Zainu-l-'ābidīn built himself a palace in the town which in the dialect of Kashmir is called *Rājdān* [i.e., Skr. *rājadhānī*]. It has twelve stories, some of which contain fifty rooms, halls and corridors. The whole of this lofty structure is built of wood." This construction of the palace would well explain the rapidity with which it was burned down by the pretender Uccala on his final attack upon Harṣa.[2] We can thus also understand why there are no particularly striking remains at the site which could be attributed to the ruins of this royal residence.

The last-named incident gives Kalhaṇa occasion to mention also some other data regarding the royal palace. Close to it was a garden in which Harṣa and his ill-fated son Bhoja enjoyed a deceptive rest before the rebels' last assault.[3] The gardens near the palace are also elsewhere mentioned. Harṣa had their trees cut down because they obstructed the view, and at a later time the besieging Ḍāmaras fed their camp-fires with wood brought from the same gardens.[4] Even at the present day there are numerous old gardens across the Kṣiptikā close to the site where the palace once stood. In front of the palace was the boat-bridge already mentioned which the king had himself constructed, and which was the scene of his last desperate struggle.[5]

Where the old palace stood which was abandoned by King Ananta, we cannot say with accuracy. It is, however, probable that its site was in the old part of Pravarapura on the right bank. Kalhaṇa mentions it twice as *purāṇarājadhānī* ('the old palace'), but gives no particulars.[6] Its deserted ground was built over with a Maṭha in Kalhaṇa's own time.

1 See *Tārīkh-i-Rashīdī*, p. 429.
2 See *Rājat.* vii. 1565 *sq.*, 1583.
3 *Rājat.* vii. 1538 *sqq.*
4 *Rājat.* vii. 1223; viii. 1056.
5 See *Rājat.* vii. 1539, 1549.
6 See *Rājat.* viii. 837, 2417.

The embankments on the left side of the river as well as the walls of Ziārats show ample remains of ancient buildings. But we have no means of identifying any particular sites. At the western extremity of this part of the city, however, we may locate with some probability the temple of *Kṣemagaurīśvara*, built by Queen Diddā's weak husband Kṣemagupta. Bilhaṇa in his description of S'rinagar mentions it as an imposing building, the 'Maṇḍapas' of which extended to a 'Saṁgama' of the Vitastā.[1] I have shown elsewhere that the confluence meant is probably that of the Vitastā with the Dugdhasindhu or Chatsᵊkul which lies opposite to the quarter of Diddāmaṭha.[2]

SECTION V. THE ENVIRONS OF S'RĪNAGARA.

101. Having completed our survey of old S'rinagara we may now proceed to examine the ancient sites of its environs. They are almost all situated to the north of the Vitastā within the Pargaṇa now known as *Phākh*, and designated as *Phākhuvā* in S'rīvara's Chronicle.[3] It comprises the tract lying between the east shore of the Anchᵊār, the range towards the Sind Valley and the hills which enclose the Ḍal on the east and south. Owing to the facility of communication across the lake and the manifold attractions of its shores, Phākh seems to have always been a favourite resort for the inhabitants of the capital. This fact is fully illustrated by the numerous places of ancient date which we find dotted around the lake.

The 'Hill of Gopa' (Gopādri)

Starting from its southernmost corner in the immediate vicinity of the city we come first to the hill popularly known as Takht-i-Sulaimān. Its bold pyramidal form and the old temple which crowns its summit, make this hill a most conspicuous object in the land-scape of S'rinagar. The present name of the hill, meaning 'Solomon's throne,' is undoubtedly of Muhammadan origin. Its alleged derivation from *Saṁdhimat*, the saintly hero of a well-known legend recorded in the Rājataraṅgiṇī, is nothing but an invention of the Bāchbaṭṭas of S'rinagar.[4]

1 *Vikram.* xviii. 23.

2 Compare *Rājat.* vi. 172-173 note.

3 *S'rīv.* iv. 306. The Lokaprakāśa writes *Phāgvā* while the modern Māhātmyas of Iśālaya or Iśᵊbar and Sureśvarī affect the form *Phālaka*.

4 The name Takht-i-Sulaimān is common enough in the local nomenclature of Muhammadan countries; compare, *e.g.*, the peak of this name in the Sulaimān

That the ancient designation of the hill was GOPĀDRI is shown beyond all doubt by an interesting passage of Kalhaṇa's Chronicle. It relates how the troops of the pretender Bhikṣācara when thrown back from the city which they had endeavoured to enter after crossing the Mahāsarit, *i.e.*, from the south-east, took refuge on the 'Gopa hill' or *Gopādri*.[1] There they were besieged by the royal troops until a diversion made by Bhikṣācara enable them to retreat to the higher hills in the east by the low neck which connects these with the Takht-i Sulaimān.

Kalhaṇa in the First Book of his Chronicle informs us that King Gopāditya built a shrine of S'iva Jyeṣṭheśvara on the Gopādri.[2] It is difficult not to connect this notice in some way with the extant temple which occupies so prominent a position on the summit of the hill. General Cunningham, it is true, on the strength of an alleged tradition had proposed to identify this temple with the Jyeṣṭharudra shrine which Kalhaṇa mentions as a foundation of Jalauka, Aśoka's son, in the ancient S'rīnagarī.[3] But Prof. Bühler has already shown that there is no genuine tradition regarding the temple among the S'rīnagar Brahmans.[4]

It is certain that the superstructures of the present temple belong to a late period.[5] But the massive and high base on which this temple is raised, and certain parts of the structure are no doubt of a far earlier date. These may well have formed part of a building which in Kalhaṇa's time,—rightly or wrongly, we have no means to judge,—was looked upon as a shrine of Jyeṣṭheśvara erected by King Gopāditya. There is no other ancient ruin on the hill. Nor would the configuration of the latter have admitted at any other point but the summit, of the construction of a shrine of any dimensions. It is of interest to note that the tradition of Abū-l-Fazl's time distinctly attributed the temple standing on 'Solomon's hill' to the time of Gopāditya.[6]

Kōh, S. of the Gumal Pass. The derivation from Saṁdhimat, referred to by Prof. BÜHLER, *Report*, p. 17, is not supported by any evidence whatever and unknown even to the most modern Māhātmyas.

1 See *Rājat.* viii. 1104–10 note. That the Takht-i-Sulaimān was called by its ancient name Gopādri, had been surmised already by Pt. Govind Kaul at the time of Prof. Bühler's visit; see *Report*, p. 17. But the decisive evidence of this passage was not known to him.

2 See i. 341 and note.

3 *Rājat.* i. 124; *Anc. Geogr.*, p. 95; also above, § 90.

4 See *Report*, p. 17.

5 See the remarks of FERGUSSON, *History of Indian Archit.*, p. 282, against Gen. Cunningham's and Major Cole's assumptions who represented the extant temple as one of the earliest buildings in Kaśmir.

6 *Āin-i-Akb.*, ii. p. 353.

Tīrtha of Jyeṣṭheśvara.

102. In my note on Rājat. i. 124 I have shown that an old tradition which can be traced back to at least the sixteenth century, connected the Ta<u>kh</u>t hill with the worship of Śiva Jyeṣṭharudra or, by another form of the name, JYEṢṬHEŚVARA (Jyeṣṭheśa).[1] And we find in fact a Liṅga known by this name worshipped even at the present day at the Tīrtha of Jyēṭhēr, scarcely more than one mile from the east foot of the hill.

This Tīrtha which undoubtedly derives its name from Jyeṣṭheśvara, lies in a glen of the hill-side, a short distance from the east shore of the Gagri Bal portion of the Ḍal.[2] Its sacred spring, designated in the comparatively modern Māhātmya as *Jyeṣṭhānāga*, forms a favorite object of pilgrimage for the Brahmans of Srinagar. Fragments of colossal Liṅgas are found in the vicinity of Jyēṭhēr and show with some other ancient remains now built into the Ziārats of Jyēṭhēr and Gupᵃkār, that the site had been held sacred from an early time.

It is in this vicinity that we may look for the ancient shrine of Jyeṣṭharudra, which Jalauka is said to have erected at Srīnagarī. But in the absence of distinct archæological evidence its exact position cannot be determined. It is highly probable that whatever the origin and the date of the temple on the Ta<u>kh</u>t hill may be, it was connected with the worship of Jyeṣṭharudra at Jyēṭhēr. No other Tīrtha is known in the immediate neighbourhood.

The distance of the shrine from the Tīrtha is scarcely greater than that of Lalitāditya's temple at Mārtaṇḍ from the sacred spring in honour of which it was erected. And in both places the distance of the temple is easily accounted for by the more prominent position which was thus secured for it. There is yet another analogy in the case of the two shrines. Both have long ago ceased to be places of popular worship. But the sacred springs, to the presiding deity of which they were dedicated, continue to attract pilgrims though shorn of all splendour of temples and images.

Gopāgrahāra; Bhūkṣīravāṭikā; Theḍā.

Kalhaṇa in the same passage which mentions the erection of King Gopāditya's shrine on the 'Gopa hill' makes that prince bestow the 'Gopa Agrahāras' on Brahman settlers from Āryadeśa.[3] The combination of the two local names suggests that by the GOPĀ-

[1] Compare Fourth Chron. 592, 853, 806.

[2] For *Jyeṣṭheśvara* > *Jyēṭhēr* we have exact analogies in *Kapaṭeśvara* > *Kōṭhēr*, *Amareśvara* > *Amburhēr*, etc.

[3] See i. 341. *Agrahāra* is the regular term designating a Jāgir or piece of land bestowed on individuals or religious corporations, etc.; see note i. 87.

GRAHĀRAS are meant the fertile lands of the present *Gup*ᵃ*kār*, between the north foot of the Ta*kh*t hill and the Ḍal. The name Gupᵃkār may be, in fact, the direct phonetic derivative of the term used by Kalhaṇa.[1]

Our surmise is supported by the reference which Kalhaṇa in the verse immediately following makes to the village BHŪKṢĪRAVĀṬIKĀ. This place is identified by the old glossator A_2 with *Buch*ⁱ*vōr*, a small hamlet situated on the narrow strip of land at the rocky north-west foot of the Ta*kh*t hill. The modern name is clearly derived from Kalhaṇa's form. Gopāditya is said to have removed to this confined and secluded spot Brahmans who had given offence by eating garlic.

The combined mention of Gopādri, Gopāgrahāra and Bhūkṣīravāṭikā in Rājat. i. 341 *sq.* suggests that Kalhaṇa has reproduced here local traditions collected from the sites immediately adjoining the hill. Whether the connection of these localities with King Gopāditya's reign was based on historical fact, or only an old popular etymology working upon the word *Gopa* found in the first two names, can no longer be decided.

Continuing our route along the eastern shore of the Ḍal we come, at a distance of about one mile from Gupᵃkār, to the large village of *Thīd*, prettily situated amid vineyards and orchards. It is the THEDĀ of the Rājataraṅgiṇī, mentioned as one of the places which the pious King Saṁdhimat or Āryarāja adorned with Maṭhas, divine images, and Liṅgas.[2] Abū-l-Fazl speaks of Thīd as "a delightful spot where seven springs unite; around them are stone buildings, memorials of by-gone times."[3] The remains here alluded to can no longer be traced, but the seven springs (*Saptapuṣkariṇī*) which are also referred to in the Haracaritacintāmaṇi (iv. 40 *sqq.*), are still pointed out.

The cluster of villages which we reach about one and a half miles beyond *Thīd*, and which jointly bear the name *Brān*, can be safely identified with BHĪMĀDEVĪ which Kalhaṇa notices along with Thedā. The Nilamata knows the sacred site of Bhīmādevī in conjunction with the Sureśvarī Tīrtha which we shall next visit, and in the Haracaritacintāmaṇi it is named with the seven springs of Thedā. The Tīrtha of Bhīmādevī is no longer known, but may be located with some probability at the fine spring near *Dāmpōr* marked now by a Muhammadan shrine.

1 *Gup*ᵃ*kār* may go back to a form * *Gup*ᵃ*gār*, with assimilation of *g* to the preceding tenuis. In Kś. the hardening of *g* to *k* is by no means unknown, see Dr. Grierson's remarks, *Z.D.M.G.*, l., p. 3. * *Gup*ᵃ*gār* could easily be traced back to *Gopāgrahāra* through Pr. forms like * *Gupagrār*.

2 See *Rājat* ii. 135 note.

3 *Āīn-i-Akb.*, ii. p. 361.

103. A sacred site of far greater fame and importance is that of the present village of *Iś^ebar* which lies about two miles further north on the Ḍal shore and a little beyond the Mughal garden of Nishāt. The site was known in ancient times as *Sureśvarīkṣetra* ('the field of Sureśvarī').[1] It was sacred to Durgā-Sureśvarī who is still worshipped on a high crag rising from the mountain range to the east of Iś^ebar village. The seat of the goddess is on a rugged rock some 3000 feet above the village, offering no possible room for any building. The numerous shrines erected in her honour were hence built on the gently sloping shore of the lake below.

Tīrtha of Sureśvarī.

The Tīrtha of Sureśvarī is often referred to in Kalhaṇa's Chronicle and other Kaśmīrian texts as a spot of exceptional holiness. It was particularly sought by the pious as a place to die at. The pilgrimage to Sureśvarī is connected with visits to several sacred springs in and about Iś^ebar. One of them, *Satadhārā*, is already mentioned by Kṣemendra.[2] It is passed in a narrow gorge some 1500 feet below the rock of Sureśvarī.

Iś^ebar derives its present name from the shrine of ĪŚEŚVARA which King Saṁdhimat-Āryarāja according to the Rājataraṅgiṇī erected in honour of his Guru Īśāna.[3] An earlier form, *Iś^ebrōr*, which is found in an old gloss of the Chronicle and evidently was heard also by Abū-l-Faẓl, helps to connect Iś^ebar and Īśeśvara.[4]

Iś^ebar is still much frequented as a pilgrimage place. The chief attraction is a sacred spring known as *Guptagaṅgā* which fills an ancient stone-lined tank in the centre of the village. This conveniently accessible Tīrtha is the scene of a very popular pilgrimage on the Vaiśākhi day and has fairly obscured the importance of the mountain seat of Sureśvarī. A ruined mound immediately behind the tank is popularly believed to mark the site of the Īśeśvara shrine. Numerous remains of ancient buildings are found around the sacred springs and elsewhere in the village. They probably belong to the various other temples the erection of which is mentioned by Kalhaṇa at the site of Sureśvarī.[5]

Ṣaḍarhadvana; Tripureśvara.

Passing round the foot of the ridge on which Sureśvarī is worshipped, we come to the small village of *Hārvan* which the old glossator of the Rājataraṅgiṇī identifies with ṢAḌARHADVANA ('the

[1] Compare for *Sureśvarī* and the site of Iś^ebar, note v. 37.

[2] See *Samay.* ii. 29.

[3] See *Rājat.* ii. 134 note.

[4] *-bar* is a modern contraction for *-brōr*, from Skr. *bhaṭṭāraka*, which in Kaśmīr local names has often taken the place of its synonym *-īśvara*; comp. *e.g.*, Skr. *Vijayeśvara* > Kś. *Vij^ebrōr*.

[5] See *Rājat.* v. 37, 40 *sq.*; viii. 3365.

wood of the six Arhats'). This place is mentioned by Kalhaṇa as the residence of the great Buddhist teacher Nāgārjuna.[1] The name Hārvan may well be derived from Ṣaḍarhadvana, but in the absence of other evidence the identification cannot be considered as certain. On the hill-side south of the village I observed already in 1888 fragments of ornamented bricks. Since then remarkable remains of ancient brick-pavements have come to light on occasion of excavations made for the new S'rīnagar waterworks.

Proceeding further up the valley of the stream which comes from the Mār Sar lake, we reach, at a distance of about three miles from the Ḍal, the village of *Triphar.* Evidence I have discussed elsewhere, makes it quite certain that it is the ancient TRIPUREŚVARA (Tripureśa).[2] The latter is repeatedly mentioned as a site of great sanctity by Kalhaṇa as well as in the Nīlamata and some Māhātmyas. But it has long ago ceased to be a separate pilgrimage place. A little stream known as the *Tripuragaṅgā* near Triphar is, however, still visited as one of the stations on the Mahādeva pilgrimage.

Kṣemendra in the colophon of his Daśāvatāracarita refers to the hill above Tripureśa as the place where he was wont to find repose and where he composed his work. In Zain-ul-'ābidīn's time Tripureśvara seems yet to have been a Tīrtha much frequented by mendicants.[3] Tripureśvara too possessed its shrine of Jyeṣṭheśvara, and to this King Avantivarman retired on the approach of death.[4] A legend related by the S'arvāvatāra connected the site of Tripureśvara with the defeat of the demon Tripura by S'iva and with the latter's worship on the neighbouring peak of Mahādeva. I have not been able to examine the site and am hence unable to state whether there are any ancient ruins near it.

The whole mountain-ridge which stretches to the south of Triphar and along the Ḍal, bore in ancient times the name of S'RĪDVĀRA.[5] On the opposite side of the Valley rises the great peak of MAHĀDEVA to a height of over 13,000 feet. Numerous references to it in the Nīlamata, S'arvāvatāra, and other texts, show that it was in old times just as now frequented as a Tīrtha.

We may now again descend the valley towards the north shore of the Ḍal. On our way we pass close to Hārvan the village of T̲s̲at̲s̲a where the convenience of modern worshippers has located a substitute for the

1 See *Rājat.* i. 173 note.

2 Compare *Rājat.* v. 46 note.

3 See *S'riv.* i. 402.

4 See *Rājat.* v. 123 note.

5 See *Rājat.* viii. 2422.

ancient Tirtha of the goddess S'āradā (see below § 127). Leaving aside the famous garden of Shālimār of which our old texts know nothing,[1] we come to a marshy extension of the Ḍal known as Tēl^abal. The stream which flows through it and which forms a branch of the river coming from the Mār Sar, bore the old name of *Tilaprasthā*.[2]

Hiraṇyapura.

104. The road which takes us from Tēl^abal to the mouth of the Sind Valley is the same which was followed by the pretender Bhikṣācara and his rebel allies on a march to Sureśvarī described in the Rājataraṅgiṇī.[3] The narrow embankment on which they fought and defeated the royal troops, leads across the Tēl^abal marshes.

At the south foot of the ridge which runs down to the opening of the Sind Valley, we find the village of *Ranyil*, the ancient HIRAṆYAPURA.[4] The place is said by Kalhaṇa to have been founded by King Hiraṇyākṣa. As it lies on the high-road from the Sind Valley to S'rīnagar it is repeatedly mentioned also in connection with military operations directed from that side against the capital. The victorious Uccala when marching upon S'rīnagar, had the Abhiṣeka ceremony performed *en route* by the Brahmans of Hiraṇyapura. It seems to have been a place of importance, since it figures in a fairy-tale related in the Kathāsaritsāgara as the capital of Kaśmīr.[5] A spring a little to the south of the village is visited by the pilgrims to the Haramukuṭagaṅgā and bears in Māhātmyas the name of *Hiraṇyākṣanāga*.

Juṣkapura; Amareśvara.

From near Raṇyil several old water-courses radiate which carry the water of the Sind River to the village lying between the Anch^iār and the Ḍal lakes. One of these canals passes the village of *Zukur*. A tradition recorded already by General Cunningham identifies this place with the ancient JUṢKAPURA. Kalhaṇa names the place as a foundation of the Turuṣka (*i.e.* Kuṣana) King Juṣka who also built a Vihāra there.[6] The Muhammadan shrines and tombs of the village contain considerable remains of ancient buildings.

[1] The first reference to this somewhat over-praised locality which I can find, is in Abū-l-Faẓl who mentions the waterfall or rather the cascades of 'Shālahmār'; see ii. p. 361. The Vitastā-, Iśālaya-, and Mahādeva-Māhātmyas which are of very modern origin, show this fact also by their references to '*Sālamāra*' and the whimsical etymologies which they give for the name (*Mārasālā*, etc.). We might reasonably expect that Jonarāja and S'rīvara in their detailed accounts of the Ḍal would have mentioned the place if it had then claimed any importance.

[2] See *Rājat.* v. 46 note; *S'rīv.* i. 421.

[3] See *Rājat.* viii. 744 note.

[4] For detailed references *see Rājat.* i. 287 note.

[5] See *Kathāsar.* lxv. 215 *sqq.*

[6] See *Rājat.* i. 168 note; *Anc. Geogr.* p. 101.

To the west of Juṣkapura and on the shore of the Anch^{i}ār lies the large village of Ạmburhǝr. It is the ancient AMAREŚVARA often mentioned in the Rājataraṅgiṇī in connection with military operations to the north of S'rīnagar.[1] This is easily accounted for by the fact that the place lay then as now on the high road connecting the Sind Valley with the capital. It took its name from a temple of S'iva Amareśvara which Sūryamatī, Ananta's queen, endowed with Agrahāras and a Maṭha. The ancient slabs and sculptured fragments which I found in 1895 in and around the Ziārat of Farrukhzād Ṣāhib, may possibly have belonged to this temple.

Continuing on the road towards S'rīnagar for about two miles further we come to the large village of Vicār Nāg prettily situated in extensive wallnut groves. A fine Nāga near the village forms the object of a popular Yātrā in the month of Caitra. It is supposed to be an epiphany of the Ailāpattra Nāga who is mentioned also in the Nīlamata. An earlier designation seems to be MUKTĀMŪLAKANĀGA which is given to the locality by S'rīvara and in the Tīrthasaṁgraha.[2] To the west of the village and near an inlet of the Anch^{i}ār are the ruins of three ancient temples now converted into Ziārats and tombs.[3]

Amṛtabhavana.

Only a quarter of a mile to the east of Vicār Nāg and on the other side of the old canal called Lach^{a}m Kul (*Lakṣmīkulyā) stands the hamlet of *Ânt^{a}bavan.* In my "Notes on Ou-k'ong's account of Kaśmīr" I have proved that Ânt^{a}bavan derives its name from the ancient Vihāra of AMṚTABHAVANA which Amṛtaprabhā, a queen of Meghavāhana, is said to have erected.[4] Ou-k'ong mentions the Vihāra by the name of *Ngo-mi-t'o-po-wan* which represents a transcribed Prakrit form *Amitabhavana or Āmitabhavana. An ancient mound with traces of a square enclosure around it, which is found between the canal and the hamlet, may possibly belong to the remains of this Vihāra.

Tīrtha of Sodara.

Proceeding to the east of Ânt^{a}bavan for about a mile we come to the large village of *Sudar^{a}bal* situated on a deep inlet of the Ḍal, known as *Sudar^{a}khun.* The name of the village and the neighbouring portion of the lake make it very probable that we have to place here the sacred spring of SODARA.[5] It formed the subject of an ancient legend related by

[1] See *Rājat.* vii. 183 note.

[2] See *S'rīv.* iv. 65. On his authority the name Muktāmūlakanāga ought to have been shown on the map.

[3] Compare for a view of these remains, COLE, *Ancient Buildings*, p. 31.

[4] See *Rājat.* iii. 9 note, and *Notes on Ou-k'ong*, pp. 9 *sqq.*

[5] See *Rājat.* i. 125-126 note. Kś. *-bal* in Sudar^{a}bal means merely 'place.'

Kalhaṇa. King Jalauka had built at S'rīnagarī his shrine of Jyeṣṭharudra whose original place of worship was at Bhūteśvara, below Mount Haramukuṭa. He then wished to have by the side of the new shrine also the Sodara spring which adjoins the site of Bhūteśvara.[1] To fulfil the king's pious desire "there broke forth from a waterless spot a spring which was alike to Sodara in colour, taste and other respects." A golden cup thrown into the original Sodara spring appeared after two and half days in its Avatāra near S'rīnagarī. This miracle removed all doubts as to their identity.

Close to the mosque of Sudarᵃbal and by the lake shore are two pools fed by perennial springs. These according to a local tradition were in old times visited by numerous pilgrims. Now all recollection of this Tīrtha has been lost among the Brahmans of S'rīnagar. But the name of a portion of the village area, *Baṭṭᵃpōr*, points to a former settlement of Baṭṭas or Purohitas. It is curious, too, that we find only half a mile from the village the Ziārat of Ḥazrat Bal, perhaps the most popular of all Muhammadan shrines in the Valley. It is supposed to be built over the remains of the miracle-working Pīr Dastagīr Ṣāhib. Is it possible that the presence of this rather ubiquitous saint at this particular spot had something to do with the earlier Hindu Tīrtha?

SECTION VI.—NORTHERN DISTRICTS OF MAḌAVARĀJYA.

105. Our circuit through the Phākh Pargaṇa has brought us back to the purlieus of the capital. We must leave them now once more and start on our tour through the outlying districts. We may direct it first to the upper half of the Valley, the ancient Maḍavarājya. This again is divided by the Vitastā into two portions, one to the north and east, the other to the south and west of the river. We shall begin with the Parganas on the right bank, starting from S'rīnagar.

District of Khaḍūvī.

The Pargaṇa which adjoins S'rīnagar from the south-east, is now known as Vihī. It extends from near Purāṇādhiṣṭhāna to the spur of Vastᵃrvan, near Vāntⁱpōr (Avantipura), and comprises a wide semi-circular tract of fertile Karēwa lands. In ancient times the district took its name from the village of KHAḌŪVĪ, the present *Khruv*.[2] The Ḍāmaras of the *Khaḍūvī* district are repeatedly mentioned by Kalhaṇa along with those of Holaḍā, the modern Vular Pargaṇa.

[1] For *Sodara*, the present Nārān Nāg, see notes i. 123; v. 56-59.

[2] Compare *Rājat.* viii. 733 note.

The site of Pāndrēṭhan or Purāṇādhiṣṭhāna has already been fully noticed. About two miles higher up the river lies Pānd^{e}chuk village, with some ancient remains and the traces of a stone bridge-head, probably of late date. The old name of the place is unknown. We pass next by the river the village of Simpōr. This may retain the name of SIṀHAPURA, founded by King Jayasiṁha in Kalhaṇa's time.[1]

Less than two miles to the north-west of Siṁpōr lies the village of *Zevan*, the ancient JAYAVANA. It was correctly identified already by Prof. Bühler on the basis of the happy and exact description given of it by Bilhaṇa.[2] The poet mentions in this "place of high-rising monuments" the "pool filled with pure water, sacred to *Takṣaka*, lord of snakes." This pool still exists in the *Takṣaka Nāga* which is visited annually by the pilgrims to Harṣeśvara.[3]

The mention made by Kalhaṇa in his history of Narapura of the pilgrimage to the Takṣaka spring proves that in old times it must have enjoyed great reputation as a separate Tirtha. It is in fact the only Kaśmir Nāga which is distinctly mentioned in the Tirtha list of the Mahābhārata (iii. lxxxii. 90). Abū-l-Fazl records the interesting fact that this spring was populary held to be the place whence the cultivation of saffron flourishing in this neighbourhood originated.[4] In Akbar's time the cultivators, undoubtedly Muhammadans, still worshipped at this fountain at spring time. It was customary to pour cow's milk into it to secure a good omen for the success of the crop. We see that the Takṣaka Nāga long retained his importance with the cultivators as a local divinity.

Khonamuṣa.

About two miles to the north-east of Zevan we come on gently rising ground to the village of *Khun^{e}moh*. It is, as already stated above, the ancient KHONAMUṢA, famous as the birthplace of Bilhaṇa. The latter in the Vikramāṅkadevacarita gives an enthusiastic description of the charms of his rural home.[5] The saffron fields which Bilhana mentions extend close to the lower of the two separate hamlets which form the village. In the upper hamlet is a sacred spring called *Dāmodaranāga* with some sculptured funeral Stèlès and a few fragmentary inscriptions.

On the hill-side above the village issues another Nāga which under

[1] See *Rājat.* viii. 2443 note.

[2] Compare *Report*, pp. 5 *sq.*; *Rājat.* vii. 607 note; *Vikram.* xviii. 70.

[3] See *Rājat.* i. 220 note.

[4] See *Āin-i-Akb.*, ii. p. 358.

[5] For a detailed and accurate account of the position and remains of Khonamuṣa, see Prof. BÜHLER's *Report*, pp. 5 *sq.* The identity of Khun^{e}moh with the Khonamuṣa of *Rājat.* i. 90, was first pointed out by Gen. CUNNINGHAM, *Anc. Geogr.*, p. 98.

the name of *Bhuvaneśvarī* is visited on the pilgrimage to HARṢEŚVARA. The latter Tīrtha lies on the summit of the high ridge which rises to the north of the village. It consists of a 'Svayambhū' Liṅga situated in a small cave and enjoys considerable popularity. I have not been able to trace its name except in the local Māhātmya and the Tīrthasaṁgraha.

The chief place of the Vihi Pargaṇa is now the town of *Pāmpar*, the ancient PADMAPURA, about four miles south-west of Khunᵊmoh.[1] It was founded in the beginning of the 9th century by Padma, the powerful uncle of the puppet king Cippaṭa-Jayāpīḍa. Padma is said by the Chronicle to have also built a temple of Viṣṇu *Padmasvāmin*. To this may possibly belong the scanty remains of an ancient temple which have been described by General Cunningham.[2] Close by is the Ziārat of Mīr Muḥammad Hamadānī, with some fine ancient columns and ornamented slabs which are likely to have been taken from this temple. Also the other Ziārats of the town show similar remains. Padmapura, owing to its central position in a fertile tract, seems to have always been a place of importance and is often mentioned by Kalhaṇa and the later Chroniclers.

Padmapura.

Proceeding north-eastwards of Padmapura we pass first *Bālᵊhōm*, a large village, which in the Lokaprakāśa and Tīrthasaṁgraha figures as *Bālāśrama*. Under a large Deodar near it Bālādevi is now worshipped in the form of an old stone-image. Numerous ancient Stêlês, showing miniature reproductions of temples, are found in the neighbouring rivulets and canals; they were apparently used in recent times as stepping-stones which would account for their preservation. At the foot of a rocky spur which descends from the mountain-range to the north, lies the picturesque village of *Uyan*, once mentioned by Kalhaṇa under the name of OVANĀ.[3] It has a large sulphurous spring visited by the sick.

About two miles further east we reach the large village of *Khruv*, the ancient KHAḌŪVĪ which, as we have seen, gave to the district its former name. There is an abundance of fine springs in and about Khruv; Abū-l-Faẓl mentions them as objects of worship and estimates their number at 360.[4] Above the village a so-called Svayaṁbhū-cakra or mystical diagram is shown on a rock.[5] It is held sacred to Jvālā-

1 For a detailed notice see *Rājat.* iv. 695 note. The old name of the place is well-known to Srīnagar Paṇḍits; VIGNE too, *Travels*, ii. p. 31, recognized it correctly.

2 See *J. A. S. B.*, 1848, p. 274.

3 See *Rājat.* vii. 295.

4 *Āīn-i-Akb.*, ii. p. 358.

5 Compare for such diagrams, also designated *Devīcakra* or *Mātṛcakra*, *Rājat.* i. 122 note.

mukhi-Durgā and largely visited by pilgrims. I am, however, unable to trace any old reference to this Tīrtha.

S'anāra.

Only a mile to the south-east of Khruv is the village of *Sār*, until recently the seat of a flourishing iron-industry. Kalhaṇa mentions it by the name of S'ANĀRA as an Agrahāra founded by King S'acīnara.[1] Whatever the historical value of this notice may be, which Kalhaṇa took from Padmamihira, the evidence detailed in my note on the passage proves that the present S'ār is intended. An intermediate form of the name is preserved in the *Snār* of an old gloss. The Ziārat of Khwāja Khiẓr which stands here near several small springs, is built with remains of a Hindu temple; among them is a Liṅga-base some six feet square.

About two miles south-west of S'ār are found the well-preserved ruins of a temple near the village of *Ladu* (not marked on Survey map). They have been described by Bishop Cowie,[2] but I am unable to trace any old reference to this shrine in the texts I have examined. It is remarkable for having a circular cella, the only one known to me in Kaśmīr. A small square cella to the east of this temple has been annexed to a neighbouring Ziārat.

Near the south end of the Vihi Pargaṇa and on the river lies the village of *Lat°pōr*. An old gloss of the Rājataraṅgiṇī identifies it with LALITAPURA, a place founded in honour of King Lalitāditya by his architect.[3] The King according to the Chronicle was not pleased with the attention; in any case no importance seems to have attached to this place. There are no old remains above ground, but the local tradition still tells of King 'Lalitādit' as the founder of a large town on the neighbouring Uḍar.

District of Holaḍā; Avantipura.

106. Passing round the foot of Mount Vast^a^rvan we enter the Pargaṇa of *Vular*, the ancient HOLAḌĀ. This identification is supported, apart from the clear phonetic evidence, by all passages of the Rājataraṅgiṇī which mention Holaḍā.[4] Its feudal barons played a great part in the troubled times of the later Hindu reigns.

Its most important place in old times was undoubtedly the town of AVANTIPURA, founded by King Avantivarman (A.D. 855–883).[5] Its position is marked by the present village of *Vạnt^i^pōr* on the Vitastā. The

[1] See note i. 100.

[2] See *J. A. S. B.*, 1866, pp. 97 *sqq.*

[3] See *Rājat.* iv. 186.

[4] See *Rājat.* i. 306 note.

[5] See *Rājat.* v. 45 *sq.* note. Its identity with Vạnt^i^pōr was first pointed out by Dr. WILSON in his note on Moorcroft, *Travels*, ii. p. 244.

conspicuous ruins of this place attracted already the attention of the early European visitors. General Cunningham did not fail to recognize in them the remains of the two great temples of *Avantisvāmin* and *Avantiśvara* which Avantivarman had built here.[1] Of the two great ruins one is at Vạnt[i]pōr itself, the other and larger one half a mile further down the river close to the hamlet of Jaubrạ̄r (map 'Jabair.') Owing to the complete destruction of the central shrines it is impossible to ascertain now which was dedicated to Viṣṇu and which to S'iva. The fine enclosing quadrangles of the temples have also suffered badly. That of Avantisvāmin was used as a temporary fortification in Kalhaṇa's own time and underwent a severe siege.[2]

The site on which Avantivarman's town was built, had apparently enjoyed some sanctity before these temples were founded, and bore the old name *Viśvaikasāra.* The great extent of the town is indicated by the traces of ruined buildings which cover the foot of the hills east of Vạnt[i]pōr for a considerable distance. The frequent references to Avantipura in the Chronicles show that the town retained some importance long after the death of its founder.

We hear but little of other old sites in Holaḍā. The great town of *Mihirapura* which King Mihirakula is said to have founded in it, can no longer be traced.[3] *Khuli*, a village situated a short distance to the south-west of Trāl, the modern headquarters of the district, may possibly be the *Khola* of the Chronicle, one of Gopāditya's Agrahāras.[4] Of *Trāl* I am unable to trace any old notice.

The identification of the village of *Būṭṣ*, about two miles south of Khuli, with the old Bhavaccheda is also uncertain.[5] It is based on a gloss of Rājānaka Ratnakaṇṭha, the writer of the Codex Archetypus of the Rājataraṅgiṇī. Still further south lies the village of *Kai*, probably the old Katika named by Kalhaṇa as a foundation of Tuñjīna I.[6] This identification is made in the old gloss on the passage and supported by the phonetic evidence of the modern name.

Of old remains in Vular the interesting temple of *Nārastān* at the northern extremity of the district (34° 3′ lat. 75° 10′ long.) deserves notice.[7] Unfortunately I am unable to find any clue as to its old name

1 See for a full description *J. A. S. B.*, 1848, pp. 275 *sqq.*; also *ib.*, 1866, 121 *sqq.*

2 See *Rājat.* viii. 1429 *sq.*, 1474 *sqq.*

3 See *Rājat.* i. 306.

4 See *Rājat.* i. 340.

5 Compare iii. 381 note.

6 *Rājat.* ii. 14.

7 See Mr. Lawrence's notice, *Valley*, p. 172. The attached photograph shows the site after my excavations. Regarding the result of the latter, see *Vienna Oriental Journal*, 1891, p. 345 *sqq.*

or history. Excavations made by me at the site in 1891 brought to light interesting sculptures, but no evidence as to its name. The large village of *Sutur* (map 'Sootoor') to the south-west of Nārastān may possibly account for the entry of *Satrava* in the Lokaprakāśa's list of Parganas.

District of Dakṣiṇapāra.

107. The eastern boundary of Vular is marked by the high spur which descends from the north towards the confluence of the Vitastā and Gambhīrā. The adjoining district to the east is one of considerable extent. It comprises besides the whole right or western side of the Lid^a^r Valley also the low-lying tract between the Vitastā and the lower course of the Viśokā. The modern name of this great Pargaṇa is *Dachünpōr* which appears in S'rīvara's Chronicle as DAKṢIṆAPĀRA. This clearly means 'the right bank' [of the Ledarī or Lid^a^r]. Another form, of the same significance, is *Dakṣiṇapārśva* found in the Lokaprakāśa and Mārtāṇḍamāhātmya. To this designation corresponds the term *Vāmapārśva*, now Khōvurpōr, which as we shall see, is applied to the left side of the Lid^a^r Valley.[1]

The junction of the Vitastā with the Gambhīrā, *i.e.*, the united Viśokā and Ramaṇyāṭavī, has already been mentioned above as a Tīrtha.[2] Not far from it lies the village of *Marhōm*, on the Vitastā, mentioned by Jonarāja under its old name of MAḌAVĀŚRAMA.[3] The first part of the name is identical with that of *Maḍavarājya.*

About two miles south-east of Marhōm and not far from the Vitastā, we find the village *Vāg^a^hōm*, with a sacred spring known by the name of HASTIKARṆA. This name seems to have applied formerly to the place itself which we find twice thus referred to by Kalhaṇa.[4] It is possibly the Hastikarṇa, where Bhoja, Harṣa's son, was treacherously murdered.

Temple of Cakradhara.

About one mile to the south of Hastikarṇa the Vitastā makes a great bend. The peninsula thus formed is occupied by a small *Uḍar* or alluvial plateau which owing to its height and isolated position is a very conspicuous object in the landscape. It was once the site of

[1] General Cunningham, *Anc. Geogr.*, p. 94, assumes that Kś. *dachün* 'right' is 'now used to denote the "north," and *kāvar*, (recte *khōvur*) or "left," to denote the "south."' This assumption, however, as well as the explanation given for the alleged change of meaning are based on some misunderstanding.

[2] See § 64.

[3] See *Jonar.* (Bo. ed.), 132.

[4] See *Rājat.* v. 23 note; also vii. 1650. Another *Hastikarṇa*, mentioned by S'rīvara, i. 441, seems to have been near S'rīnagar on the west.

one of the oldest and most famous shrines of the Valley, the temple of Viṣṇu CAKRADHARA.

The plateau is still known as *Ṯsakᵃdar* Uḍar.[1] Brahman tradition is aware of the derivation of this name from *Cakradhara*. It was first brought to the notice of European scholars by Prof. BÜHLER who had duly recognized the antiquarian importance of the site.[2] The shrine of Cakradhara is often mentioned as a Tīrtha of great sanctity.[3] It was also closely connected with the legends regarding the burned city of *Narapura*, localized as we shall see in its close vicinity. But the only detailed notice of the temple we owe to a historical incident which occurred there during the civil wars of Sussala's reign.[4]

The royal troops having been forced to evacuate the neighbouring town of Vijayeśvara or Vijᵊbrōr, the inhabitants of the latter place and the neighbouring villages took refuge in the temple of Cakradhara. This, by its position on the high and steep Uḍar, was naturally well-adapted for defence. The temple filled by the crowd of fugitives and routed soldiers, was soon besieged by the rebel troops of Bhikṣācara. The temple courtyard was protected by massive wooden ramparts and gates. When these had been set on fire by the assailants a mighty conflagration ensued in which the whole mass of people inside perished. Kalhaṇa vividly describes this great catastrophe which he believes to have provoked divine vengeance and thus to have brought about the downfall of the pretender.

The account here given is of topographical interest. It shows that the temple actually stood on the flat top of the Uḍar, and also explains the scarcity of stone-remains in this locality. The absence of conspicuous ruins had already been noticed by Prof. Bühler. When visiting in 1895 the Ṯsakᵃdar Uḍar, I found only traces of a quadrangular enclosure, about forty yards square. They are marked by hollows at the northern end of the Uḍar which is separated from the rest by a dip in the ground. These hollows may possibly be the last indications of the wooden ramparts which enclosed the shrine.

The temple seems to have been subsequently restored, and Jonarāja mentions the statue of Cakradhara among those chief divine images which Sikandar Butshikast destroyed.[5] Jayadratha in his

[1] See *Rājat.* i. 38, 201 notes.

[2] See *Report*, p. 18.

[3] See *Rājat.* vii. 258, 261, 269; *Jonar.* (Bo. ed.), 763; *Śrīkaṇṭhac.* iii. 12; *Nīlamata*, 1170.

[4] See *Rājat.* viii. 971–995. The date of the burning of Cakradhara seems to have been the 12th Śrāvaṇa śudi, A.D. 1121.

[5] See *Jonar.* (Bo. ed.), 763.

Haracaritacintāmaṇi devotes a separate canto, vii., to the relation of the legend which localized the disc-wielding god at the Tīrtha of Cakradhara. The latter is still referred to in a general way in the old Vijayeśvaramāhātmya (No. 87, Poona MSS.). Now, however, Cakradhara is no longer visited by the pilgrims to Vijayeśvara though the Purohitas of the latter place still retain a recollection of the former sanctity of the site.

108. There can be no doubt that at the foot of the Cakradhara Uḍar there stood once an ancient town of considerable importance. From the low ground towards the river on the east and from the river-bed itself, ancient coins going back to Greek and Indo-Scythian rule are annually extracted in considerable quantities. Popular tradition still asserts that this site was once occupied by a great town. This tradition existed already in the time of Kalhaṇa who records it in the interesting legend of the burned city of Narapura.[1] This is told at great length in a poetic episode of the First Book.

Legend of Narapura.

King *Nara* is said to have founded a splendid capital, called after himself NARAPURA, on the sandy bank of the Vitastā close to the shrine of Cakradhara. "There in a grove was a pond of limpid water, the habitation of the Nāga Suśravas." A young Brahman who had found occasion to assist the Nāga and his two daughters when in distress, was allowed to marry in reward one of the latter. He lived in happiness at Narapura until the beauty of the Nāga lady excited the passion of the wicked king. When Nara found his advances rejected with scorn, he endeavoured to seize the beautiful Candralekhā by force. The couple fled for protection to their father's habitation.

The Nāga then rose in fury from his pool and "burned the king with his town in a rain of fearful thunderbolts." Thousands of people were burned before the image of Viṣṇu Cakradhara to which they had fled for protection. Ramaṇyā, the Nāga's sister, came down from the mountains carrying along masses of rocks and boulders. These she dropped, as we have seen, along the bed of the Ramaṇyāṭavī or Rembyār*, when she found that Suśravas had already wreaked his vengeance. The Nāga himself feeling remorse at the carnage he had caused, removed to a lake on a far-off mountain. There "he is to the present day seen by the people on the pilgrimage to Amareśvara."[2] "To this day," thus closes Kalhaṇa's narration, "that tale is remembered by the people when they behold close to Cakradhara that town destroyed by fire and that pond which has become a dry hollow."

[1] See *Rājat.* i. 201–274.

[2] Compare regarding the lake of the Nāga *Suśravas* on the route to Amburnāth, above, § 59.

Whatever the origin of the legend here told may have been, it is clear that popular tradition in Kalhaṇa's time looked upon the barren ground which stretches along the river between Tsak^{a}dar and the present Vij^{a}brōr as the site of an ancient city. The ruins which in the 12th century were pointed out as the remains of the burned Narapura, may have supplied the immediate starting point of the legend.

What these remains were we cannot say. As the ground referred to is subject to annual inundation it is possible that the remains meant have since disappeared under alluvial deposits. The habitation of the 'Suśram' Nāga was still shown to me in a hollow, generally dry, close to the south-east foot of the Uḍar. The name of Narapura and its king are no longer remembered. But the main features of the legend as heard by Kalhaṇa, still live in the local tradition.

Vijayeśvara.

109. The ancient town which once stood in the position indicated, was evidently succeeded by VIJAYEŚVARA, the present *Vij^{a}brōr*. The latter place, situated less than two miles above Cakradhara, received its name from the ancient shrine of Śiva *Vijayeśvara* (Vijayeśa, Vijayeśāna).[1] This deity is worshipped to the present day at Vij^{a}brōr. The site has evidently from early times been one of the most famous Tirthas of Kaśmīr. It is mentioned as such in the Rājataraṅgiṇī and many old Kaśmīrian texts.[2] The tradition regarding Aśoka's connection with it supplies historical proof for its antiquity. According to Kalhaṇa's account which may well have been based on genuine local tradition or even inscriptional evidence, Aśoka had replaced the old stuccoed enclosure of the temple by one of stone. The great king was also credited with having erected within this enclosure two temples called *Aśokeśvara.*

This old temple which is often mentioned by Kalhaṇa and was the scene of many a historical incident, has now completely disappeared. According to the tradition of the local Purohitas it stood at a site close the river-bank and nearly opposite to the bridge over the Vitastā. When I first visited Vij^{a}brōr in 1889 I still found some ancient slabs and fragments at this spot. It was then some 15 feet below the level of the surrounding ground,[3] and has since been partly built over. Stone materials are said to have been removed from here for the new temple

[1] Compare for detailed references, *Rājat.* i. 38, 105 notes.

[2] The legend of the Tīrtha is given at length in the x. Prakāśa of the *Haracaritacintāmaṇi.*

[3] General Cunningham who saw these remains in 1847, rightly attributes them to the temple of Vijayeśa, but calls the place 'Vijayapāra.' He justly points to the difference of level as an indication of the antiquity of the structure; see *Anc. Geogr.*, p. 98.

of Vijayeśvara which was built by Mahārāja Raṇbīr Singh some thirty years ago higher up on the river-bank.

It is probable that a temple so much frequented had undergone more than one restoration in the course of the fifteen centuries which lie between the time of Aśoka and the end of Hindu reign in Kaśmīr. Some time before A.D. 1081, while King Ananta was residing at the Tīrtha of Vijayeśvara, the temple was burned down in a general conflagration, caused by his son Kalaśa. The latter, however, subsequently restored the shrine. The old Liṅga of S'iva Vijayeśvara seems to have fallen a victim to the iconoclasm of Sikandar Butshikast.[1]

The town of Vijayeśvara is ascribed by Kalhaṇa to King Vijaya.[2] But nothing else is recorded of this ruler, and this may cause a doubt as to his historical existence. It is significant that the town is designated either simply *Vijayeśvara* or as *Vijayakṣetra*, which is abbreviated from *Vijayeśvarakṣetra*. The modern name *Vij*ᵊ*brōr* is the Kś. equivalent of Vijayeśvara, *-brōr* (from Skr. *bhaṭṭāraka* 'god') having replaced the more specific *-īśvara*, the usual designation of S'iva.[3]

That the town had acquired importance at a comparatively early date, is indicated by the mention of a thousand Agrahāras said to have been granted here by King Mihirakula to a settlement of Gandhāra Brahmans.[4] It was large enough to accommodate the whole court and army of King Ananta when the latter removed his residence to Vijayeśvara.[5] The narrative of the civil wars which fills the last Book of Kalhaṇa's Chronicle shows the importance of the town by frequent references to the military operations of which it was the object.[6] One of these passages proves that there was a bridge over the Vitastā here already in the twelfth century, just as there is one still.

Vijᵊbrōr has remained a town of some importance and still boasts of a considerable number of Brahmans, mostly Purohitas of the Tīrtha. The latter being conveniently situated on the pilgrims' way to Mārtāṇḍa

[1] See *Jonar.* (Bo. ed.), 762; for an earlier mention of this emblem see *ib.*, 127.

[2] *Rājat.* ii. 62.

[3] Compare *Rājat.* i. 38 note; also ii. 134. In the same way *Iśᵊbrōr* represents *Iśeśvara*; with the feminine *-brᵊr* for *bhaṭṭārikā* we have *Sundᵊbrᵊr* for *Saṁdhyādevī*, *Budᵊbrᵊr* for *Bheḍādevī*, etc.

The forms 'Bijbiāra,' 'Bijbihara,' 'Bijbehara,' etc., under which the local name figures in European books, are all based on a faulty Panjābī pronunciation. A fanciful etymology of the name which sees in the first part of the word *vidyā* 'learning' and in the second '*Vihāra*,' has found favour in the guide-books and may be mentioned here for curiosity's sake.

[4] See *Rājat.* i. 317.

[5] See *Rājat.* vii. 336 *sqq.*

[6] *Rājat.* viii. 746 *sqq.*, 969 *sqq.*, 1140, 1509 *sqq.*, etc.

and Amaranātha is much frequented even at the present day. The Māhātmyas of Vijayeśvara do not fail to name a considerable number of minor Tīrthas to be visited along with the main site now marked by the new temple above referred to. But apart from *Cakradhara* and *Gambhīrasaṁgama* I am unable to trace any of these in the older texts.

Turning to that portion of the Dachünpōr district which lies in the Lid^a^r Valley we have but few old localities to notice. The village of *Liv^a^r*, some ten miles to the north-west of Vijayeśvara, is the LEVĀRA of the Rājataraṅgiṇī, mentioned as an Agrahāra established by King Lava.[1] *Kular*, about four miles higher up the Valley, is identified by an old gloss with KURUHĀRA, said to have been an Agrahāra of Lava's son Kuśa.[2]

Close to Pah^a^lgām where the Lid^a^r Valley divides into two branches, lies the hamlet of Māmal. A small temple of the usual Kaśmīr style built by the side of a fine spring is visited by the pilgrims to Amaranātha. It is designated in the Māhātmya called Amareśvarakalpa as MAMMEŚVARA. It is in all probability identical with the shrine of this name mentioned in the Rājataraṅgiṇī.[3]

110. As we have already before noticed the several sacred sites of the Amaranātha pilgrimage, we may now turn back and descend to the left or eastern portion of the Lid^a^r Valley. It forms the modern Pargaṇa of *Khōvurpōr*. The latter name meaning 'left side' reproduces the earlier designation VĀMAPĀRŚVA, of the same significance, found in Jonarāja's Chronicle, the Lokaprakāśa and elsewhere.[4] In the upper portion of the Pargaṇa I am not able to identify any particular old locality, though ancient remains in the form of sculptures of some interest are found near several Nāgas of this tract, *e.g.*, at Loknt^i^pūr and Ṣāli (*Pāpaharaṇanāga*).

District of Vāmapārśva.

The large village of *Hut^a^mar* is undoubtedly an old site. Its modern name seems to identify it with the ŚAKTAMAṬHA which Kṣemendra names as one of the stations in the peregrinations of his heroine Kaṅkālī. The chief mosque of the place is built with the remains of a Hindu temple and preserves in its walls some sculptured fragments of remarkable beauty.[5]

1 See *Rājat*. i. 87.

2 *Rājat*. i. 88.

3 See viii. 3360.

4 *Jonar*. (Bo. ed.) 79,1232.

5 See *Samay*. ii. 43. The change of *Śākta* > *Hut^a^* is in accordance with the phonetic laws of Kaśmīrī; *mar* is the regular derivative of *maṭha*, see above, § 56. [When preparing my map, I had not noticed the local name of Kṣemendra's text; it is hence not shown on the map].

Shrine of Bhīmakeśava.

About one mile below Hut^a^mar and on the bank of a branch of the Lid^a^r, lies the hamlet of *Bum^a^zu*, which contains an ancient structure of considerable historical interest. The Ziārat of Bāba Bām^a^dīn Ṣāḥib is nothing but a well-preserved temple, converted, with a liberal use of plaster, into the supposed resting place of a Muhammadan saint. I have shown elsewhere that there is good reason to identify this shrine with the BHĪMAKEŚAVA temple which *Bhīma Sāhi*, king of Kābul, the maternal grandfather of Queen Diddā, is said to have erected during the rule of her husband Kṣemagupta (A.D. 950–958).[1]

The legendary of the Ziārat relates that the saint was originally a Hindu and bore before his conversion to Islām the name of *Bhīma Sādhī.* It is easy to recognize in this name an adaptation of Bhīma S'āhi. Also the name of the locality Bum^a^zu which the Mārtāṇḍa-māhātmya renders by *Bhīmadvīpa*, is clearly derived from the old name of the shrine. *Bhīma* is an abbreviation of *Bhīmakeśava* to which Kś. *zu*, 'island,' has been added with reference to the several islands formed here by the Lid^a^r immediately in front of the hamlet.

Kalhaṇa tells us a curious anecdote regarding the fate of Bhīma S'āhi's temple in King Harṣa's time who confiscated the great treasures, with which it was endowed.[2] Close to the present Ziārat of Bām^a^dīn Ṣāḥib is a small cave in the cliff containing a well-preserved little temple which is still used for Hindu worship. Another smaller shrine outside has been turned into the tomb of Rishī Ruknu-d-dīn Ṣāḥib.

Tīrtha of Mārtāṇḍa.

111. About one mile south of Bum^a^zu we reach the Tīrtha sacred to *Mārtāṇḍa* which has from early times to the present day enjoyed a prominent position among the sacred sites of Kaśmīr. It is marked by a magnificent spring traditionally represented as two, *Vimala* and *Kamala.* An ancient legend connects them with the birth of the sun-god MĀRTĀṆḌA.[3] The Tīrtha is visited at frequent intervals by crowds of pilgrims and is well-known also in India proper.

The popular name of the Tīrtha, *Bavan*, is derived from Skr. *bhavana*, '[sacred] habitation.' This somewhat general appellation seems to have come into use already at an early date, as S'rīvara employs it,[4] and is in itself an indication of the great popularity of the Tīrtha. A

[1] See *Rājat.* vi. 178 note. For an accurate description of the temple, see Bishop COWIE's paper, *J. A. S. B.*, 1866, pp. 100 *sq.*

[2] See *Rājat.* vii. 1081 *sqq.*

[3] Compare for a detailed account of the Tīrtha, *Rājat.* iv. 192 note. The Vimala Nāga is named by the *Nīlamata*, 963 ; *S'riv.* i. 377, etc.

[4] *S'riv.* i. 376, 387.

more specific designation is *Matsᵃbavan*, Skr. '*Matsyabhavana*'; this owes its origin to the abundance of sacred fish which swarm in the large basins filled by the spring.[1]

The ancient remains at the sacred spring itself are very scanty. All the more imposing are the ruins of the great temple which King Lalitāditya erected at a short distance in honour of the presiding deity of the Tīrtha.[2]

They are situated a little over a mile to the south-east of 'Bavan,' near the northern edge of the Uḍar which stretches towards Anatnāg. It can scarcely be doubted that the site was chosen with a view to the prominent position it assured to the great temple. Kalhaṇa duly praises "the wonderful shrine of *Mārtāṇḍa* with its massive walls of stone, within a lofty enclosure." Its ruins though much injured by the ravages of time and earthquakes, form still the most impressive specimen of ancient Kaśmīr architecture. They have been much admired by European travellers and often described. They are the earliest ruins in Kaśmīr the date of which is fixed with approximate accuracy.[3]

The name Mārtāṇḍa, in the form of *Mārtaṇḍ* or Maṭan, still attaches to the ruins though they have long ago ceased to be an object of religious interest. King Kalaśa had sought this great fane at the approach of death and expired at the feet of the sacred image (A.D. 1089). Harṣa, his son, respected this temple in the course of the ruthless confiscations to which he subjected the other rich shrines of the country. Subsequently in Kalhaṇa's time the great quadrangular courtyard of the temple with its lofty walls and colonnades was used as a fortification. The destruction of the sacred image is ascribed to Sikandar Butshikast.

Kalhaṇa distinctly mentions the town "swelling with grapes" which Lalitāditya founded near his temple; but of this no trace remains now. It is probable that at that time a canal supplied water from the Lidᵃr to the naturally arid plateau on which the temple stands. This canal seems to have been repaired by Zainu-l-'ābidīn whose irrigation works on the Mārtaṇḍ Uḍar are described at length by Jonarāja.[4] The

[1] Comp. *Āīn-i-Akb.*, ii. p. 358.

[2] See *Rājat.* iv. 192 and for details my note on the passage. For a description of the temple compare, *e.g.*, CUNNINGHAM, *J. A. S. B.*, 1848, pp. 258 *sqq.*; COLE, *Ancient Buildings*, pp. 19 *sqq.* FERGUSSON, *Ind. Architecture*, pp. 285 *sqq.*

[3] Lalitāditya's rule falls in the first half of the eighth century. Gen. Cunningham's assumption that the temple was built by the earlier King Raṇāditya, and only the enclosure by Lalitāditya, rests on a misinterpretation of the Rājatar. passages iv. 192 and iii. 462.

[4] See *Jonar.* 1245 *sqq.*

plateau has since become once more an arid waste though the course of the old canal can still be traced above Hut^{a}mar.

The town of Mārtāṇḍa had left its name to the small Pargaṇa of Maṭan which comprised this plateau as well as the villages situated along the foot of the hills further east. It is referred to as *Mārtāṇḍadeśa* by Jonarāja.[1] Abū-l-Fazl notices the large temple of *Maṭan* and the well or pit close by, which a Muhammadan legend represents as the place of captivity of the 'angels Hārūt and Mārūt.'[2]

SECTION VII.—SOUTHERN DISTRICTS OF MAḌAVARĀJYA.

Anantanāga.

112. At the foot of the western extremity of the Mārtāṇḍa plateau lies the town of Islāmābād or by its Hindu name *Anatnāg*. The latter is derived from the great spring of the ANANTANĀGA which issues at the southern end of the town. The Nāga, though no Tīrtha of particular repute, is mentioned in the Nīlamata, Haracaritacintāmaṇi and some Māhātmyas.[3] Of the town, however, I cannot find any old notice, and it is in all probability, as its Muhammadan name implies, a later foundation. To the north of the town and on the way to Bavan is the *Gautamanāga*, named by the Nīlamata and the Mārtāṇḍamāhātmya.

The modern name of the small district which comprised besides Anatnāg the tract immediately south and west of it, is *Anyech*. This is represented in some Māhātmyas of recent composition by *Anekākṣa*. This name occurs also once in Śrīvara's Chronicle, but the locality there meant is not certain.[4]

Tīrtha of Kapateśvara.

The valley of the Ār^{a}path or *Harṣapathā* which opens to the east of Islāmābād, forms the Pargaṇa of *Kuṭ^{a}hār*. This name is in all probability connected with that of the ancient Tīrtha of KAPAṬEŚVARA, situated on the southern side of the valley close to the village of *Kōṭhēr*.[5] The name of the latter is undoubtedly a derivative of *Kapaṭeśvara*, as the analogy of Jyeṭhĕr < Jyeṣṭheśvara, Triphar < Tripureśvara, etc., clearly shows.

1 *Jonar.* 1310.

2 See *Āīn-i-Akb.*, ii. p. 358. For the Muhammadan story, see also VIGNE i. p. 361.

3 See *Nīlamata*, 902; *Vitastā,-Trisaṁdhyāmāhātmya*, etc., also *Haracar.* x. 251 *sqq.* (Anantabhavana).

4 *Śrīv.* iii. 184.

5 See for a detailed account, *Rājat.* i. 32 note.

The place of pilgrimage is the sacred spring of *Pāpasūdana* ('sin-removing'), situated a short distance above Kōṭhēr. In it S'iva is believed to have shown himself in the disguise (*kapaṭa*) of pieces of wood floating on the water. The legend is related at length in the Nīlamata, and the author of the Haracaritacintāmaṇi devotes to it a separate canto which has now become the official Māhātmya of the Tīrtha.[1] The importance of the latter is shown by the fact that Kalhaṇa mentions it in his Introduction first among the sacred sites of Kaśmīr.

Before him already Albērūnī had heard of the story that pieces of wood sent by Mahādeva appear annually "in a pond called *Kūdaishahr* to the left of the source of the Vitastā, in the middle of the month of Vaiśākha."[2] *Kūdaishahr* (كوديشهر), is an easily explained corruption for كوديشور *i.e.*, **Kavadēśvar*, a prakritized form of the name. The map shows that the description of the position of the Tīrtha is accurate enough with reference to the Nīlanāga as the Vitastā's traditional source. The date named by Albērūnī is identical with that prescribed for the Kapaṭeśvara Yātrā.

The sacred spring rises in a large circular tank, enclosed by an ancient stone-wall with steps leading into the water. According to Kalhaṇa's account this enclosure was constructed about a century before his own time at the expense of the well-known King Bhoja of Mālava. The latter is said to have taken a vow to always wash his face in the water of the Pāpasūdana spring which he caused to be regularly supplied to him in jars of glass.[3] In my note on the passage I have shown that local tradition at Kōṭhēr still retains a recollection of this story though in a rather legendary form. A small temple which stands to the east of the tank, and some other remains probably belong to the period of Bhoja. Abū-l-Faẓl too knows, "in the village of Kōtihār, a deep spring surrounded by stone temples. When its water decreases an image of Mahādeva in sandal wood appears."

Śamāṅgāsā.

About four miles to the north-east of Kōṭhēr and on a branch of the Ārapath river lies the populous village of *Sāṅgas*, the ancient S'AMĀṄGĀSĀ.[4] The modern name can be traced back to S'amāṅgāsā through a course of regular phonetic conversion, one stage of which is preserved in the form *Svāṅgas* supplied by the old glossator of the Chronicle.[5] Some old

1 *Haracar.* xiv.
2 See *India*, ii. p. 181.
3 See *Rājat.* vii. 190 *sqq.*
4 See *Rājat.* i. 100; viii. 651.
5 Compare *Rājat.* i. 100 note and the analogy of *S'anāra* > *Sār*.

carved slabs built into the chief Ziārat of the place attest its antiquity. A short distance above S'āngas we come to another old place. It is the present village of *Vutᵊrus* which on the authority of the same glossator and the name itself we can safely identify with Kalhaṇa's *Utrāsa.*[1] Uccala and Sussala in their flight from Harṣa's court found a temporary refuge with the Ḍāmara who resided there.

Turning back to the west we find in the middle of the valley the village of *Khondur.* An old gloss enables us to identify it with the ancient SKANDAPURA mentioned by Kalhaṇa as an Agrahāra of King Gopāditya.[2] More important is *Achᵃbal,* a large village at the west foot of the ridge which lines the Kuṭᵃhār Pargaṇa from the south. It is mentioned in the Chronicle under the name of AKṢAVĀLA. The beautiful springs of the place have often been described since Abū-l-Faẓl's time, also by Bernier.[3] The park around them was a favourite camping ground of the Mughal court. The Nīlamata calls the spring *Akṣipālanāga.*

113. The Kuṭᵃhār Pargaṇa is adjoined on the south by the district of Bring which coincides with the valley of the Bring stream. Its old name cannot be traced; the Lokaprakāśa transcribes the modern designation by *Bhṛṅga.*

Pargaṇa of Bring.

At the western end of the Pargaṇa and about 5 miles to the south-west of Achᵃbal is the village of *Lōkᵃbavan* which an old gloss identifies with the LOKAPUṆYA of the Rājataraṅgiṇī.[4] The numerous passages which mention the place agree with this location. The name Lōkᵃbavan applies also to the fine Nāga adjoining the village, and this explains the second part of the present name *-bavan* (Skr. *bhavana*).[5] King Lalitāditya is said to have built a town here. A small garden-palace erected in Mughal times near the spring is partly constructed of old materials.

Ascending the Bring valley we come again to an old site at the large village of *Biḍᵃr.* It is certainly the BHEḌARA of Kalhaṇa who notices here a wealthy Agrahāra of King Bālāditya.[6] A ruined mound in the village and some old sculptures at the neighbouring Brahman village of Hāngalgūnd are the only ancient remains now above ground.

[1] Compare vii. 1254.

[2] See *Rājat.* i. 340.

[3] Compare *Rājat.* i. 338. In the translation of the *Āīn-i-Akb.* the name appears as 'Acch Dal', ii. p. 358; see BERNIER, *Travels,* p. 413.

[4] See *Rājat.* iv. 193 note.

[5] See above, § 111.

[6] *Rājat.* iii. 481.

Tīrtha of Ardhanārīśvara.

From Biḍ^a^r we may pay a passing visit to a small Tīrtha which though I cannot find it mentioned in any old text, may yet claim some antiquity. About 1½ miles to the south-east of Biḍ^a^r lies the village of Nāṛu in the low hills flanking the valley. It contains a small temple of ancient date which was restored forty years ago by a pious Dogrā official. It stands by the side of a small Nāga at which, according to the local Māhātmya I acquired from the resident Purohita, Śiva is worshipped as ARDHANĀRĪŚVARA, that is, in conjunction with his consort Pārvatī. Inside the temple is an ancient image of Viṣṇu with a short Sanskrit inscription said to have been found in a miraculous way at the restoration of the temple. About half a mile to the south-west is a sacred spring known as *Svedanāga* which seems to have risen originally within a large temple. The remains of the latter lie in shapeless heaps around the spring. The latter is still visited by pilgrims.

It appears to me likely that it is this spot which Abū-l-Faẓl wishes to describe in the following notice. After mentioning the Kuk^a^r Nāg and Sund^ə^brāṛ (see below) among the sacred places of Bring, he says: "At a little distance in the midst of a beautiful temple, seven fountains excite the wonderment of the beholder. In the summer-time self-immolating ascetics here heap up a large fire around themselves and with the utmost fortitude suffer themselves to be burned to death."[1] He then mentions a lofty hill containing an iron mine to the north of this spot. This can only be the hill above *Sōp*, on the northern side of the Valley and nearly opposite Nāṛu, from which iron is still extracted at the present time. There is no other Nāga within Bring to which Abū-l-Faẓl's description would apply so closely as to the Svedanāga.

The *Kuk^a^r Nāg*, mentioned by Abū-l-Faẓl for its good water inciting a healthy appetite, lies about a mile above Biḍ^a^r. It is a spring of very great volume, referred to in the Trisaṁdhyāmāhātmya as Kukkuṭeśvara.

Tīrtha of Trisaṁdhyā.

Bring contains one of the holiest of Kaśmīr Tīrthas in the sacred spring of the goddess SAṀDHYĀ, also called *Trisaṁdhyā*, the modern *Sund^ə^brāṛ*.[2] It is situated in a side valley opening to the south of the village of Devalgōm, circ. 75° 22′ long. 33° 32′ lat. The spring of Saṁdhyā derives its fame as well as its appellation from the fact that during uncertain periods in the early summer it flows, or is supposed to flow, intermittently, three times in the day and three times in the night. Owing to the analogy thus presented to the three-fold recitation of the Gāyatrī

[1] See *Āin-i-Akb.*, ii. p. 356.

[2] See *Rājat.* i. 33 note.

(Saṁdhyā), it is held sacred to the goddess Saṁdhyā. At the season indicated it is visited by a considerable concourse of people.

The small spring, which is usually dry for the greater part of the year, has owing to the curious phenomenon above indicated always enjoyed great fame as one of the 'wonders' of the valley. Kalhaṇa duly mentions it immediately after Kapaṭeśvara. The Nilamata too knows it. Abū-l-Faẓl describes it in detail, and Dr. Bernier made it a special point to visit this 'merveille de Cachemire.'[1] He has observed the phenomenon with his usual accuracy. The ingenious explanation he has recorded of it, shows how closely he had examined the topographical features of the little valley.

Close to the Trisaṁdhyā spring there is another Nāga, sacred to the Seven Ṛṣis, but not sharing the former's peculiar nature. There are no ancient remains in the neighbourhood deserving special notice.

Nīlanāga.

114. To the south of Bring lies the valley of the Sāṇdraṇ River which forms the Pargaṇa of Shāhābād. This name is of comparatively modern origin, as Abū-l-Faẓl still knows the tract as *Vēr.*[2] This designation still survives in the designation Vērnāg, *i.e.*, 'the Nāga of Vēr,' popularly given to the fine spring which we have already noticed as the habitation of the NĪLANĀGA and the traditional source of the Vitastā. Abū-l-Faẓl saw still to the east of it 'temples of stone.' These have now disappeared, their materials having been used probably for the construction of the fine stone-enclosure which Jahāngīr built round the spring. The deep blue colour of the water which collects in the spring-basin, may possibly account for the location of the Nīlanāga in this particular fountain. Kalhaṇa's reference to the "circular pond" from which the Vitastā rises, shows that the spring had also in ancient times an artificial enclosure similar to the present one.[3]

Vitastātra.

Reference has already been made to the sacred spring of *Vithavutur* only about one mile to the north-west of Vērnāg. The small village near by is mentioned by Kalhaṇa as a town under the name of VITASTĀTRA.[4] Aśoka is said to have erected there numerous Stūpas. Within the *Dharmāraṇya* Vihāra there stood a lofty Caitya built by him, but of these structures no remains can now be traced above ground. *Vitastātra* could never have been a large town as the ground is too confined. But some importance is assured to the site by the Bānahāl route which leads past

[1] Compare *Āin-i-Akb.*, ii. pp. 355 *sq.*; BERNIER, *Travels*, pp. 410 *sqq.*

[2] See *Āin-i-Akb.*, ii. pp. 361, 370.

[3] See *Rājat.* i. 28.

[4] See *Rājat.* i. 102 note.

it. This pass and its ancient name *Bāṇaśālā* we have already spoken of.[1]

Of other old localities PAÑCAHASTĀ, the present *Pānzath*, has already been referred to as the site of one of the traditional sources of the Vitastā. Kalhaṇa mentions it in connection with a Maṭha which S'ūravarman, Avantivarman's minister, built here.[2] A pretty valley which opens to the south of Pānzath, is now known by the name of its chief village *Ruzul*. The latter is mentioned by Jonarāja as RĀJOLAKA.[3] About three miles higher up this valley is the Nāga of VĀSUKI. It is mentioned in the Nīlamata and other old texts, but does not appear to have ever been an important Tīrtha.[4]

District of Devasarasa.

115. The Pargaṇa of *Div^asar* which adjoins Shāhābād-Vēr on the west, may be roughly described as comprising the tract of alluvial plain drained by the Veśau (Viśokā). By its ancient name of DEVASARASA it is often mentioned in the Rājataraṅgiṇī and other Chronicles.[5] Being extensively irrigated by canals drawn from the Viśokā it is very fertile. This accounts for the great part which the Ḍāmaras or feudal landholders of Devasarasa played during the weak reigns of the latter kings. No certain reference to a specific locality within this tract can be traced in our old texts. But it seems probable that *Pāreviśoka*, repeatedly named in Kalhaṇa's Chronicle, must be looked for within Devasarasa; the name means literally 'beyond the Viśokā.'[6]

The fertile valleys descending to the right bank of the Viśokā from that portion of the Pīr Pantsāl Range which lies between the Kōns^ar Nāg Peak and the Mohi Pass, form a small district of their own, known in recent times by the double name *Khur-Nār^avāv*. The first part of this name is taken from the large village of Khur situated about two miles from the Viśokā, circ. 74° 56′′ 45″ long. 33° 37′ lat. It is marked as 'Koori' on the larger Survey map. The name KHERĪ which we find used by Kalhaṇa and S'rīvara for the designation of the tract, is in all probability the older form of Khur.[7] It seems that in later Hindu times the administration of Kherī, perhaps as a royal allodial domain, formed a special charge. Kalhaṇa often refers to the *Kherīkārya* as a high state-office. The Sikhs and Dogrās who established Jāgīrs for members

1 Compare above, § 41.

2 See *Rājat.* v. 24.

3 See *Jonar.* (Bo. ed.), 90.

4 See *Nīlamata*, 901.

5 Compare *Rājat.* viii. 504 note.

6 Compare *Rājat.* iv. 5 note.

7 Compare regarding the identification of *Kherī*, *Rājat.* i. 335 note.

of the reigning family in Khur-Nārᵃvāv, may thus have followed an earlier arrangement.

Godharā-Hastiśālā.

The only localities in this little district that are known to us by their old names, are GODHARĀ and HASTIŚĀLĀ, the present *Gudar* and *Ast'hēl*.[1] These two villages are situated close together, on a branch of the Viśokā near the eastern limits of Khur-Nārᵃvāv. Kalhaṇa mentions the 'Agrahāra of Godharā-Hastiśālā' as a foundation of King Godhara. The old gloss which transcribes these local names by *Godhar-Astihil* enabled me to identify the places intended.

A small stream which falls into the Viśokā at Gudar is known by the name of Godāvarī and forms a Tīrtha of some repute among the Brahmans of the neighbouring districts. In the Māhātmya of the Tīrtha the site of the village is called *Godara*, and its name connected with the legend of the appearance of the *Godāvarī*. The local tradition heard by me on the spot tells of a town which King Gudar is supposed to have founded here. It is possible that the name of King Godhara, which we know Kalhaṇa took indirectly from Helārāja's 'List of Kings,' rests on no better foundation than this long-surviving local tradition.[2] There are no ancient remains traceable above ground at Gudar, and the locality is far too confined for a larger settlement.

The Naubandhana Tīrtha and the Kramasaras or Kōnsᵃr Nāg south of this district have already been previously noticed.

District of Karāla (Ardhavana).

116. To the north of Divᵃsar lies the considerable district of Āḍᵊvin extending from the western end of Khur-Nārᵃvāv to the lower course of the Viśokā. Its present name is derived from that of the large village of *Āḍᵊvin*, which lies on the left bank of the Viśokā, about three miles south-west of Vijᵊbrōr. In the form of *Ardhavana* this name is found already in a passage of Jonarāja's Chronicle, supplied by the new edition.[3] The ancient designation of the district, however, was KARĀLA. This is used by Kalhaṇa when speaking of the *Suvarṇamaṇikulyā*, the present Sunᵊmaṇⁱ Kul, which has already been referred to as irrigating part of Āḍᵊvin.[4]

In the lower portion of the district and on the left bank of the Viśokā, we have the ancient *Katīmuṣa*, the present village of *Kaimuh.*

[1] For details compare *Rājat.* i. 96 note.

[2] Regarding the unhistorical character of the royal names which Kalhaṇa inserted on Helārāja's authority, see *Rājat.* i. 86 note. They seem to be all of an eponymic character.

[3] See *Jonar.* (Bo. ed.) 1330.

[4] See *Rājat.* i. 97 note, and above, § 78.

The place is mentioned by Kalhaṇa as an Agrahāra founded by Tuñjina I., and contains some old remains built into its chief Ziārat.[1]

Part of Āḍᵊvin lies on an alluvial plateau. The northernmost portion of this Uḍar seems to have been formed into a separate Pargaṇa after Zainu-l-'ābidīn had constructed there extensive irrigation channels. From the small town of *Jainapurī* founded by him the new subdivision took the name of Zainᵊpōr or JAINAPURA.[2] At the east foot of the Zainᵊpōr Uḍar lies the village of *Vachⁱ* (map 'Woochi') which on the authority of an old gloss may be identified with VAŚCIKĀ (or Vaścika), an Agrahāra founded by Gopāditya.[3]

The Pargaṇa which joins on to Āḍᵊvin in the north-east, is now known as *Bōṭ* (map 'Batoo'). Its ancient name is unknown. The only old locality I can trace in it is the village of *Sidau*, 74° 51′ long. 33° 41′ lat., the ancient SIDDHAPATHA.[4] It has given its name to the route previously mentioned which leads to the Būdil and Kōnsᵃr Nāg Passes.

It is curious that we find no old mention whatever of *Śupiyạn*, a considerable town, which is now the trade emporium for the Pīr Panṭsāl route. In this character Śupiyạn has replaced the ancient Śūrapura or Hürᵊpōr, but the change must be a comparatively recent one.

Śūrapura.

ŚŪRAPURA which we have already noticed as the Kaśmīr terminus of the Pīr Panṭsāl route, lies some seven miles higher up on the Rembyārᵊ.[5] It received its name from the minister Śūravarman who built it in the time of Avantivarman and transferred to it the watch-station or 'Draṅga' of the route. The position of the latter is marked by a spot known as Ilāhī Darwāza, a short distance above Hürᵊpōr.[6] Śūrapura must have been a place of considerable extent as ruins of old habitations can be traced on the river banks for over two miles below the present Hürᵊpōr. It evidently retained its importance down to Akbar's time. For it is regularly mentioned by all the later Chronicles in connection with marches and traffic by the Pīr Panṭsāl route. The ancient remains of the place have been described by me in my notes on the latter.[7]

Our previous account of the old localities on the way to the Pīr

[1] Compare *Rājat.* ii. 55 note.

[2] See *Jonar.* (Bo. ed.) 1144 *sq.*; *Śrīv.* iii. 194; Fourth Chron. 360, 383.

[3] Compare *Rājat.* i. 343 note.

[4] See *Rājat.* viii. 557.

[5] Regarding Śūrapura and its old sites, compare Rājat. Note *D* (iii. 227); v. 39 note; also *J. A. S. B.*, 1895, pp. 381 *sqq.*

[6] See above, § 42.

[7] See *J. A. S. B.*, 1895, p. 385.

Pantsal Pass makes it unnecessary for us to proceed now further in this direction. Descending, then, by the Rembyār[2] we come on its left bank to the village of *Dēgām* situated about one and a half miles to the west of S'upiyan. It is the DEGRĀMA of the Rājataraṅgiṇī and the site of the *Kapālamocana* Tīrtha.[1] At the spring of the latter S'iva is supposed to have cleaned himself from the sin attaching to him after the cutting-off of Brahman's head (*kapāla*). The Tīrtha is old, because the Haracaritacintāmaṇi mentions it twice.[2] There are but few ancient remains at the sacred site, and the extant Māhātmya is evidently not of old date. It calls the village by the name of *Dvigrāma* and knows the modern S'upiyan by the name of *S'ūrpāyaṇa*.

117. The villages which lie at the foot of the pine-clad spurs descending into the valley west and north-west of S'upiyan, formed until recent times a small distinct Pargaṇa known as *Sūparsāmün*. Abū-l-Fazl mentions it (Sōparsāman), but I am not able to trace it in our older texts.

To the north of this tract and of Bōṭ extends the Pargaṇa of *S'ukru*.

Kalyāṇapura.

Its old name is unknown. Here at the foot of the hills, we have the ancient KALYĀṆAPURA, represented by the present village of *Kalampōr*, situated 74° 54′ long. 33° 48′ lat. It was founded by Kalyāṇadevī, a queen of Jayāpīḍa.[3] Being on the high road from the Pīr Pantsal Pass to S'rīnagar, it was repeatedly the scene of battles fought with invaders from that direction.[4]

At Kalyāṇapura there was in Kalhaṇa's time the splendid country-seat of a powerful Ḍāmara.[5] The large village of *Drābagām*, some three miles north of Kalampōr, is mentioned as DRĀBHAGRĀMA by S'rīvara, along with Kalyāṇapura, in the description of a battle which was fought between the two places.[6]

High up in the valley of the Birnai stream which debouches at Drābagām from the south-west, is the site of an ancient Tīrtha which though now completely forgotten must have ranked once amongst the most popular in Kaśmīr.

Tīrtha of Bheḍā.

In Kalhaṇa's introduction there is named, along with Trisaṁdhyā, Svayaṁbhū, S'āradā and other famous sites, "the hill of Bheḍa (*Bheḍa-giri*) sanctified by the Gangodbheda spring." There the goddess Sarasvatī

1 Compare *Rājat.* vii. 266.

2 See *Haracar.* x. 249; xiv. 111.

3 See *Rājat.* iv. 483 note.

4 See *Rājat.* viii. 1261 *sqq.*; *S'rīv.* iv. 466 *sqq.*

5 See *Rājat.* viii. 2348 *sqq.*

6 See *S'rīv.* iv. 467. For a miniature temple extant at Drābagām, compare Bishop Cowie's note, *J. A. S. B.*, 1866, p. 117.

was believed to have shown herself as a swan in a lake situated on the summit of the hill. This Tīrtha has long ago ceased to be visited by pilgrims, and all recollection regarding its position has been lost to Paṇḍit tradition. Fortunately the old Māhātmya of the sacred lake has survived in a single copy. With the help of some indications furnished by it and an opportune notice of Abū-l-Faẓl, I was able to make a search for this ancient Tīrtha which ultimately led to its discovery at the present Buḍ^ᵊbrā̤r in the valley above indicated.

For the detailed evidence regarding this identification I must refer to my note on Kalhaṇa's passage.[1] Here a brief reference to the topographical peculiarity of the site will suffice. The Māhātmya describes the lake sacred to the goddess Sarasvatī-*Bheḍā* as situated on the summit of a hill, and *Gaṅgodbheda* as a spring flowing from it. At *Buḍ^ᵊbrā̤r*, a small Gujar hamlet, which occupies the position marked by BHEḌAGIRI on the map, I found an ancient stone-lined tank fed by a spring on the top of a small hillock. The latter rises about seventy feet above the level of the narrow valley in which it is situated. From the side of the hillock issues a spring which is the natural outflow of the tank and exactly corresponds to the description given of Gaṅgodbheda. The name *Buḍ^ᵊbrā̤r* is the direct derivative of *Bheḍādevī*, 'the goddess Bheḍā,' the popular designation of the Tīrtha found in the Māhātmya; *-brā̤r* < Skr. *bhaṭṭārikā* is the equivalent of *devī* as in Sund^ᵊbrā̤r, Har^ᵊbrā̤r and other names.

The water of the spring which fills the tank, is said to keep warm in the winter. This accounts evidently for the story told in the Māhātmya that snow never lies on the ground around the sacred tank. Also Abū-l-Faẓl's notice of the Tīrtha mentions this particular feature: "Near Shukroh (S'ukru) is a low hill on the summit of which is a fountain which flows throughout the year and is a place of pilgrimage for the devout. The snow does not fall on this spur."[2]

Also S'rīvara helped to guide my search in the direction of Buḍ^ᵊbrā̤r and to confirm the subsequent identification. He mentions the route through *Bheḍāvana*, 'the forest of Bheḍā,' as the line of retreat taken by the troops who after their defeat in the above-mentioned engagement near Drāb^ᵃgām were fleeing towards Rajaurī.[3] A glance at the map shows that the thickly wooded valley of Buḍ^ᵊbrā̤r is meant here. For a force beaten near Drāb^ᵃgām it affords the most direct and safest retreat to the Pīr Pantsāl Pass and hence to Rajaurī. The route leading through the valley joins the 'Imperial Road' at Dubji and is shown on the map.

1 See *Rājat.* i. 35, Note *A.*

2 See *Āīn-i-Akb.*, ii. p. 362.

3 Compare *S'rīv.* iv. 496 and the preceding narrative.

Returning once more to the plain we have yet to notice two other old localities of S'ukru. *Bilau* (map 'Belloh') about four miles north-east of Drāb^{a}gām is probably the 'village of BILĀVA' once mentioned by Kalhaṇa.[1] Within a mile of it lies the village *Sun^{a}sāmil* which we may safely identify with the SUVARṆASĀNŪRA of the Rājataraṅgiṇī, in view of the resemblance of the names and the repeated mention of the latter place together with Kalyāṇapura.[2]

Districts of Sāvur and Chrāṭh.

118. East of S'ukru towards the Vitastā stretches the Pargaṇa of *Sāvur* (map 'Showra'). The earlier form of its name cannot be traced. Its northern part is formed by the alluvial plateau known as the *Naunagar Uḍar*. This latter is twice referred to as NAUNAGARA in Kalhaṇa's Chronicle.[3] The village of *Pāyer* which lies at the foot of the Uḍar at its north-western end contains a well-preserved little temple often described by European travellers.[4] Nothing is known regarding the original name of the locality.

To the north of S'ukru we have the district of *Chrāṭh* (shown by name on the larger survey map). It extends from the hills above Rāmuh in a north-easterly direction to the left bank of the Vitastā. Its old name is restored in Paṇḍit Sāhibrām's Tīrthasaṁgraha as * *S'rīrāṣṭra*, but I do not know on what authority. *Rāmuh*, first correctly identified by Prof. Bühler with Kalhaṇa's RĀMUṢA,[5] is a considerable village on the high road from S'upiyan to S'rinagar. It is first mentioned as an Agrahāra, founded by a queen of Tuñjina I. A small spring at the northern end of the village, called *Dhananāga*, is visited as a Tīrtha and contains some fragments of ancient sculptures. The temple erected by the Brahman family of the Dars which now holds Rāmuh as a Jāgīr, does not seem to mark an old site.

A short distance to the north of Rāmuh rises an alluvial plateau which is crossed by the road to S'rinagar. It is known as *Gūs Uḍar*, from the village of *Gūs* situated at its eastern foot, about two miles from Rāmuh. The place is mentioned as GUSIKĀ in S'rīvara's

1 See *Rājat.* vii. 1016.

2 See *Rājat.* vii. 1519 note; *sun^{a}* 'gold' is the regular Kś. derivative of Skr. *suvarṇa*.

3 See *Rājat.* vii. 358.

4 Compare, *e.g.*, CUNNINGHAM, *J. A. S. B.*, 1848, pp. 254 *sqq.* I am unable to explain why the place figures in all European accounts as Pâyech, Pā Yech, etc. VIGNE, ii. 41, first uses this form which is locally quite unknown, and does not fail to explain it by one of his naïve etymologies.

5 *Rājat.* ii. 55; *Report*, p. 7. Medial *ṣ* becomes in Kś. regularly *h*; comp. *Katīmuṣa* > *Kaimuh*, *Khonamuṣa* > *Khun^{a}moh*, etc.

Chronicle which also knows the plateau by the name *Gusikoḍḍāra*.[1] At the other end of Chrāṭh towards the Vitastā lies the large village of *Ratanpōr*, 75° 1′ long. 33° 55′ lat., which in all probability represents the RATNĀPURA of the Rājataraṅgiṇī.[2] The latter was founded in Kalhaṇa's time by Queen Ratnādevī who also constructed there a fine Maṭha.

With Chrāṭh may be mentioned two localities on the left bank of the Vitastā though in recent times they were counted with the riveraine Pargaṇa of Sāiru-l-Mawāẓiʻ Bālā. *Gūrⁱpūr*, a small village opposite to the foot of Mount Vastᵃrvan, is identified by an old gloss with GOPĀLAPURA which, according to Kalhaṇa, was founded by Queen Sugandhā (A.D. 904-6).[3]

Lower down on the river is the large village Kākᵃpōr which forms as it were the riverside station or port for S'upiyaṇ. A note from the hand of Paṇḍit Rājānaka Ratnakaṇṭha who wrote about the middle of the 17th century the Codex Archetypus of the Rājataraṅgiṇī, identifies UTPALAPURA with Kākᵃpōr.[4] Utpalapura was founded by Utpala, an uncle of King Cippaṭa-Jayāpīḍa, in the early part of the 9th century. If this identification is correct, one of the ruined temples extant at Kākᵃpōr and noticed already by Gen. Cunningham, may be the shrine of Viṣṇu *Utpalasvāmin* mentioned by Kalhaṇa in connection with the foundation of Utpalapura. Jonarāja also knows the latter place and records a late restoration of its Viṣṇu temple.[5]

Districts of Nāgām and Yech.

119. North of Chrāṭh we come to the district of Nāgām which is one of considerable extent. Its old name NĀGRĀMA is often mentioned in the later Chronicles.[6] The only old locality which I can trace in it, is the village of *Ārⁱgōm*, situated 74° 45′ long. 33° 56′ lat. It is the HĀḌIGRĀMA of Kalhaṇa, mentioned as an Agrahāra of Gopāditya and as the scene of several fights in the Chronicler's own time.[7]

[1] *Śrīv.* iv. 532, 465, 592 *sqq.*; *-uḍḍāra* is the Skr. original of the Kś. term *uḍar*, see *Rājat.* note viii. 1427.

[2] See *Rājat.* viii. 2434.

[3] See *Rājat.* v. 244 note.

[4] See *Rājat.* iv. 695 note. The learned copyist's note is in a copy of the *Kṣetrapālapaddhati* seen by me in 1895 in the possession of a Kaśmīr Brahman resident at Lahore.

[5] See *Jonar.* (Bo. ed.) 111 *sqq.*, 369, 1142.

[6] Compare *Jonar.* (Bo. ed.) 661; *Śrīv.* ii. 10; iii. 24, 430; iv. 340; Fourth Chron. 258, etc.

[7] See *Rājat.* i. 340 note. The old glossator on this passage renders Hāḍigrāma correctly by *Āḍegrām*.

Some remains of old buildings are reported to exist at this place; I have not seen it myself.

About five miles due south of Ār[i]gōm we find a small lake known as Nil[a]nāg, situated in a valley between low spurs descending from the Pīr Pantsāl Range. It appears to have been formed by an old landslip which blocked a narrow defile in the Valley. This lake does not appear ever to have enjoyed any particular sanctity. But Abū-l-Fazl by some curious misapprehension transfers to it the legends of the famous Nīlanāga (at Vērnāg). He adds to them what appears like a garbled version of the story of the city submerged in the Mahāpadma or Volur lake.[1]

Nāgām is adjoined on the north by the Pargaṇa of *Yech* which extends to the immediate vicinity of S'rīnagar. Its old name is given as IKṢIKĀ by S'rīvara.[2] In the centre of the tract lies an arid alluvial plateau known as *Dām[a]dar Uḍar*, where an ancient popular tradition surviving to the present day has localized the legend of King *Dāmodara.*

Dāmodara's Uḍar.

The story as related by Kalhaṇa, represents the king as having built a town on the Uḍar which latter was called after him DĀMODARASŪDA.[3] In order to bring water to it he had a great dam, called GUDDASETU, constructed by supernatural agency. Once hungry Brahmans asked the king for food, just as he was going to bathe. The king refused to comply with their request until he had taken his bath. The Brahmans thereupon cursed him so that he became a snake. Ever since the unfortunate king is seen by people in the form of a snake "rushing about in search of water far and wide on the Dāmodara-Sūda." He is not to be delivered from the curse until he hears the *whole* Rāmāyaṇa recited to him in a single day, a task which renders his release hopeless.

The modern name Dām[a]dar Uḍar is the exact equivalent of Kalhaṇa's *Dāmodara-Sūda*, the old Skr. term *sūda* meaning a 'place where the soil is barren.' The local name *Guddasetu* still lives in that of the small village *Guḍ[a]suth* situated at the south foot of the Uḍar. Just at this point the latter shows its greatest relative elevation and falls off towards the valley with a steep bank over one hundred feet high. The wall-like appearance of this bank probably suggested the story of an embankment which was to bring water to the plateau. In view of the configuration of the ground no serious attempt at irrigation by means of an aqueduct could ever have been made in this locality.

1 Compare *Āīn-i-Akb.*, ii. p. 363. It is possible that of the two Nīlanāgas which the Nīlamata, 903, mentions besides the famous spring of that name, one was located in the Nāgām lake.

2 *S'rīv.* iii. 25.

3 Compare for detailed references, *Rājat.* i. 156 note.

The Uḍar stretches in a north-westerly direction, for about six miles from the village of Vahᵊtōr, with a breadth varying from two to three miles. It bears only scanty crops of Indian corn in patches. Being entirely devoid of water, it is a dry and barren waste, a haunt of jackals as in the days when King Kṣemagupta hunted over the '*Dāmodarāraṇya*.'[1] The main features of the legend regarding it are well known to popular tradition throughout Kaśmīr. The inhabitants of the neighbouring villages also point to a spot on the Uḍar known as *Satᵊrās Tēng*, as the site of Dāmodara's palace. A spring called *Dāmodar-Nāg* in the village of Lālgām, is believed to have served for the king's ablutions.

To Yech belongs also the small village of *Somarᵊbug* on the left bank of the Vitastā which according to the note of the old glossator A_2 marks the site of the temple of Viṣṇu Samarasvāmin mentioned by Kalhaṇa.[2] Another old locality in Yech is probably marked by the hamlet of *Halᵊthal* to which Abū-l-Fazl refers. It is not shown on the Survey map, and I have not been able to ascertain its exact position. Halᵊthal is evidently a derivative of Śālāsthala, the name given by Kalhaṇa to a locality where a fight took place in the time of King Ananta.[3] Abū-l-Fazl mentions 'Halthal' for its quivering tree. "If the smallest branch of it be shaken, the whole tree becomes tremulous."

Section VIII.—Southern Districts of Kramarājya.

Districts of Dūnts, Bīru, Māñchᵊhōm.

120.—To the west of Yech and reaching close up to the capital, lies the Pargaṇa now called *Dūnts* (map 'Doonsoo'). Its ancient name is uncertain; possibly it is intended by the name *Dvāviṁśati* in the Lokaprakāśa's list of 'Viṣayas.' In Abū-l-Fazl's table of Pargaṇas Dūnts ('Dūnsū') is already counted with Kamrāz. An old locality in it is *Sīlᶦpōr*, a large village situated circ. 74° 45′ long. 34° 1′ lat. (map 'Shalipoor'). We may safely recognize in it the Selyapura of the Rājataraṅgiṇī which is referred to as a place on the direct route from the Tōsᵊmaidān Pass and the Kārkotadraṅga to Śrīnagar.[4]

Hukhᵊlitᵊr (map 'Haklitri') can safely be identified, in view of the name and the evidence of an old gloss, with Śuskaletra mentioned in the

[1] Compare *Rājat.* vi. 183.

[2] See note v. 25.—The ending *-bug* is not rare in Kaśmīr village names. According to Paṇḍit tradition, it is derived from Skr. *bhoga* in the sense of 'property granted for the usufruct [of a temple].'

[3] See note vii. 159; *Āīn-i-Akb.*, ii. p. 363.

[4] See *Rājat.* vii. 494 note; viii. 200.

Rājataraṅgiṇi as a place where Stūpas were erected by King Aśoka.[1] I have not visited the village myself and am hence unable to say whether there are any remains in the vicinity which could be attributed to Stūpas. Kalhaṇa locates at S'uṣkaletra the fierce battle in which King Jayāpīḍa recovered his kingdom.

West of Dūṇṭs and towards the mountains of the Pīr Pantsāl lies the Pargaṇa of *Bīru*. Its old designation BAHURŪPA is derived from the spring of that name which is situated at the present village of Bīru, 74° 39′ long. 34° 1′ lat., and is already referred to as a Tīrtha in the Nīlamata.[2] Abū-l-Faẓl knows the village and spring by an intermediate form of the name, *Bīruwā*, and mentions the miraculous power of the spring to heal leprosy.[3] Close to the village of Bīru is *Sunapāh* in which we may, with an old glossator of the Rājataraṅgiṇī, recognize SUVARṆAPĀRŚVA, an Agrahāra of Lalitāditya.[4]

About four miles to the south-west of Bīru we reach *Khāg*, a considerable place. It is undoubtedly the KHĀGI or KHĀGIKĀ mentioned by Kalhaṇa as an Agrahāra both of King Khagendra and of Gopāditya.[5]

Some miles north of Khāg an isolated spur known as *Pōṣkar* projects into the level plain from the slopes of the Pīr Pantsāl Range. At its eastern foot is the *Puṣkaranāga*, referred to as a Tīrtha in the Nīlamata and several older Māhātmyas, and still the object of a regular pilgrimage.[6] Of the route which leads down into Bīru from the Tōsa-maidān Pass, and of KĀRKOṬADRAṄGA, the watch station on it, we have already spoken above.

Bīru and Dūnts are adjoined on the north by the Pargaṇa of *Māñchahōm* which extends eastwards as far as the Vitastā. It is probably intended by the name of *Mākṣāśrama* found in a single passage of S'rīvara and in the Lokaprakāśa.[7] The village of *Ratasun*, situated 74° 38′ long. 34° 4′ lat., is probably, as indicated by an old gloss, the

[1] Compare *Rājat.* notes i. 102; iv. 473; Kś. *Hukhalitar* is the direct phonetic derivative of the Skr. form.

[2] See *Nīlamata*, 948, 1180, 1341 *sq*. The name Bahurūpa is given to the tract by *Jonar.* (Bo. ed.) 286, 840; *S'rīv.* ii. 19, iii. 159; iv. 620, and ought to have been shown on the map.

[3] *Āīn-i-Akb.*, ii. p. 363.

[4] See *Rājat.* iv. 673.

[5] Compare *Rājat.* i. 90, 340.

[6] See *Nīlamata*, 1021, 1347. There were several other Puṣkara Tīrthas in Kaśmīr. One was connected with the Sureśvarī pilgrimage and probably situated in Phākh; see *Sarvāv.* v. 56 *sqq*.

[7] See *S'rīv.* iv. 351.

ARIṢṬOTSĀDANA of the Rājataraṅgiṇī.[1] From this form the modern name of the village can be derived without difficulty. A temple is said to have been erected there by a queen of Bālāditya.

On the Vitastā some six miles below S'rinagar is the small village of *Malur* which on the authority of Rājānaka Ratnakaṇṭha may be identified with MALHĀṆAPURA, a foundation of King Jayāpīḍa.[2] *Zainəkōṭh*, situated near marshy ground about two miles south-east of it, preserves the name of Zainu-l-'ābidīn, its founder, and is mentioned as JAINAKOṬṬA by Jonarāja.[3]

Parihāsapura.

121. The Pargaṇa of *Parəspōr* (map 'Paraspoor') which lies next to Māñchəhōm, is one of small extent, but contains a site of great historical interest. It has received its name from the ancient PARIHĀSAPURA, which King Lalitāditya had built as his capital.[4] The identity of the name *Parəspōr* and *Parihāsapura* is evident on phonetic grounds and was well-known to the authors of the Persian abstracts of the Rājataraṅgiṇī. Yet curiously enough the site of Parihāsapura had remained unidentified until I visited the spot in 1892 and traced the ruins of Lalitāditya's great structures as described by Kalhaṇa, on the plateau known as the 'Parəspōr Uḍar.'

This plateau rises south-east of Shādipūr, between the marshes of Panzinōr on the east and those of Hārətraṭh on the west. Its length is about two miles from north to south, and its greatest breadth not much over a mile. On the north this plateau is separated from the higher ground of Trigām by the Badrihēl Nāla which, as I have shown above, represents the old bed of the Vitastā previous to Suyya's regulation.[5] On the other sides it is surrounded by marshes which for a great part of the year are still accessible by boats. Its general elevation is about one hundred feet.

A broad ravine which cuts into the plateau from the south, and in which the village of *Divar* (map 'Diaraṇ') nestles, divides it into two parts. On the south-western portion are the ruins of two large temples, much decayed, but still showing dimensions which considerably exceed those of the great temple of Mārtāṇḍa. On that part of the Uḍar which lies to the north-east and towards the Badrihēl Nāla, there is a whole

1 *Rājat.* iii. 482.

2 Compare *Rājat.* iv. 484.

3 *Jonar.* (Bo. ed.), 1248.

4 For a detailed account of the site of Parihāsapura and its identification, compare Note *F*, Rājat. iv. 194–204. The large scale map added to Note *I* shows the position of the several ruins in detail.

5 See § 70.

series of ruined structures. Among these three great buildings attract attention. As an indication of their size it may be mentioned that the ruined mound which marks the central shrine of the northernmost building has a diameter of nearly 300 feet. Though it consists now only of a confused heap of massive blocks it still rises to a height of over 30 feet from the ground. The enclosing quadrangle which can also be traced, measures about 410 feet square. At some distance from this group of ruins there is another smaller one at the south-eastern extremity of the plateau now known as *Gurdan*.

I must refer for a more detailed account of these ruins and their relative position to the Note on Parihāsapura, *F*, appended to my translation of the Chronicle. Here it will suffice to point out that the four great temples of Viṣṇu Parihāsakeśava, Muktākeśava, Mahāvarāha, Govardhanadhara as well as the *Rājavihāra* with its colossal image of Buddha, which Kalhaṇa mentions as Lalitāditya's chief structures at Parihāsapura, must all be looked for among these ruins. Their extremely decayed condition makes an attempt at detailed identification difficult.

Still less we can hope to trace now the position of the numerous shrines, Liṅgas, Vihāras, etc., which are mentioned by Kalhaṇa as having been erected at the king's favourite residence by his queens and court.[1] One of the great ruins of the northern group shows features characteristic of a Vihāra and may be the Rājavihāra. Some clue is also furnished by the name *Gurdan* attaching to the isolated ruins above mentioned. Gurdan is the common Kaśmīrī form of the name *Govardhana*, and hence points to these ruins being the remains of the temple called GOVARDHANADHARA.

History of Parihāsapura.

The state of utter destruction in which the ruins of Parihāsapura, are now found, is easily accounted for by the history of the site. Parihāsapura ceased to be the royal residence already under the son of its founder. The Chronicle distinctly records of King Vajrāditya that he withdrew the various foundations which his father Lalitāditya had made there.[2] When a century later King Avantivarman effected his great regulation of the Vitastā, the bed of the river and its junction with the Sindhu was diverted to Shạd[1]pūr, nearly three miles away from Parihāsapura.[3] This change must have still more seriously diminished the importance of the latter. The ruinous condition into which Parihāsapura must have fallen only one and a half centuries after its foundation,

[1] See *Rājat.* iv. 207–216.

[2] *Rājat.* iv. 395.

[3] See above, §§ 70, 71.

is shown by the fact that Śaṁkaravarman (A.D. 883–902) carried away from it materials for the construction of his new town and temples at *Puttana* (Paṭan).[1]

Some of the shrines of Parihāsapura, however, survived to a later period. Thus we find the colossal copper statue of Buddha at the Rājavihāra mentioned as one of the few sacred images which escaped being melted down in the reign of King Harṣa (A.D. 1089–1101). Also a great religious festival established at Parihāsapura by Lalitāditya seems to have been held still in Kalhaṇa's time.[2] In the rising which led to the downfall of Harṣa, Pārihāsapura was occupied by the pretender Uccala.[3] The steep slopes of the plateau and the marshes around made it a position of military value. When Uccala had suffered a defeat some of the routed rebels threw themselves into the Rājavihāra, which was subsequently burned down. After this, Harṣa carried away and broke up the famous silver statue of Viṣṇu which had been placed by Lalitāditya in the temple of Parihāsakeśava.

The final destruction of the temples is attributed by Abū-l-Faẓl and the Muhammadan chroniclers to Sikandar Būtshikast. The former records the tradition that after the destruction of the lofty temple of 'Paraspūr' a copper tablet with a Sanskrit inscription was discovered which predicted its destruction 'after the lapse of eleven hundred years' by one Sikandar.[4] This prophecy *post factum* shows that its author, whoever he may have been, was rather weak in historical chronology. Parihāsapura had been founded only about six and a half centuries before Sikandar Butshikast's time.[5] At the beginning of the eighteenth century the ruins seem still to have been in a somewhat better condition than now. Both Muḥammad 'Aẓim and Nārāyaṇ Kaul mention them and speak particularly of fragments of a large monolithic column. Tradition seems to have connected these fragments with the pillar of Garuḍa which Kalhaṇa mentions as having been set up by Lalitāditya.[6] The huge square block of stone still visible on the top of the northernmost mound is perhaps one of them.

1 See *Rājat.* v. 161.

2 See *Rājat.* iv. 242 *sq.* For the temple of Rāmasvāmin which was seen empty in Kalhaṇa's time, compare iv. 275, 334 *sq.*

3 *Rājat.* vii. 1326 *sqq.*

4 See *Āīn-i-Akb.*, i. p. 364.

5 Exactly the same tradition is now current among the Purohitas of Vijᵊbrōr about the destruction of the Vijayeśvara image. This alleged inscription is said to have run: *Ekādaśaśatam varṣam Sikendaramahābala* । *bismilla iti mantreṇa naśyante Vijayeśvarāḥ* ॥ The curious Sanskrit of this doggrel is an indication that its author may probably have belonged himself to the noble guild of the Bāchbaṭṭas.

6 Compare Wilson, *Essay*, p. 50; also footnote 16 to Note *F*, on Parihāsapura.

The ruins of Parihāsapura have served ever since S'aṁkaravarman's time as quarries for stone-material. Their position near to navigable water-channels made them particularly convenient for this purpose. Since 1892 when I first saw the ruins, till 1896 many large stone-blocks have found their way as road metal into the new Tonga Road which passes the plateau on the south. On my report steps were subsequently taken by the Darbār to stop this vandalism and prevent its recurrence.

Trigrāmī; Phalapura.

122. We have already above when describing the old bed of the Vitastā near Parihāsapura, had occasion to refer to the village of *Trigām*, the ancient TRIGRĀMĪ. It lies about one and a half miles to the north-east of the Parᵊspōr ruins. The place is mentioned already in Lalitāditya's time in connection with an affray which took place at Parihāsapura.[1] The *Bōnᵃsar* (* Bhavanasaras ?) lake to the west of Trigām is visited as a subsidiary Tīrtha on the Kapālamocana pilgrimage. The ruined temple south of Trigām which I believe may be identified with the VAINYASVĀMIN temple, has already been mentioned in our remarks on the site of the old confluence.

A ruined site which lies opposite to Vainyasvāmin on the western side of the Trigām swamp, may for reasons set forth elsewhere be taken for the old *Viṣṇusvāmin* temple.[2] This is named by Kalhaṇa as having been situated opposite to the Vainyasvāmin shrine on the other side of the old confluence. The passage of the Chronicle describes the temple of Viṣṇusvāmin as belonging already to Phalapura, while Vainyasvāmin was counted with Parihāsapura.

From this and some other indications I conclude that PHALAPURA was the designation of a small territorial subdivision which probably extended along the present left bank of the Vitastā near Shạdⁱpūr.[3] The site at which I locate the Viṣṇusvāmin temple, was included in recent times in the riveraine Pargaṇa of Sāiru-l-mawāẓiʻ Pāyīn (map 'Salimozapaieen'). This, we know from Abū-l-Faẓl, was created already before Akbar's time and probably absorbed Phalapura as well as other minor tracts.[4] Phalapura had received its designation from a locality of that name which Lalitāditya had founded apparently before Parihāsapura,[5] just as the latter gave its name to the Parᵊspōr Pargaṇa.

[1] See *Rājat.* iv. 323 *sqq.*

[2] Compare *Rājat.* Note *I*, v. 97–100, § 12.

[3] See *Rājat.* Note *I*, § 13.

[4] See *Āīn-i-Akb.*, ii. p. 367.

[5] Compare *Rājat.* iv. 184, 673.

Jayapura.

Descending by the left bank of the Vitastā for about five miles below Shādipūr, we approach the site of king Jayāpīḍa's capital, the ancient JAYAPURA.[1] It is marked by the present village of *Andᵊrkōṭh*. This consists of two distinct parts. One lies on an island in the marshes opposite Sạmbal and the other facing the former on the strip of land which separates these marshes from the Vitastā. On the island there are conspicuous remains of ancient temples which have been first examined and described by Prof. Bühler.[2] They are attributed by the local tradition to King 'Jayāpiḍ.' The identity of Andᵊrkōṭh with King Jayāpīḍa's town is also well-known to the S'rīnagar Paṇḍits. As S'rīvara still uses the term Jayapura or Jayāpīḍapura for the designation of the present Andᵊrkōṭh, we can easily understand the survival of the tradition.

Kalhaṇa's description of the town indicates clearly the situation of the latter and also accounts for its modern name. Jayāpīḍa according to this notice had the castle (*koṭṭa*) of Jayapura built in the middle of a lake, after having the ground required for it filled up, as the legend asserts, by the help of Rākṣasas. There he constructed a large Vihāra with Buddha images, a temple of Keśava (Viṣṇu), and several other shrines; other sacred structures were erected by his ministers. Besides Jayapura the king built on ground recovered from the lake another place, called DVĀRAVATĪ, in imitation of Kṛṣṇa's famous town by the sea-shore. Kalhaṇa notes that in his own time Jayapura was popularly designated as the 'Inner Castle' (*ābhyantara koṭṭa*) while Dvāravatī was known as the 'Outer Castle' (*bāhya koṭṭa*).

The present name ANDᵊRKŌṬH (from Skr. **Antarakoṭṭa*) is the direct derivative of this popular designation of Jayapura. It has in the course of time been extended also to the site on which originally Dvāravatī stood. In my note on the passage I have shown that Jayapura must be identified with the island portion of Andᵊrkōṭh, while the remains in that part of the village which lies on the lake shore opposite, belong to Dvāravatī. These remains are far less extensive than those on the island. This is in full agreement with the fact that Kalhaṇa men-

1 For a detailed note on the position of the twin towns Jayapura-Dvāravatī, see *Rājat.* iv. 501-511. For a map showing the site on a larger scale refer to Note *I*, v. 97-100.

2 See *Report*, pp. 13 *sqq.* where the topography and ruins of Andᵊrkōṭh are described in detail. General Cunningham had already heard of the identity of Andᵊrkōṭh with Jayāpīḍa's town but he does not seem to have visited the place; *Anc. Geogr.*, p. 101. Owing to the erroneous location of Parihāsapura on the *right* bank of the Vitastā opposite Sạmbal, there is a good deal of confusion in his notes on the two capitals.

tions great religious buildings only in Jayapura and not in Dvāravatī. The latter is, indeed, referred to only in connection with the foundation of Jayapura and does not appear ever to have been a place of importance. We can thus understand why its original name Dvāravatī and its subsequent designation 'Outer Castle' have both completely disappeared. The distance between the island and the opposite lake shore being only about four hundred yards at the narrowest point, the name of the far more important 'Inner Castle' was naturally extended also to this outlying suburb.

The term *koṭṭa* which Kalhaṇa repeatedly applies to Jayapura, and which is contained also in its popular designation, is justified by its position surrounded on all sides by water.[1] The limited extent of the island precludes the belief of Jayapura ever having been a populous place. But it retained a certain importance far longer than Parihāsapura and served occasionally as a royal residence even in late times. Queen Koṭā, the last of the Hindu rulers of Kaśmīr, retired to Jayapura, and there she was murdered by her husband, the adventurer Shāhmīr (A.D. 1339).[2] Zainu-l-'ābidīn restored the town which had fallen into decay and built there a new palace on the lake-shore.[3]

We have no distinct information as to the old course which the Vitastā followed in the neighbourhood of Jayapura previous to Avantivarman's regulation. If our views on the subject as above indicated are right, the main channel of the river must then have passed through the marshes west of Jayapura. Notwithstanding the change subsequently effected, Jayāpīḍa's town did not lose its convenient access to river communication. The great canal known as *Nōr* which, as we saw, is in reality nothing but an old river-bed, runs but a short distance to the south-west of Andᵊrkōṭh. A branch of it which is much used by boats even at the present day though not shown on the map, passes still actually along the old Ghāṭs on the south side of the Andᵊrkōṭh island. It seems probable that Jayapura owed its preservation from the fate of Parihāsapura in part at least to the retention of a convenient waterway.

In Abū-l-Faẓl's time Andᵊrkōṭh gave its name to a separate small Pargaṇa.

District of Bhāṅgila; Paṭṭana.

123. From the marshy tracts south of the Volur which we have approached at Andᵊrkōṭh, we may return once more to Parᵊspōr. Crossing the swamps formed west of the Parᵊspōr plateau by the

[1] *Rājat.* iv. 506, 512; vii. 1625. S'rīvara, iv. 540, 545, applies to Jayapura the expression *durga*, 'fort.'

[2] See *Jonar.* 300.

[3] See *S'rīv.* i. 250 *sqq.*

Sukhnāg and other hill streams, we come to the considerable district of *Bāngil*. It is often referred in the Rājataraṅgiṇi and the other Chronicles by its ancient name of BHĀṄGILA.[1] No old localities belonging to it are mentioned in our texts, unless we may count with Bāngil the closely adjacent *Paṭan* situated on the shore of the Pambasar marsh, circ. 74° 37′ long. 34° 10′ lat.

This large village occupies the site chosen by King S'aṁkaravarman (A.D. 883–902) for the town which was to bear his name.[2] Kalhaṇa, however, informs us that *Saṁkarapura* "subsequently lost its proper appellation and became known only by the name PATTANA, 'the town.'"[3] This somewhat general designation still survives in the present *Paṭan*. Kalhaṇa sees in this disappearance of the original appellation the just retribution of fate for the king's cruelty and other bad qualities. Yet the old name must have long lingered on by the side of the popular 'Pattana.' For Kṣemendra mentions S'aṁkarapura, and Kalhaṇa himself speaks of the 'town of S'aṁkaravarman' when subsequently referring to events of his own time.[4] Paṇḍit tradition too has retained a recollection of the founder of Pattana and its original name.

S'aṁkaravarman is said to have carried off "whatever was of value at Parihāsapura," in order to raise the fame of his own town. At the same time Kalhaṇa plainly tells us that "what gave fame to that town was only what is still to be found at Pattana,—manufacture of woollen cloths, trade in cattle, and the like."[5]

The only ancient remains of any pretension which can now be found at Paṭan, are, in fact, the ruins of the two temples which were erected there by S'aṁkaravarman and his queen Sugandhā.[6] These shrines which bore the names of *Saṁkaragaurīśa* and *Sugandheśa* are structures of no great dimensions and are without the fine quadrangular courts which enclose all more important Kaśmīrian temples. They have been fully described by General Cunningham and others. Kalhaṇa when mentioning these buildings ironically alludes to kings who like bad poets take the materials for their works from others' property. This combined with the immediately following mention of S'aṁkaravarman's exploitation of Parihāsapura, makes it probable that the building materials for these very temples were taken from the ruins of Parihāsapura. This could have easily been done, owing to the convenient water-

1 See *Rājat.* vii. 498 note.

2 See *Rājat.* v. 156 note.

3 Compare v. 213.

4 Compare *Samay.* ii. 13; *Rājat.* viii. 2488, 3130.

5 *Rājat.* v. 161 *sq.*

6 Compare *Rājat.* v. 158 note.

route offered by the marshes which stretch between Parᵉspōr and Paṭan, a distance of only seven miles.

Though Śaṁkarapura owed thus to its founder but little that could secure distinction, yet the site he had chosen for it was one likely to retain some importance. Paṭan still lies on the direct road between Śrīnagar and Bārāmūla, reckoned at two daily marches, and has probably always just as now been the half-way station between the two places. Considering that Bārāmūla is the starting point of the route to the west, traffic and trade were thus sure to be attracted to Śaṁkaravarman's town. We find it referred to as a local centre still in Kalhaṇa's time, and it has remained to the present day a large and thriving place.

Paṭan figures as a separate Pargaṇa in Abū-l-Faẓl's list. A popular tradition has it that when Tōdar Mal, Akbar's minister, was arranging for the redistribution of Pargaṇas, he inadvertently omitted the Paṭan village at which he was just then encamped. To remedy the mistake Paṭan with its immediate vicinity was made into an additional Pargaṇa.[1] However this may be, we find Paṭan subsequently named as the chief place of the Tilᵃgām Pargaṇa.[2] At the last settlement it became the headquarters of one of the new Taḥsīls.

The Pambạsar lake which stretches to the east of Paṭan as far as the 'Gond Ibrahim' and 'Adin River' of the map, is referred to by Kalhaṇa under the name of PAMPĀSARAS. King Harṣa seems to have extended or regulated it.[3] The Karēwa ground to the west of Paṭan with the deep valleys which intersect it, forms the Pargaṇa of Tilᵃgām. It is mentioned in the Fourth Chronicle, 780, by the name of TAILAGRĀMA.

Pratāpapura.

About four miles to the north-west of Paṭan and on the high road to Bārāmūla lies *Tāpar*, a considerable village. On the evidence of an old gloss and several passages of the Chronicles, it can be safely identified with the ancient PRATĀPAPURA.[4] The latter was founded by King Pratāpāditya-Durlabhaka, the father of Lalitāditya, probably in the second half of the seventh century. When visiting the place in 1892 I found close to the road two ruined mounds covered with large slabs and architectural fragments evidently marking the sites of old temples. Since then, I am informed, most of these remains have been turned into road metal by the native contractors employed in the construction of the new cart-road to Śrīnagar.

[1] See BATES, *Gazetteer*, p. 2.

[2] See MOORCROFT, ii. p. 113; VIGNE, ii. 166.

[3] See *Rājat.* vii. 940 note.

[4] Compare *Rājat.* iv. 10 note.

124. The district through which the Vitastā flows immediately before leaving the Valley, bears now the name of *Kruhin.* The ancient form of this name is unknown unless the Lokaprakāśa's 'Krodhanaviṣaya' may be connected with the tract. Kruhin extends along both sides of the river, but its greater portion lies on the left bank.

District of Kruhin.

Proceeding on the road towards Bārāmūla and at a distance of about six miles from the latter place, we pass on our right the village of *Kạnispōr.* It is identified by an old glossator of the Rājataraṅgiṇī and by the Persian Chroniclers with the ancient KANIṢKAPURA. The latter is mentioned in the Rājataraṅgiṇī as a town founded by the Turuṣka king Kaniṣka,[1] whom we know as the great Indo-Scythian or Kuṣaṇa ruler from the coins and Buddhist tradition. There are no conspicuous remains above ground at Kạnispōr, but old coins and carved stones are occasionally extracted from an old mound near the village.

We have already had occasion to speak of the important position occupied by the ancient twin towns HUṢKAPURA and VARĀHAMŪLA. Built on the banks of the Vitastā immediately above the gorge through which the river leaves the Valley, they form the starting-point on the great route of communication to the west. It is unnecessary to refer here again to the commercial and other advantages which have made this site one of great importance from ancient times to the present day.

Varāhamūla.

Varāhamūla, situated on the right river-bank, has left its name to the present town of *Varahmul,* usually called *Bārāmūla* by Panjābīs and other foreigners.[2] The name Varāhamūla or Vārāhamūla—both forms occur in our texts—is itself derived from the ancient Tīrtha of Viṣṇu Ādi-Varāha who was worshipped here evidently since early times. From it the site of the town and its whole neighbourhood received also the designation of *Varāhakṣetra.* Various legends related at length in the Varāhakṣetramāhātmya and often alluded to in the Nīlamata and the other Māhātmyas, connect this sacred site and the Tīrthas of the immediate neighbourhood with the Varāha or Boar incarnation of Viṣṇu. An abstract of these legends as well as an accurate description of the scanty remains of ancient date to be found at the several Tīrthas, has been given by Prof. Bühler.[3]

1 Compare *Rājat.* i. 168 note. General Cunningham's suggested identification of Kaniṣkapura with 'Kāmpōr,' on the road from Śrīnagar to Śupiyạn, is unsupported by any evidence. The place is really called Khāmpōr and has no ancient remains whatever.

2 For detailed references regarding *Varāhamūla* and *Varāhakṣetra,* see *Rājat.* vi. 186 note.

3 See *Report*, pp. 11 *sqq.*

Temple of Varāha.

The ancient temple of Varāha which seems to have been one of the most famous shrines of Kaśmīr, is repeatedly mentioned by Kalhaṇa. According to the tradition of the local Purohitas it stood near the site of the present *Koṭitīrtha*, at the western extremity of the town and close to the river-bank. Some ancient Liṅgas and sculptures found at the Koṭitīrtha may have originally belonged to the temple. The destruction of its sacred image is noted by Jonarāja in the reign of Sikandar Būtshikast.[1] A short distance below this site where a steep spur runs down to the river-bed, stood the ancient watch-station, still known as *Drang*, which has already been described. A bridge over the Vitastā existed at Varāhamūla already in old times.[2]

It cannot be doubted that Varāhamūla is a very ancient place. It enjoyed the advantage of being on the right river-bank, which is followed by the old route down the Vitastā Valley. But on the other hand the contracted nature of the ground which it occupies, between the hill-side and the river, did not favour the development of a large town. On this account we find that the twin town of HUṢKAPURA built on the open plain of the opposite bank was in ancient times the larger of the two places.

Huṣkapura.

Huṣkapura is mentioned by Kalhaṇa as the town built by King Huṣka, the Turuṣka, and is often referred to in his subsequent narrative.[3] Its name survives in that of the small village of *Uṣkür*, situated about two miles to the south-east of the present Bārāmūla. The identity of Uṣkür and Huṣkapura, correctly noted already by General Cunningham,[4] is well-known to S'rīnagar Paṇḍits, and is indicated also by an old glossator of the Rājataraṅgiṇī. Kalhaṇa in one passage distinctly includes Huṣkapura within Varāhakṣetra, *i.e.*, the sacred environs of the Varāha Tīrtha,[5] and the same location is implied by numerous other references in the Chronicle.

King Huṣka of the Rājataraṅgiṇī has long ago been identified with the Indo-Scythian ruler who succeeded Kaniṣka, the Huviṣka of the inscriptions and the OOHÞKI of the coins. The foundation of Huṣkapura falls thus probably within the first century of our era. Hiuen Tsiang, as we saw, spent his first night after passing through the western entrance of the kingdom, in a convent of *Hu-se-kia-lo* or Huṣkapura. Albērūnī too knows 'Ūshkārā' opposite to Bārāmūla.

1 Compare *Jonar.* 600.

2 See *Rājat.* viii. 413.

3 For detailed references as to Huṣkapura: Uṣkür, see *Rājat.* i. 168 note.

4 See *Anc. Geogr.*, pp. 99 *sq.*

5 See vi. 186.

Kalhaṇa mentions Huṣkapura far more frequently than Varāhamūla. The conclusion to be drawn herefrom as to the relative importance of the two places in Hindu times, is confirmed by the frequent references which the Chronicle makes to religious buildings erected in Huṣkapura. Of King Lalitāditya-Muktāpīḍa it is recorded that he built there the great temple of Viṣṇu *Muktasvāmin* and a large Vihāra with a Stūpa.[1] Kṣemagupta who sought the sacred soil of Vārāhakṣetra in his fatal illness, had founded two Maṭhas at Huṣkapura.[2]

At present foundations of ancient buildings can be traced at numerous points of the plain which stretches from the left river-bank towards the low hills behind Uṣkür. These remains as well as two colossal Liṅgas still *in situ* have already been noted by Bishop Cowie.[3] About 400 yards to the west of the village are the much-damaged remains of a Stūpa, which had been found still intact by Bishop Cowie and photographed in that condition by Major Cole (1870). Subsequently it was dug into and partly levelled down "by some Ṣāhib's order," as the villagers told me. Of this excavation I have not been able to trace a report. But General Cunningham refers to an ancient coin of the Taxila type which was found in this Stūpa and had come into his possession.[4]

It is possible that this Stūpa was identical with the one which King Lalitāditya erected at Huṣkapura. Of the Vihāra which Kalhaṇa mentions in connection with the king's Stūpa, I have shown elsewhere that it was in all probability the same convent which Ou-k'ong refers to under the name of *Moung-ti* Vihāra.[5] The *Moung-ti* of the Chinese transcription seems to represent a prakritized form of the shortened name *Mukta* or *Muktā*. The latter forms which are abbreviations (*bhīmavat*) for *Muktāpīḍa*, occur also in the designations of other religious buildings erected by that king (Muktākeśava, Muktasvāmin).

As we do not meet with the name of Huṣkapura in any of the later Chronicles it may be assumed that its importance did not survive the time of Hindu rule.

1 See *Rājat.* iv. 188.

2 *Rājat.* vi. 186.

3 See *J. A. S. B.*, 1866, p. 123.

4 See *Coins of Anc. India*, p. 62.

5 Compare *Notes on Ou-k'ong*, pp. 5 *sqq.*; *Rājat.* iv. 188 note.

SECTION IX.—THE NORTHERN DISTRICTS OF KRAMARĀJYA.

125. The ancient localities in the Vitastā Valley below Varāhamūla have been noted by us already in connection with the route which leads through it. We may therefore proceed now to those Parganas of the ancient Kramarājya which lie to the north of the river and the Volur lake.

District of Śamālā.

The district which adjoins Kruhin in this direction, is known as *Hamal* (map 'Hummel'). Its ancient name was S'AMĀLĀ from which the former designation is the direct phonetic derivative.[1] S'amālā is very frequently mentioned in the last two Books of the Rājataraṅgiṇī, particularly on account of its feudal chiefs or Ḍāmaras who played a prominent part in all the civil wars of the later reigns. The pretender Bhikṣācara in particular had his most powerful adherents in S'amālā and often took refuge with them. The village of VANAGRĀMA which is mentioned on one of these occasions, is probably identical with the present *Vangām*, situated circ. 74° 25′ long. 34° 19′ lat.[2] *Kākaruha*, another place in S'amālā, referred to in connection with Bhikṣācara's campaigns, can no longer be traced.

Tīrtha of Svayaṁbhū.

To the north of Hamal we reach the Pargaṇa of Maċh[i]pūr (map 'Mochipoora.') Its ancient name is nowhere mentioned. In it lies the sacred site of SVAYAṀBHŪ which owing to the apparently volcanic phenomenon there observed has from early times been renowned as a Tīrtha. Kalhaṇa in his introduction duly notes the 'Self-created Fire' (*Svayaṁbhū*), which "rising from the womb of the earth, receives with numerous arms of flame the offerings of the sacrificers." [3]

The spot meant is still known as *Svayaṁbhū*, or to the villagers as *Suyam*. It lies on a low ridge about half a mile south-west of the village of Nich[a]hōm (not shown on map) and about one and a half miles north of Tsak[a]vaḍar (map 'Sheikwadda.') Visiting it in 1892 I found there in a shallow hollow the soil bright red like burned clay and furrowed by narrow fissures. In certain years steam has been known to issue from these fissures. The ground then becomes sufficiently hot to boil the S'rāddha offerings of the pilgrims who at such times flock to the site in great numbers. The phenomenon which may be either truly volcanic or, according to a modern authority, be caused by hidden seams of coal taking fire, was last observed in the year 1876. Occurrences at

1 See *Rājat.* vii. 159 note.

2 See *Rājat.* viii. 1438.

3 See *Rājat.* i. 34, and for further references the note thereon.

the beginning of the present century are referred to by Mr. Vigne and Dr. Falconer.[1] Abū-l-Fazl too mentions the phenomenon at 'Soyam.'[2]

Considering the rarity of the occasions when this manifestation of the 'Self-created Fire' is observed and the pilgrimage performed, the total absence of ancient remains cannot surprise us. There is, however, a Māhātmya of the Tīrtha, and the latter is also referred to in the Nīlamata. A pilgrimage which King Uccala (A.D. 1101–11) made to Svayaṁbhū gives Kalhaṇa occasion to acquaint us with some localities of the neighbourhood.[3] The king who was stopping in Kramarājya, is said to have started for the village of VARHAṬACAKRA with a small retinue to see the miracle there. On his way which took him past the village of KAMBALEŚVARA, he was set upon in a deep mountain gorge by robbers from whom he escaped only with difficulty.

I believe, the places mentioned in connection with this adventure, can still be identified without difficulty. Varhaṭacakra is probably the present *Tsakᵃvaḍar*, *tsakᵃ* being the ordinary Kś. form for Skr. *cakra* and *vaḍar* the phonetic derivative of *Varhaṭa-*.[4] Cases of village names in which the two component parts, being originally distinct names, can alternate in their position, are by no means unfrequent in Kaśmīr. Thus we have now *Dārā-Sādᵃpōr* and *Sādᵃpōr-Dārā*, etc.

In *Kambaleśvara* we may safely recognize the present village of *Krambhar*, situated about six miles north-east of Svayaṁbhū; for the ending *-har* as the derivative of Skr. *-eśvara*, compare *Triphar* < *Tripureśvara*, etc.[5] The way from Krambhar to Svayaṁbhū leads through the valley of the Panjtar stream. The latter as I convinced myself by personal inspection on a tour in 1892, passes above Rājpōr a narrow thickly-wooded gorge. The path which follows the tortuous course of the stream at the bottom of the gorge, offers excellent opportunities for an ambuscade such as described by Kalhaṇa.

Badᵃrkāl, a small village, about four miles south-east of Krambhar, has a small local Tīrtha marked by a spring and some old Liṅgas. It is visited on the pilgrimage to Svayaṁbhū and mentioned by the name of BHADRAKĀLĪ in the Māhātmya of the latter.

District of Uttara.

126. The Pargaṇa of Uttar stretching along the foot of the range towards the Kiṣangaṅgā, forms the extreme north-west of the Kaśmīr Valley. A passage

[1] See VIGNE, *Travels*, ii. p. 280; LAWRENCE, *Valley*, p. 42.

[2] *Āīn-i-Akb.*, ii. p. 365.

[3] Compare *Rājat.* viii. 250 *sq.* note.

[4] For medial Skr. *r* > Kś. *ḍ*, compare *e.g.*, *Bhaṭṭāraka[maṭha* > *Braḍⁱ[mar* for *ṭ* > *r*, *e.g.* *Kāṣṭhavāṭa* > *Kaṣṭᵃvār*.

[5] For detailed evidence on the phonetic points alluded to, see *Rājat.* viii. 250 note.

of the Rājataraṅgiṇī records its ancient name UTTARA, and refers also to GHOṢA as a locality situated in it.[1] The place meant is undoubtedly the present *Guṣ* situated in the centre of Uttar, near the confluence of the Kāmil River and the stream coming from Lōlau. It is the starting-point for the Śāradā pilgrimage and is mentioned correctly as *Ghoṣa* in the Śāradāmāhātmya.

About ten miles higher up the Kāmil river lies the village of Pạnzⁱgām, circ. 74° 7′ long. 34° 29′ lat. I take its position from Major Bates' Gazetteer; the 'Atlas of India' map does not show the place. It is in all probability identical with PAÑCIGRĀMĪ, mentioned by Kalhaṇa in connection with the surrender of the pretender Bhoja.[2] I have not been able to visit this portion of the district, and Major Bates' reference to Pạnzⁱgām attracted my attention only after the preparation of my map.[3]

In the extreme north-east of Uttar and within a mile of each other, we have the old villages of *Drang* and *Hāyᵃhōm*, referred to by Kalhaṇa under their ancient designations of DRAṄGA and HĀYĀŚRAMA.[4] The latter place, as its name shows, marks the position of an old frontier watch-station towards the Kiṣangaṅgā. We have already seen that there is a route leading past it to Śardi, the ancient Tīrtha of Śāradā situated on that river.

Draṅga and Hāyāśrama are both mentioned by Kalhaṇa in connection with the siege of the Śiraḥśilā castle which took place in his own time. A brief reference may therefore be made here both to this stronghold and the neighbouring shrine of Śāradā, though they are both situated outside the limits of the Kaśmīr Valley.

127. The introduction of the Rājataraṅgiṇī mentions the temple of the goddess Śāradā amongst the foremost Tīrthas of Kaśmīr.[5] It was well known even far beyond the frontiers of Kaśmīr. Albērūnī had heard of it,[6] and a story recorded in a Jaina life of the great grammarian Hemacandra proves that its fame had spread even to far-off Gujrāt.

The Tīrtha of Śāradā.

1 See *Rājat.* vi. 281.

2 See *Rājat.* viii. 3124.

3 There seems to be good reason to suspect that TĀRAMŪLAKA, a place repeatedly referred to in connection with Bhojā's last campaign, lay somewhere in or near Uttar. Unfortunately this locality which is of importance also for other portions of Kalhaṇa's narrative, has not yet been identified; see note vii. 1307.

4 For *Hāyāśrama*, see *Rājat.* viii. 2937 note; for *Draṅga*, viii. 2507 note, also Note *B*, i. 37.

5 The position and history of the temple of Śāradā have been fully discussed in Note *B*, i. 37.

6 See *India*, i. p. 117.

Notwithstanding this former celebrity the S'āradā shrine is now almost completely forgotten by the Paṇḍits of S'rīnagar and the great mass of the Brahman population of the Valley. Fortunately, however, tradition had been more tenacious in the immediately adjoining tracts of Kamrāz. Guided by it I was able to ascertain the position of the ancient Tīrtha at the present *Sardi*, situated circ. 74° 15′ long. 34° 48′ lat., on the right bank of the Kiṣangaṅgā.

My note on Rājat. i. 37 (*B*) gives a detailed account of the tour which in 1892 led me to the Tīrtha as well as a description of the ancient temple still extant at the site. The situation of the shrine corresponds exactly to Kalhaṇa's description. Immediately in front of it the sacred stream of the MADHUMATĪ falls into the Kiṣangaṅgā, while another confluence, that with the SARASVATĪ river coming from the north, is also visible from the temple.

In Jonarāja's time the shrine was still sufficiently popular to attract a visit even from Sultān Zainu-l-'ābidīn.[1] Soon afterwards apparently the miracle-working image of the goddess was destroyed. Abū-l-Faẓl, however, still notes the sanctity of the site and correctly indicates its position on the bank of the Madhumatī.[2]

The subsequent neglect of this Tīrtha must be ascribed chiefly to the obstacles to the pilgrimage which arose from the troubled political condition of the Upper Kiṣangaṅgā Valley. The Bomba chiefs of the latter had made themselves independent in the later Mughal and Paṭhān times. Their predatory inroads often threatened the adjacent tracts of Kaśmīr while their own territory became practically inaccessible to peaceful pilgrims. It is only since the advent of the Sikhs that the pilgrimage to S'āradā's seat was revived. It is probable that the difficulties here briefly indicated must be held to account for the several substitute Tīrthas of S'āradā which are now to be found in various parts of Kaśmīr proper.

Śirahśilā Castle.

My visit to the old 'S'āradāsthāna' also enabled me to identify with certainty the site of the S'IRAHŚILĀ Castle. The latter had been the scene of a memorable siege by King Jayasiṁha's troops which Kalhaṇa describes at length.[3] The accurate topographical data furnished in this account prove clearly that the castle occupied the top of the steep ridge which projects into the Kiṣangaṅgā valley about two and a half miles below the S'āradā temple.

1 *Jonar.* (Bo. ed.) 1056–71. This visit apparently took place A.D. 1422.

2 *Āīn-i-Akb.*, ii. pp. 365 *sq.* Abū-l-Faẓl places S'āradā's stone temple "at two days' distance from Hāchāmūn," *i.e.* Hāyᵊhōm.

3 *Rājat.* viii. 2492–2709. The position of *S'irahśilā* and the evidence for its identity with the 'Gaṇeś Ghāṭī' hill have been fully discussed in my Note *L*, viii. 2492.

The several incidents of the siege, in particular those connected with the attempted escape of the pretender Bhoja, became at once easily intelligible on a close inspection of this site. The ridge bears now the name of *Gaṇeś Ghāṭi*, from a curious rock formation on its side which resembles the head of an elephant and is accordingly worshipped as a 'Svayaṁbhū' representation of the elephant-faced god. It is very probable that the older name *Siraḥśilā* which means literally 'the rock of the head,' owed its origin also to this very rock.

Districts of Lōlau, Zain°gīr.

128. Returning from our excursion to the Kiṣangaṅgā and the confines of the Dard country, we enter immediately to the east of Drang-Hāy°hōm the Pargaṇa usually called *Lōlāb*. Its proper Kaśmīrī name is *Lōlau*, derived from Skr. LAULĀHA.[1] In the picturesque valley which forms this district, no old localities can be specified.

Lōlau is adjoined on the south by the Pargaṇa of Zain°gīr which comprises the fertile Karēwa tract between the Volur and the left bank of the Pohur River. It received its present name from Zainu-l-'ābidīn who is credited with having carried irrigation canals from the Pohur to the Uḍar ground of JAINAGIRI.[2] The earlier name of this tract can no longer be traced.

The chief place in it is the town of *Sōpūr*, the ancient SUYYAPURA, the foundation of which by Suyya, Avantivarman's engineer, has already been mentioned.[3] Sōpūr which lies a short distance below the point where the Vitastā leaves the Volur, has retained its importance to this day, and is still a town of over 8000 inhabitants. It has during recent times been the official head-quarters for the whole of Kamrāz. From a passage of S'rīvara it appears that this had been the case already at an earlier period.[4] Relating a great conflagration which destroyed Suyyapura in Zainu-l-'ābidīn's time, this Chronicler tells us that in it perished the whole of the official archives relating to Kramarājya. The royal residence, however, escaped and the town itself was again built up by the king in great splendour. Of this, however, nothing has remained; nor does the town now show older remains of any interest.

The suggested identity of the village *Zōlur* (map 'Zohlar') in the north-west part of Zain°gīr with JĀLORA once mentioned as a foundation of King Janaka,[5] is doubtful, resting only on the resemblance of

1 Compare *Rājat.* vii. 1241 note.

2 See *Jonar.* (Bo. ed.) 1449–56; also *S'rīv.* i. 562 sq.; iii. 59, 78.

3 Compare for Suyyapura, *Rājat.* v. 118 note.

4 Compare *S'rīv.* i. 560 *sqq.*

5 See *Rājat.* i. 98.

the names. The large village of *Bumai* (map 'Bamhai'), situated 74° 30′ long. 34° 22′ lat., may be Kalhaṇa's BHĪMATIKĀ. The name Bumai can be traced back without difficulty to the older form; but the context of the single passage in which Bhīmatikā is mentioned, does not supply any evidence as to its location.[1]

District of Khūyāśrama.

Round the north shore of the Volur lake there stretches in a semicircle the district of Khuy^{a}hōm. Its ancient name is given by Kalhaṇa as KHŪYĀŚRAMA while S'rīvara and the Lokaprakāśa, with a slight variation, call it Khoyāśramā.[2] The old route which led up to the *Madhumatī* stream and over the Pass of DUGDHAGHĀTA or Dud^{a}khut into the Darad territory on the Kiṣangaṅgā, has been already fully described.[3]

In connection with a Darad invasion which was directed into Kaśmīr by this route, we read of MĀTṚGRĀMA as the place where the invading force encamped.[4] This is certainly the present village of *Mātr^{a}gōm* situated close to the foot of the Trāg^{a}bal Pass, circ. 74° 43′ long. 34° 28′ lat. It lies just at the point where the route along the Madhumati debouches into an open valley, and is the first place where a larger camp could conveniently be formed.

The tract on the north-east shore of the Volur appears in old times to have formed a separate small sub-division called EVENAKA. It is once mentioned by Kalhaṇa, and also referred to in the Tīrthasaṁgraha.[5] But the evidence is not sufficient for a certain location. To it may possibly have belonged also the village of *Sud^{a}rkōṭh*, circ. 74° 43′ long. 34° 18′ lat., which S'rīvara refers to by the name of SAMUDRAKOṬA.[6]

District of Lahara.

129. We have now reached the vicinity of the Sind Valley which forms the largest of the Parganas of Kaśmīr. The district now known as *Lār* comprises the whole of the valleys drained by the Sind and its tributaries as well as the alluvial tract on the right bank of that river after its entry into the great Kaśmīr plain.

Its ancient name was LAHARA, and by this it is mentioned in very

1 Compare *Rājat.* vii. 6; as to the relation of *Bumai* < *Bhīmatikā* comp. *Bum^{a}zu* : *Bhīma*[*keśava*.

2 See *Rājat.* viii. 2695–98 note.

3 See above, § 56.

4 See *Rājat.* viii. 2775.

5 Compare *Rājat.* viii. 2695–98 note.

6 See *S'riv.* i. 400.

numerous passages of the Rājataraṅgiṇī and the later Chronicles.[1] The lands of the district seem to have been from early times in the hands of great territorial nobles. One family of Ḍāmaras resident in Lahara was powerful enough for its members to play the part of true kingmakers during a succession of reigns following after Harṣa.[2] It is probable that the great trade-route to Ladākh and Central Asia which passes through the district, added already in old times to its wealth and importance.

In the midst of the wide water-logged tract of the Sind Delta we find the ancient Tīrtha of TŪLAMŪLYA at the village now known as *Tul*ᵊ*mul*, situated 74° 48′ long. 34° 13′ lat. The Purohita corporation of Tūlamūlya is represented as a well-to-do and influential body already under King Jayāpīḍa.[3] The large spring of Tūlamūlya is sacred to Mahārājñī, a form of Durgā, and is still held in great veneration by the Brahman population of S'rīnagar. It is supposed to exhibit from time to time miraculous changes in the colour of its water, which are ascribed to the manifestation of the goddess. Owing to its convenient position the Tīrtha attracts large numbers of pilgrims from the capital. Abū-l-Faẓl notices the place and its marshy surroundings.[4] About two and a half miles to the east of Tulᵊmul lies the village of Dudᵊrhōm, on the main branch of the Sind which becomes here navigable. It is repeatedly spoken of by S'rīvara under its old name of DUGDHĀS'RAMA.[5]

Ascending the valley we come to the large village of *Maṇ*ⁱ*gām*, situated a short distance from the right bank of the river, 74° 52′ long. 34° 17′ lat. It is the MAYAGRĀMA of Kalhaṇa's Chronicle, mentioned in connection with a campaign of Bhikṣācara in Lahara.[6] In the time of King Saṁgrāmarāja (A.D. 1003–28) Mayagrāma gave its name to a separate fund (*Mayagrāmīṇagañja*) which Queen S'rīlekhā had established evidently with the revenue assigned from this village.[7] Maṇⁱ-gām-Mayagrāma still owns a large area of excellent rice-fields. The village itself contains no ancient remains; but a short distance above it, at the foot of the spur which descends from a high alp known as

1 Compare for the identification of *Lār* and *Lahara*, note *Rājat.* v. 51. The authors of the St. Petersburg Dictionary were already aware of it; see P. W. s. v. LAHARA.

2 Compare regarding the political part played by Janakacandra, Gargacandra and their descendants, *Rājat.* viii. 15 *sqq.*, 354 *sqq.*, 502 *sqq.*, etc. For an earlier instance of Ḍāmara power in Lahara, see v. 51 *sqq.*

3 See *Rājat.* iv. 638 note.

4 *Āīn-i-Akb.*, ii. p. 364.

5 *S'rīv.* iv. 110, 136, 263.

6 See *Rājat.* viii. 729.

7 Compare *Rājat.* vii. 126.

Mohand Marg, there is an ancient stone-lined tank filled by a fine spring known as Vuṭᵃśan Nāg. This is visited as a Tīrtha by the Brahmans of the neighbourhood and is also mentioned under the name of *Uccaiḥśirṇa Nāga* in the Haramukuṭa and several other Māhātmyas. About a mile above the village the high-road leading up the valley passes a shapeless mound of large slabs which undoubtedly belonged to an ancient temple.

Tīrtha of Cīramocana.

130. About four miles above Maṇⁱgām on the left bank of the Sind we reach a site which has enjoyed sanctity from an early period. Close to the village of Prang (not shown on map) situated circ. 74° 55′ 30″ long. 34° 16′ 45″ lat., a small branch of the Kānkᵃnai River (*Kanakavāhinī*) flows into the Sind. This confluence is now visited by the pilgrims proceeding to the Haramukuṭa lakes as one of the chief Tirthas on the route. In the modern Haramukuṭa Māhātmya it is designated as *Karaṅkatīrtha.* But I have shown that it is in reality identical with the ancient Tirtha of CĪRAMOCANA mentioned in the Rājataraṅgiṇī, the Nīlamata and the old Nandikṣetramāhātmya.[1]

The Kānkᵃnai or Kanakavāhinī which is always named together with Cīramocana, is a sacred river as it carries down the waters of the holy Gaṅgā-lake below the Haramukuṭa Peaks.[2] This explains the importance attached to this 'Saṁgama.' The Haramukuṭa Māhātmya which shows its comparatively recent origin by many of its local names, metamorphoses the old Kanavāhinī into *Karaṅkanadī* and consequently also changes the name of its confluence into *Karaṅkatīrtha.*[3] King Jalauka, the son of Aśoka, whom the Chronicle represents as a fervent worshipper of S'iva Bhūteśa and of Nandīśa, is said to have ended his days at Cīramocana.

Tīrthas of Bhūteśa, Jyeṣṭharudra.

Our survey has already taken us to the sacred sites of BHŪTEŚA and JYEṢṬHARUDRA marked by the ruined temples at the present *Buthⁱśēr* high up in the Kānkᵃnai Valley. They are closely connected with the Tīrthas of NANDIKṢETRA below the Haramukuṭa glaciers which have also been described.[4] The village of *Vāngath*, which is the highest permanently inhabited place in the valley, lies about two miles below Buthⁱśēr. It is named VASIṢṬHĀŚRAMA in the Māhātmyas and believed to mark the residence of the Ṛṣi Vasiṣṭha. Allusions in the Rājataraṅgiṇī and Nīlamata show that this legendary location is of old date.[5]

[1] See *Rājat.* i. 149-150 note.

[2] See above, § 57.

[3] Regarding the local nomenclature of this Māhātmya, see above, § 31.

[4] See above, § 57; also *Rājat.* notes i. 36, 107, 113; v. 55-59.

[5] Compare *Rājat.* viii. 2430 note.

At the mouth of Kānkᵃnai Valley, and about two miles to the north-east of Ciramocana, is the hamlet of *Bāravul* which Kalhaṇa mentions as an Agrahāra of King Jalauka under the name of VĀRABĀLA.[1] A large sculptured Liṅga base which I found here in 1891, shows the antiquity of the place.

Upper Sind Valley.

131. Returning to the main valley we come, about three miles above Ciramocana, to the large village of *Kangan* situated on the right bank on the Sind. It is, perhaps, identical with KAṄKAṆAPURA which Queen Diddā is said to have founded in commemoration of her husband Kṣemagupta, known by the epithet of 'Kankaṇavarṣa.'[2] No old localities can be identified with certainty in the Sind Valley until we reach the village of *Gagangīr*, situated two marches above Kangan, circ. 75° 15′ long. 34° 18′ lat. This is undoubtedly the GAGANAGIRI of Jonarāja, and the Fourth Chronicle.[3] The place is mentioned in both texts in connection with invasions which were made into Kaśmīr over the Zōji-Lā Pass. The first was that of the Bhauṭṭa Riñcana, the second the famous inroad of the Mughal leader Mirzā Ḥaidar (A.D. 1532).[4] The account which the latter himself has left us of his exploit, fully explains the special reference made to Gaganagiri by the Hindu Chronicler.

Defile of Dhuḍāvana.

About three miles above Gagangīr two rocky spurs descend from opposite sides into the valley and reduce it to a narrow gorge (see map). The passage of this defile was until recent improvements of the road distinctly difficult, as large fallen rocks blocked the narrow space between the right bank of the river and the high cliffs rising above it. It is at this point of the valley which Mirzā Ḥaidar calls 'the narrow defile of Lār,' that the Kaśmīr chiefs vainly attempted to stop the brave Turks of the invader's advanced guard.

Kalhaṇa's Chronicles shows that the defile here indicated had witnessed fighting already at an earlier epoch. When King Sussala's forces had driven Gargacandra, the great feudal chief, from his seats in Lahara, we are told that the Ḍāmara with his followers retired to the mountain called DHUḌĀVANA. There he was long besieged by the troops

[1] See *Rājat.* i. 121 note.

[2] See *Rājat.* vi. 301.

[3] Compare *Jonar.* (Bo. ed.), 197, and Fourth Chron. 316. The old name of the locality ought to have been entered in the map. The Bombay edition of the Fourth Chron. wrongly reads *gamananiryanta* for *gaganagiryanta* of the MSS.

[4] See *Tārīkh-i Rashīdī*, p. 423. Mr. ELIAS in his note on the passage has quite correctly identified the defile meant by his author. The Fourth Chronicle names the autumn of the Laukika year [460]8 as the date of the event which agrees exactly with Mirzā Ḥaidar's A.H. 939 Jamād II (December, 1532 A.D.).

"of the king who was encamped at the foot of the mountain." In my note on the passage I have shown that the name *Dhuḍāvana* survives in *Dūrün Nār* (map 'Darnar'), the appellation of the high spur which descends into the Sind Valley from the south between Gagangīr and Sunᵃmarg.[1] It is exactly at the foot of this spur that the river passes through the gorge above described. The position taken up by the king's opponent is thus fully explained.

Gagangīr being already 7400 feet above the sea, is the last permanently inhabited place in the valley. Some twenty-five miles higher up we arrive at the Zōji-Lā Pass. Here we have reached the limits of Kaśmīr as well as the end of our survey.

[1] See *Rājat.* viii. 595 *sqq.*—*Dūrün* is the direct phonetic derivative of *Dhuḍāvana*. *Nār*, the Kś. equivalent of Skr. *nāḍa*, the Anglo-Indian 'Nullah,' is often found as the second part in names of high hill-ranges in Kaśmīr; compare, *e.g.*, the 'Soornar' and 'Baibnar' of the map, east of the Haramukh Peaks.

SUPPLEMENTARY NOTE *AA*.—§ 29.

Māhātmyas of Kaśmīrian Tīrthas.

The following is a complete list of the Māhātmya texts acquired by me in Kaśmīr. The numbers in the fourth column refer to the manuscripts representing these texts in my collection. Where the same text is found in several Manuscripts, the number of the best copy has been shown first. In the column of Remarks the Tīrtha to which the Māhātmya refers has also been indicated, as well as the paragraph of the present Memoir in which it has been discussed.

Serial No.	Name of text.	Alleged source.	Nos. of MSS. in my collection.	Remarks.
1	Amaranāthamāhātmya ...	Bhṛṅgīśasaṁhitā ...	8, 7	Amaranātha, § 59.
2	Amareśvara Kalpa ...	Vāthulatantra ...	214	Ditto. (Copied from Poona MS. No. 49).
3	Ardhanārīśvaramāhātmya	Ādikalpa ...	251	Ardhanārīśvara, § 113.
4	Iśālayamāhātmya ...	Bhṛṅgīśasaṁhitā ...	43	Iśeśvara, § 103.
5	Kapaṭeśvaramāhātmya ...	Haracaritacintāmaṇi	43	Kapaṭeśvara (Pāpasūdana), § 112.
6	Kapālamocanamāhātmya	Bhṛṅgīśasaṁhitā ...	43, 19, 20, 21, 22	Kapālamocana, § 116.
7	Kedāratīrthamāhātmya...	Bhṛṅgīśasaṁhitā ...	49	Tīrtha in Varāhakṣetra.

Serial No.	Name of text.	Alleged source.	Nos. of MSS. in my collection.	REMARKS.
8	Kedārapurāṇa ...	......	215	Doubtful (copied from Poona MS. No. 54).
9	Koṭitīrthamāhātmya ...	Bhṛṅgīśasaṁhitā ...	50	Koṭi Tīrtha, § 124.
10	Gaṅgodbhedamāhātmya	Ādipurāṇa ...	216	Bheḍā Tīrtha, § 117 (copied from Poona MS. No. 56.)
11	Gayāmāhātmya ...	......	55	Gayā (near Shādipūr).
12	Gayāmāhātmya ...	Bhṛṅgīśasaṁhitā ...	54	Ditto.
13	Godāvarīmāhātmya ...	Bhṛṅgīśasaṁhitā ...	43	Godāvarī (Godharā), § 115.
14	Jaṭāgaṅgāmāhātmya ...	......	43	Tīrtha at Gaṅgajatan, Pargaṇa Bīru.
15	Jyeṣṭhādevīmāhātmya ...	Bhṛṅgīśasaṁhitā ...	43	Jyeṣṭheśvara, § 102.
16	Tripurāprādurbhāva ...	Bhṛṅgīśasaṁhitā ...	43	Small Tīrtha near the Kanye Kadal, S'rīnagar.
17	Trisaṁdhyāmāhātmya ...	Ādipurāṇa, Nandīśvarāvatāra.	43	Trisaṁdhyā, § 113.
18	Trisaṁdhyāmāhātmya ...	Nandīśvarāvatāra by S'ivasvāmin.	67	Ditto.
19	Dhyāneśvaramāhātmya...	......	75	Tīrtha in hills of Khuyahōm.
20	Nandikṣetramāhātmya ...	S'arvāvatāra ...	77	Tīrthas of Nandikṣetra, § 57.
21	Naubandhanamāhātmya	......	43, 85, 86	Naubandhana, § 41.
22	Piṅgaleśvaramāhātmya...	Haracaritacintāmaṇi	43, 88	Tīrtha at Pingilyun, Chrāṭh Pargaṇa.
23	Puṣkaramāhātmya ...	Bhṛṅgīśasaṁhitā ..	43	Puṣkara Tīrtha, § 120.

Serial No.	Name of text.	Alleged source.	Nos. of MSS. in any collection.	REMARKS.
24	Bahurūpakalpa ...	Kaśmīratīrthamāhātmyasaṅgraha.	95, 96	Bahurūpa Nāga, § 120.
25	Bhadrakālīprādurbhāva	Mahābhārata, Vanaparva.	97	Bhadrakālī Tīrtha, § 125.
26	Mahādevagirimāhātmya	Bhṛṅgīśasaṁhitā ...	104	Mount Mahādeva, § 103.
27	Maheśvarakaṇḍamāhātmya.	Bhṛṅgīśasaṁhitā ...	43	Said to be in Shāhābād Pargaṇa.
28	Mārtāṇḍamāhātmya ...	Bhṛṅgīśasaṁhitā ...	43	Mārtāṇḍa, § 111.
29	Mārtāṇḍamāhātmya ...	Brahmapurāṇa, Kaśmīrakhaṇḍa.	217, 110	Ditto. (Copied from Poona MS. No. 78).
30	Mārtāṇḍamāhātmya ...	Bhaviṣyatpurāṇa ...	109	Ditto.
31	Mitrapathāmāhātmya ...	Ādipurāṇa ...	218	Uncertain. (Copied from Poona MS. No. 80).
32	Yogyālaṅkaraṇamāhātmya.	......	43	Tīrtha on Ḍal, in Rāṇivōr quarter.
33	Rājñīprādurbhāva ...	Bhṛṅgīśasaṁhitā ...	43, 211	Tūlamūlya, § 129.
34	Rājñīmāhātmya ...	Bhṛṅgīśasaṁhitā ...	43	Ditto.
35	Varāhakṣetramāhātmya	Varāhapurāṇa ...	219, 143, 144	Varāha Tīrtha, § 124 (also in Poona MS. No. 85).
36	Vardhamāneśamāhātmya	......	142	Vardhamāneśa; see § 31, note.
37	Vijayeśvaramāhātmya ...	Ādipurāṇa ...	220	Vijayeśvara, § 109. (Copied from Poona MS. No. 77).
38	Vijayeśvaramāhātmya ...	Bhṛṅgīśasaṁhitā ...	152	Ditto.
39	Vitastāmāhātmya ...	Bhṛṅgīśasaṁhitā ...	156, 153, 154	Tīrthas on Vitastā.
40	Vitastāmāhātmya ...	Ādipurāṇa, Kaśmīrakhaṇḍa.	252, 155	Ditto. (Copied from Poona MS. No. 88).

Serial No.	Name of text.	Alleged source.	Nos. of MSS. in my collection.	Remarks.
41	S'arvāvatāra... ...	......	213	Copied from Poona MS. No. 94.
42	S'āradāpuramāhātmya ...	Vitastāmāhātmya ...	160	'Prayāga' at Shādipūr, § 68.
43	S'āradāmāhātmya ...	Bhṛṅgīśasaṁhitā ...	43, 161	S'āradā Tīrtha, § 127.
44	S'āradāmāhātmya ...	Ādipurāṇa ...	43	Ditto.
45	S'ārikāpariccheda ...	Bhṛṅgīśasaṁhitā ...	163, 162, 204	S'ārikā Hill, § 95.
46	S'vetagaṅgāmāhātmya ...	Bhṛṅgīśasaṁhitā ...	43	Dugdhagaṅgā (Chatsakul), § 67.
47	Sureśvarīmāhātmya ...	Bhṛṅgīśasaṁhitā ...	43, 176, 177	Sureśvarī, § 103.
48	Svayaṁbhvagnimāhātmya	Bhṛṅgīśasaṁhitā ...	43, 183, 184	Svayaṁbhū, § 125.
49	Haramukuṭagaṅgāmāhātmya.	Bhṛṅgīśasaṁhitā ...	185, 186, 210, 211	Haramukuṭa Lakes, § 57.
50	Haridrāgaṇeśamāhātmya	Bhṛṅgīśasaṁhitā ...	43	Said to be in Dachünpōr Pargaṇa.
51	Harṣeśvaramāhātmya ...	......	194, 195, 196	Harṣeśvara § 105.

SUPPLEMENTARY NOTE *BB.*—§ 86.

THE LISTS OF KAŚMĪR PARGAṆAS.

The following table shows the names of Kaśmīr Pargaṇas as contained in the lists of Abū-l-Faẓl, Moorcroft, Von Hügel, Vigne and Major Bates. The list of the latter (*Gazetteer*, p. 2) is the fullest and also indicates the division of the Pargaṇas between Marāz and Kamrāz as shown in the table.

The arrangement of the Pargaṇa names conforms to the topographical order followed in Chapter IV. of this Memoir. The second column gives the Pargaṇa names according to their present Kaśmīrī pronunciation, without regard to the often curiously distorted forms in which these names are presented by the earlier lists. The third column shows the authorities in whose lists each particular name is found. In the fourth column the Sanskrit name of the district has been indicated, whenever known, together with the text in which it first occurs. In the last column references have been given to the paragraphs of the Memoir specially dealing with the historical topography of the several districts.

Besides the Pargaṇas shown in the table, Abū-l-Faẓl counts with Kaśmīr the Pargaṇas of '*Maru Aḍwin*' (Maḍivāḍvan), '*Banihāl*' (Bānᵃhāl), and '*Dachhin Khāwarah*' (*i.e.*, Dachün-Khōvur, the valley on both banks of the Vitastā below Bārāmūla). In the same way Moorcroft adds the Pargaṇas of '*Durbid*' (*i.e.*, Dvārbidi in the Vitastā Valley, comp. § 53), '*Karnao*' and '*Tahirabad*'; of the position of the last-named tract I am not certain.

[The list of Kaśmīr Pargaṇas given by P. JOSEPH TIEFFENTHALER, *Description de l'Inde*, p. 77, is only a defective reproduction of Abū-l-Faẓl's list. RITTER, *Asien*, ii. pp. 1136 *sq.*, has endeavoured to elucidate

Tieffenthaler's queer names with whatever materials were then available].

List of Abbreviations.

AF.	ABŪ-L-FAẒL, *Āīn-i Akb.*, ii. pp. 368–371.
Mo.	MOORCROFT, *Travels*, ii. p. 113.
Hü.	VON HÜGEL, *Kaschmir*, ii. 206 *sq.*
Vi.	VIGNE, *Travels*, i. p. 272.
Ba.	BATES, *Gazetteer*, p. 2.

Serial No.	Modern name.	Shown in Pargaṇa list of	Sanskrit name.	REMARKS AND REFERENCES.
		PARGAṆAS OF MARĀZ (MAḌAVARĀJYA).		
1	Phākh ...	AF. Mo. Hü. Vi. Ba.	PHĀKHUVĀ (S'rīv.) ...	§ 101.
2	Atshan ...	Mo. Hü. Ba.	......	These small districts, formed apparently during the Sikh administration, comprised groups of villages in the immediate vicinity of S'rīnagar, to the west, south and north, respectively.
3	Balada ...	Mo. Hü. Ba.	......	
4	Ārvai ...	Ba.	......	
5	Vihī	AF. Mo. Hü. Vi. Ba.	KHAḌŪVĪ (Rāj.) ...	§ 105.
6	Vular ...	AF. Mo. Hü. Vi. Ba.	HOLAḌĀ (Rāj.) ...	§ 106.
7	Dachünpōr ..	AF. Mo. Hü. Vi. Ba.	DAKṢIṆAPĀRA (S'rīv.)	§ 107.
8	Khōvurpōr ...	AF. Mo. Hü. Vi. Ba.	VĀMAPĀRS'VA (Jonar.)	§ 110.
9	Maṭan ...	AF. Mo. Hü. Vi. Ba.	MĀRTĀṆḌA (Jonar.)	§ 111.
10	Anyech (Anatnāg)	AF. Mo. Hü. Vi. Ba.	......	§ 112. Also called Islāmābād (Mo. Hü). Anyech appears in AF. misspelt as Ītch.
11	Kuṭ[a]hār ...	AF. Mo. Hü. Vi. Ba.	[KAPAṬES'VARA, Rāj.]	§ 112. Skr. name found only as that of Tīrtha.

Serial No.	Modern name.	Shown in Pargaṇa list of	Sanskrit name.	REMARKS AND REFERENCES.
12	Bring ...	AF. Mo. Hü. Vi. Ba.	*BHṚṄGA (Lokapr.)	§ 113.
13	Shāhābād (Vēr) ...	AF. Mo. Hü. Vi. Ba.	......	§ 114. Mo. calls the Pargaṇa "Bannahal."
14	Divᵃsar ...	AF. Mo. Hü. Vi. Ba.	DEVASARASA ...	§ 115.
15	Ādᵊvin ...	AF. Mo. Hü. Vi. Ba.	KARĀLA (Rāj.) ... ARDHAVANA (Jonar.)	§ 116.
16	Zainᵊpōr ...	AF. Mo. Hü. Vi. Ba.	JAINAPURA (Jonar.)...	do.
17	Bōṭ	AF. Mo. Hü. Vi. Ba.	......	§ 116. Hü. Vi. call the district after "S'upiyan Shahr," its headquarters.
18	Sūparsāmün ...	AF. Mo. Hü. Vi. Ba.	......	§ 117.
19	S'ukru ...	AF. Mo. Hü. Vi. Ba.	......	do.
20	Sāvur ...	Hü. Vi. Ba.	......	§ 118.
21	Chrāṭh ...	Vi. Ba. ...	......	do.
22	Sāiru-l-mawāẓi' Bālā.	AF. Mo. Hü. Vi. Ba.	......	do.
23	Nāgām ...	AF. Mo. Hü. Vi. Ba.	NĀGRĀMA (Jonar.)	§ 119.
24	Yech ...	AF. Mo. Hü. Vi. Ba.	IKṢIKĀ (S'rīv.) ...	do.

PARGAṆAS OF KAMRĀZ (KRAMARĀJYA.)

Serial No.	Modern name.	Shown in Pargaṇa list of	Sanskrit name.	REMARKS AND REFERENCES.
25	Dūnts ...	AF. Mo. Hü. Vi. Ba.	*DVĀVIṀS'ATI (Lokapr.)	§ 120.
26	Bīru ...	AF. Mo. Hü. Ba.	BAHURŪPA (Jonar.)	do.
27	Māñchᵊhōm ...	Mo. Hü. Vi. Ba.	MĀKṢĀS'RAMA (S'RĪV.)	do.
28	Parᵊspōr ...	AF. Mo. Hü. Ba.	PARIHĀSAPURA (Rāj.)	§ 121.

Serial No.	Modern name.	Shown in Pargaṇa list of	Sanskrit name.	REMARKS AND REFERENCES.
29	Sāiru-l-mawāẓi' Pāyīn.	AF. Mo. Hü. Vi. Ba.	......	§ 122.
30	Andᵊrkōṭh ...	AF. Mo. ...	[ABHYANTARAKOṬṬA] (Rāj.)	do.
31	Bāngil ...	AF. Mo. Hü. Vi. Ba.	BHĀṄGILA (Rāj.) ...	§ 123.
32	Paṭan ...	AF. ...	PAṬṬANA (Rāj.) ...	do.
33	Tilᵊgām ...	AF. Mo. Vi. Ba.	TAILAGRĀMA (Fourth Chron.)	do.
34	Khuy ...	AF. Mo. Hü. Ba.	......	A small tract ('Quihi' on map) to the north of Paṭau and Tilᵊgām.
35	Kruhin ...	AF. Mo. Hü. Ba.	*KRODHANA (Lokapr.)	§ 124.
36	Hamal ...	Mo. Vi. Ba.	S'AMĀLĀ (Rāj.) ...	§ 125.
37	Maçhᶤpūr ...	Mo. Vi. Ba.	......	do.
38	Uttara ...	Vi. Ba. ...	UTTARA (Rāj.) ...	§ 126.
39	Lōlau ...	Mo. Hü. Vi. Ba.	LAULĀHA (Rāj.) ...	§ 128.
40	Zainᵊgīr ...	AF. Mo. Hü. Vi. Ba.	JAINAGIRI (Jonar.)	do.
41	Khuyᵊhōm ...	AF. Mo. Hü. Vi. Ba.	KHŪYĀS'RAMA (Rāj.)	do.
42	Lār	Mo. Hü. Ba.	LAHARA (Rāj.) ...	§ 129.

ADDITIONAL NOTE.—§ 14.

Mr. W. MERK, C.S.I., C.S., at present Deputy Commissioner of the Hazāra District, to whom I submitted the above-printed remarks on Albērūnī's route to Kaśmīr (p. 23) and on the town of *Babrahān* mentioned by him, has kindly supplied me in a letter, dated 25th April, 1899, with the interesting information that "the basin formed by the three Nullahs which unite at *Chamhad* is called the '*Babarhān*' tract." Chamhad is shown on the map as a village in the Mian Khaki Nullah, south-west of Abbottabad, circ. 34° 7′ lat., 73° 7′ long.

Mr. Merk believes that the position of Albērūnī's "town *Babrahān*, half-way between the rivers Sindh and Jailam" is marked by the present 'Babarhān' which practically retains the same name. There is much to support this identification. The Nullah called Mian Khaki on the Survey map forms a convenient route from the central plain of Hazāra, about Mīrpur, towards the Siran Valley through which the Indus could conveniently be gained at Torbela. The latter has remained a favourite crossing place to the present day, being situated just where the Indus debouches from the mountains.

The 8 *Farsakh* or about 39 miles which Albērūnī counts from Babrahān to "the bridge over the river," *i.e.*, according to my explanation, the present Muẓaffarābād, would well agree with the actual distance between the latter place and Babarhān. In calculating this distance it must be kept in view that the old road from the Indus to Kaśmīr, according to Mr. Merk's information, descended to Garhi Habībullā, on the Kunhār River, through the Doga Nullah, *i.e.*, by a more direct route than that followed by the modern cart-road *viâ* Mansahra.

I am further indebted to Mr. Merk for the very interesting notice that the plain near Mīrpur, about 5 miles north-northwest of Abbottabad, is popularly known by the name of *Urash* or *Orash*. There can be no doubt as to this local name being the modern representative of the ancient *Uraśā*. Its survival in that particular locality strikingly confirms the conclusion indicated above in § 83, and also in my note on Rājat. v. 217, as to the position of the old capital of Uraśā. The designation of this capital was undoubtedly *Uraśā*.

TABLE OF CONTENTS.

CHAPTER I.—INTRODUCTORY.

CHAPTER II.—ACCOUNTS OF OLD KAŚMĪR.

SECTION I.—CLASSICAL NOTICES.

SECTION II.—CHINESE RECORDS.

SECTION III.—MUHAMMADAN NOTICES.

SECTION IV.—INDIAN NOTICES.

SECTION V.—THE KAŚMĪR CHRONICLES.

SECTION VI.—THE NĪLAMATA AND MĀHĀTMYAS.

SECTION VII.—LOCAL TRADITION.

CHAPTER III.—GENERAL GEOGRAPHY.

SECTION I.—POSITION AND CONFIGURATION OF KAŚMĪR VALLEY.

SECTION II.—THE PĪR PANTSĀL RANGE.

SECTION III.—THE VITASTĀ VALLEY.

SECTION IV.—NORTHERN AND EASTERN MOUNTAIN RANGES.

SECTION V.—UPPER COURSE OF THE VITASTĀ.

SECTION VI.—LOWER COURSE OF THE VITASTĀ.

SECTION IV.—ANCIENT SITES OF ŚRĪNAGARA.

SECTION V.—THE ENVIRONS OF ŚRĪNAGARA.

SECTION VI.—NORTHERN DISTRICTS OF MAḌAVARĀJYA.

SECTION VII.—SOUTHERN DISTRICTS OF MAḌAVARĀJYA.

LIST OF ABBREVIATIONS.

Āin-i Akb. The Āīn-i Akbarī by Abū-l-Faẓl 'Allāmī, translated from the original Persian, by Col. H. S. Jarrett. Vol. II. (Bibliotheca Indica). Calcutta, 1891.

BATES, *Gazetteer.* A Gazetteer of Kashmir and the adjacent districts of Kishtwar, Badrawar, etc., compiled (for political and military reference), by Charles Ellison Bates, Captain, B.S.C., and Brevet-Major. Calcutta. 1873.

BERNIER, *Travels.* Travels in the Mogul Empire A.D. 1656–1668, by François Bernier, M.D. A revised and improved edition, etc., by Archibald Constable. Westminster, Archibald Constable and Co., 1891.

BÜHLER, *Report.* Detailed Report of a tour in search of Sanskrit MSS. made in Kaśmīr, Rajputana and Central India. By G. Bühler. Journal of the Bombay Branch of the Royal Asiatic Society, 1877.

COLE, *Anc. Buildings.* Illustrations of Ancient Buildings in Kashmir. Prepared under the authority of the Secretary of State for India. By Henry Hardy Cole, R.E., Superintendent, Archæological Survey of India, N.-W. P. London, 1869.

CUNNINGHAM, *Anc. Geogr.* The Ancient Geography of India, I. The Buddhist period, including the campaigns of Alexander and the Travels of Hwen-Thsang. By Alexander Cunningham, Major-General, R.E. London, 1871.

DREW, *Jummoo.* The Jummoo and Kashmir Territories. A Geographical Account. By Frederic Drew, F.R.G.S. London, 1875.

FORSTER, *Journey.* A Journey from Bengal to England, through the Northern part of India, Kashmire, etc. By George Forster. Vols. I, II. London, 1808.

Fourth Chron. Rājāvalipatāka of Prājyabhaṭṭa and Śuka. [Fourth Sanskrit Chronicle of Kaśmīr. Quoted according to the editio princeps, Calcutta, 1835; compare below, p. 41].

Haracar. The Haracaritacintāmaṇi of Rājānaka Jayadratha. Kāvyamālā, Bombay, 1897 [compare below, p. 48].

HÜGEL, *Kaschmir.* Kaschmir und das Reich der Siek. Von Carl Freiherrn von Hügel. Vols. I.–IV. Stuttgart, 1840.

India. Albērūnī's India. An account of the religion, philosophy, literature, geography, etc., of India about A.D. 1030. An English edition, by Dr. E. C. Sachau. Vols. I., II. London, 1888.

Jonar. The Rājataraṅgiṇī of Jonarāja. [Compare below, p. 41. Quoted according to Calcutta edition, 1835, except for additional verses found in Prof. Peterson's edition, Bombay Sanskrit Series, 1896].

LASSEN, *Ind. Alt.* Indische Alterthumskunde, von Christian Lassen. [Vols. I, II., quoted in second edition]. Leipzig, 1866–71.

LAWRENCE, *Valley.* The Valley of Kashmir, by Walter R. Lawrence, I.C.S., C.I.E., Settlement Commissioner, Kashmir and Jammu State. London, 1895.

Life. The Life of Hiuen-Tsiang. By the Shamans Hwui Li and Yen-Tsung. With a Preface, etc., by Samuel Beal. London, 1888.

Māh. Māhātmya [compare below, p. 49. The several texts are quoted from MSS.].

MOORCROFT, *Travels.* Travels in the Himālayan Provinces of Hindustan and the Panjab; in Ladakh and Kashmir; etc., by Mr. William Moorcroft and Mr. George Trebeck, from 1819 to 1825. Prepared for the press by Horace Hayman Wilson. Vols. I, II. London, 1841.

Nīlamata. The Nīlamatapurāṇa. [Compare below, p. 46. Quoted from MSS.].

Rājatar. Kalhaṇa's Rājataraṅgiṇī, or Chronicle of the Kings of Kashmir. Edited by M. A. Stein. Sanskrit Text with critical notes. Education Society's Press, Bombay, 1892. [Notes quoted will be found in my annotated translation of the Chronicle, in course of publication by Messrs. A. Constable & Co., London].

RITTER, *Asien.* Die Erdkunde von Asien, von Carl Ritter. Berlin, 1833.

Samayam. The Samayamātṛkā of Kṣemendra. Kāvyamālā, Bombay, 1888. [Compare below, p. 44].

Si-yu-ki. Si-yu-ki. Buddhist records of the Western World. Translated from the Chinese of Hiuen Tsiang, by Samuel Beal. Vols. I, II. London, 1884.

Śrīkaṇṭhac. The Śrīkaṇṭhacarita of Maṅkha. Kāvyamālā, Bombay, 1887.

Śrīv. The Jaina-Rājataraṅgiṇī of Śrīvara. [Compare below, p. 42. Quoted according to the editio princeps, Calcutta, 1835].

STEIN, *Notes on Ou-k'ong.* Notes on Ou-k'ong's account of Kaçmīr. By M. A. Stein. Proceedings of the Imperial Academy of Sciences, Vienna, 1896.

STEIN, *Notes on the Pīr Pantsāl.* Notes on the ancient topography of the Pīr Pantsāl Route. By M. A. Stein. Journal of the Asiatic Society, Bengal. Calcutta, 1895.

Tārīkh-i Rashīdī. The Tārīkh-i Rashīdī of Mirzā Muḥammad Ḥaidar. An English version, edited with commentary, etc., by N. Elias; the translation by E. Denison Ross. London, 1895.

TROYER.	Râdjataraṅgiṇî. Histoire des Rois du Kachmîr, traduite et commentée par M. A. Troyer. Vols. I–III. Paris, 1840–52.
VIGNE, *Travels*.	Travels in Kashmir, Ladak, etc. By G. T. Vigne, Esq. Vols. I, II. London, 1842.
Vikram.	The Vikramâṅkadevacharita. Life of King Vikramāditya of Kalyāṇa, composed by his Vidyāpati Bilhaṇa. Edited, with an Introduction, by Dr. G. Bühler. Bombay, 1875.
WILSON, *Essay*.	An Essay on the Hindu History of Cashmir. By Horace Hayman Wilson. Asiatic Researches, xv. Calcutta, 1825.
YULE, *Cathay*.	Cathay and the Way Thither; being a collection of medieval notices of China, translated and edited by Colonel [Sir] Henry Yule, C.B., R.E. With a preliminary Essay, etc. Vols. I, II. London, 1866.

NOTE.

The transcription of Sanskrit, Persian and Arabic words in the present Memoir conforms to the system approved by the International Oriental Congress of 1894. In the phonetic rendering of Kaśmīrī words the lines adopted by Dr. G. A. Grierson, in his analysis of Paṇḍit Īśvara Kaula's Kaśmīrī Grammar (*J. A. S. B.*, 1897-98) have been closely followed.

CORRIGENDA.

Page.	Line.				
10	7	For	*expect*	read	*except.*
40	27	„	*-brā̤r*	„	*-bra̤r.*
55	35	„	*Rāshidī*	„	*Rashīdī*
88	1	„	NORTHERN	„	NORTHERN AND EASTERN.
93	21	„	*Rāshidī*	„	*Rashīdī.*
98	29	„	*Nā̤rᵘ*	„	*Nā̤ru.*
103	14	„	Vastarvan	„	Vastᵃrvan.
103	17	„	Rā̤muṣa	„	Rā̤muṣ.
104	17	„	*Bhattāra°*	„	*Rhaṭṭāra°.*
105	21	„	*Śureśvari*	„	*Śureśvarī.*
110	2	„	*larger-*	„	*large.*
123	1	Add heading: SECTION VIII.—ETHNOGRAPHY.			
126	6	For	*Karnāv*	read	*Karnau.*
168	36	„	*Rā̤nī*	„	*Rā̤nⁱ.*
206	18	„	*latter*	„	*former.*